International
Environmental Politics

International Environmental Politics

THE LIMITS OF GREEN DIPLOMACY

Lee-Anne Broadhead

LYNNE
RIENNER
PUBLISHERS

BOULDER
LONDON

Published in the United States of America in 2002 by
Lynne Rienner Publishers, Inc.
1800 30th Street, Boulder, Colorado 80301
www.rienner.com

and in the United Kingdom by
Lynne Rienner Publishers, Inc.
3 Henrietta Street, Covent Garden, London WC2E 8LU

Library of Congress Cataloging-in-Publication Data
Broadhead, Lee-Anne, 1960–
  International environmental politics : the limits of green diplomacy /
  Lee-Anne Broadhead.
     p. cm.
  Includes bibliographical references and index.
  ISBN 1-58826-092-5 (alk. paper)—ISBN 1-58826-068-2 (pbk. : alk. paper)
    1. Environmental management. 2. Environmental policy—International
cooperation. 3. Nature—Effect of human beings on. I. Title.
GE300 .B756 2002
363.7'0526—dc21   2002018879

British Cataloguing in Publication Data
A Cataloguing in Publication record for this book
is available from the British Library.

Printed and bound in the United States of America

The paper used in this publication meets the requirements
∞ of the American National Standard for Permanence of
Paper for Printed Library Materials Z39.48-1984.

5 4 3 2 1

For Sean

Contents

Preface

ANOTHER BOOK ON GLOBAL ENVIRONMENTAL PROBLEMS HARDLY seems necessary, given the number to be found in any bookshop or library. There are books chronicling the increasing role of the United Nations and books about the range of actors now involved in collaborating on the mighty task of finding solutions to the problems facing us. There are countless volumes celebrating the role of nongovernmental organizations and social activists. The concept of *sustainable development* also provides a topical framing device for authors interested in international relations and the environment. The shelves are full, too, with books that set out the details of specific crises—ozone depletion, global warming, and the loss of biodiversity—and proposed solutions. The stories have been told of the proliferation of the so-called regimes—the rules, norms, and governing arrangements—that have been cooperatively agreed upon by participating states to ensure the long-term health and well-being of the natural environment. So why another book?

My interest in adding to the list stems from a deepening concern that the very way environmental issues are thought about and the negotiations that result from their common framing are themselves leading to the further deterioration of the natural environment. Governments around the world send out diplomats—adroit negotiators with an eye to national interest—to bargain over details with their counterparts in the hope of establishing rules to govern behavior in areas deemed to be suffering as a result of human action. I have called this practice *green diplomacy,* and throughout the book it becomes a kind of shorthand for a way of seeing the world from a managerial perspective: a style of negotiating a solution to the problems facing the world that takes as its starting point a view of nature solidly based in Enlightenment thought. In this manner of considering the natural world, everything can be divided into component parts for inquiry with no thought given to the possible impact on other, even related, aspects. One problem of atmospheric deterioration, for example, can be studied in splendid isolation from any other aspect in the confidence that the various components can be discrete topics of investigation. All issues are suitable for management and for control; nature is considered instrumentally (i.e., in terms of its use as a means to an end) and humans are most certainly seen as being outside nature and able to fix any problem arising by developing ever more advanced technologies. Incremental progress thus defined is to be celebrated for setting us on a path to a supposedly blissful future where our total understanding yields us a pacified natural environment that will sustain us for all eternity.

There is a fundamental problem with this instrumental view of nature, the underpinnings of which allow for one group of green diplomats to negotiate international action on, for instance, ozone depletion without recognizing that their actions are deepening the problems of global warming. But the limitations of green diplomacy do not end with this limited view of the natural world, which encourages confidence in the face of deterioration.

For while governments send out their green diplomats to consider the environmental state of the world, they also dispatch teams of negotiators to a very different sort of international gathering: meetings and conferences to determine the rules and norms for international economic arrangements. There is no concern here that the resource extraction, the burning of fossil fuels, the commodification of all parts of the natural world, or any of the other essential components of a growth-based economy could have any negative impact on the environment. Quite the contrary. The economists and government officials tell us that these negotiations to "free" trade are to be celebrated for ensuring that environmental standards (along with human rights and social standards) will rise as more and more governments lead their people into the family of nations encompassed by the World Trade Organization and the economic policies enshrined in its agreements and policies. It is a critique of the widely held belief that these two forms of multilateral activity will assist us in reversing environmentally destructive practices that is central to this book.

The insights offered by the first generation of Frankfurt School scholars (notably Max Horkheimer, Theodor Adorno, and Herbert Marcuse) assist me in my task. This is not a book specifically about critical theory, and it does not deal with some very important debates about the changing and sometimes contradictory arguments of the Frankfurt School writers. Instead, I highlight the major line of argument as devised in the early years of the school and set out the theoretical tools I use. I subsequently allow the tools to guide the critique without feeling the need to be explicit about who said what in the many debates both within the school and between its members and its detractors. In a sense this is a book inspired by a theory rather than a book of theoretical application. Critical theory's methodological point of view, as summed up concisely by Douglas Kellner, "is at once to *comprehend* the given society, *criticize* its contradictions and failures, and to *construct* alternatives."[1] It has been my goal throughout the book to fulfill this requirement.

Chapter 1 establishes the foundation upon which the rest of the argument stands. I consider the way in which the natural environment came to be regarded through Enlightenment thought and demonstrate the way in which this mind-set is reproduced within the discipline of international relations. It is here that I introduce the major arguments of the Frankfurt School and set out explicitly the tools I utilize for the critique that follows.

Chapter 2 depicts the advent of green diplomacy and presents a history of the major conferences and diplomatic initiatives that established a type of containment field around the demands made by alternative movements and nongovernmental organizations seeking to question the absence of linkage between economics and environment. The concept of sustainable development as presented by the Brundtland Commission and as incorporated into the arsenal of green diplomacy is subjected to a critical investigation. I explore both the manner in which the concept has been utilized in an effort to impose closure on debates surrounding the relationship between environmental issues and economic orthodoxy, as well as the logical inconsistency that is immediately revealed through such action, for it is impossible to hermetically seal any such vague concept. Once exposed, the illogic of the claims made provides the impetus for the reclamation of the concept in support of very different policies and programs of action. Directions this reclamation may take are explored further in Chapter 5.

The other essential subject for consideration, in order that the given society be adequately *comprehended,* is the development of an increasingly transnationalized marketplace and the resulting impact that actions allowed within the constantly developing economic structures have on the natural environment. By beginning with the origins of the economic model of progress accepted as the backdrop to green diplomacy, I endeavor in Chapter 3 to lay bare the costs of the neoliberal orthodoxy that is given practical force through the numerous trade deals currently operational. My basic argument is that the current efforts to "liberalize" trade serve only to globalize unsustainable environmental practices and more deeply embed a dangerously destructive way of seeing nature. The language of "globalization" used by the cheerleaders of free market logic is designed, I argue, to mystify the operation of the international marketplace and to encourage the belief that the direction of international economic policies and agreements is not a matter of choice or ideological policy but is rather the result of inexorable forces outside the control of mere mortals. Here again I will draw on the evident contradictions and the failure of the promises made by defenders of the status quo to demonstrate the enormous environmental costs resulting from the neoliberal economic policies and the attendant extension of capitalist economic dictates to every corner of the world.

Green diplomacy receives its practical intent with the activity known as *regime formation,* and Chapter 4 sets out both the claims made for the practice by its advocates and the intellectual understanding of the phenomenon provided by so-called regime theorists. Through an in-depth examination of two case studies—ozone depletion and climate change—it is possible to see the failed promise of the activity. Focusing on the intersection of economic and environmental interests, it is possible to view the very powerful corporate interests at play that necessarily impede the green diplomats from fulfilling their stated aim.

Chapters 2 through 4, therefore, can be regarded as constituting an effort to destabilize the given understanding of the existing society by holding it to account for the failure to produce a reality that lives up to the promises made. Because critical theory demands that any critique of existing society begin but not end with such *negation,* Chapter 5 considers the need to identify alternatives and points to the possibilities that are immanent in the current system, but that are contained or denied by those who wish to maintain the status quo. By considering a range of concrete suggestions for the ways that development could indeed be made sustainable or that international trade really could be designed to operate in the interests of the majority of people rather than a select few, I offer insight into alternative realities.

The image of demonstrably viable alternatives is premised on the need for a reformulated scientific view, the basis of which exists in the writings of a small and often marginalized group of scientists aware of the limitations of the dominant scientific method. Of equal import is the re-imagining of international economic structures that has as its basis a commitment to social justice and the true democratic principle of participation. The extent to which these myriad protests and sites of resistance could potentially become a more coherently structured transnationalized movement of counter-hegemonic struggle remains to be seen. However, we must consider the cross-cultural and transnational efforts being made by resistance groups in the Western Hemisphere to form a coherent alternative to the proposals made by the power elites for a so-called Free Trade Area of the Americas. In this movement can be glimpsed the ability of groups to work through the difficulties of the vastly different interests and expectations of people in overdeveloped and underdeveloped parts of the world. It is the clear recognition that alternative policy choices would be more environmentally sustainable as well as more beneficial to the vast majority of people in the hemisphere that underlies the efforts of the Hemispheric Social Alliance, and it is the clear articulation of what those alternative policies could be that gives them the credibility necessary to destabilize the spurious claims that the only path open to us is that encompassed in the vision of a global free trade system. Whether or not the illogic of the current system will be exposed sufficiently that the neoliberal orthodoxy will be shaken to its foundations by such efforts remains to be seen.

In Chapter 6 I draw conclusions, not entirely optimistically, about the chances for the radical rethink necessary to stem the tide of destruction. One thing is certain: if the current economic project continues to advance its cause to all corners of the globe, the oppression of both people and the natural world will continue apace. It may already be too late to reverse the destructive consequences of neoliberal economic policies, but it is essential that we try.

NOTE

1. Kellner, *Herbert Marcuse and the Crisis of Marxism,* pp. 122–123 (emphasis in original).

Acknowledgments

I AM NOT SURE IF IT IS POSSIBLE FOR ANYONE TO WRITE A BOOK in "splendid isolation." I do know that this book certainly did not spring from my mind alone and was both conceived and written in splendid association.

The impetus for the book came from the classroom. Faced with probing, intelligent questions and insights from students in my environmental politics class at the University of Bradford, UK, I willingly undertook the task of setting down the arguments contained here. The students in my classes at the University College of Cape Breton have continued to keep me on my toes with their own fresh perspectives and have cheerfully helped me to clarify my own thoughts and nudged me toward the completion of this book. It is with heartfelt thanks that I remember them here, and I only hope that they realize how much they have assisted me in my own intellectual development.

I am also indebted to the library staff of both the University of Bradford and University College of Cape Breton. Without these superb professionals, my task would have been much more difficult.

To my very close friend and outstanding research assistant, Toby Zanin, I owe special thanks. His tracking down of obscure material on short notice was an enormous help, and his analytical skills and deep understanding of this project have undoubtedly made a better book. His encouragement and warm sense of humor have been greatly appreciated, and it is also the case that without his input this book would not have been as much fun to write.

Lynne Rienner must rank as the world's most patient and understanding publisher. I cannot express the extent to which I have appreciated the encouragement received through all my requests for extensions. Special thanks to Richard Purslow for his help in getting the project going in the first place and his encouragement throughout the long years since, to Karen Williams for overseeing the final stages, and to Jason Cook for his intelligent and diligent copyediting.

I am blessed beyond measure with caring and supportive friends and family, all of whom have understood when I have failed in my own goal not to let this book intrude on my personal life. I'm pleased to say the list is far too long to include here, but I would like to acknowledge especially Jane and Bruce Barrett for all their support over many years, and Gayle Fraser, who, aside from being a good friend, saved me from nervous exhaustion by agreeing to help with the index. To Carol Aikenhead, David MacDonald, Wendy Reynolds, and Maureen, Jim, and Emma Howard—many thanks for encouragement throughout.

My parents—Bill and Fran Broadhead—have been a constant source of encouragement, enthusiasm, and love throughout the project and they, along with Steve, Lori, and Simon Broadhead, have my gratitude and love for all their support.

But the principal debt of gratitude is to my husband, Sean Howard, whose support—practical, intellectual, and emotional—has been unwavering throughout the entire process. His engagement with, and extraordinarily deep thinking about, the issues central to this book have had an enormous impact on the development of my own thinking. The long, fascinating, and inspiring conversations we engage in about the world around us are as enjoyable for me as they are intellectually nourishing. Words cannot express what he means to me, and this book is for him. *Chinese Lantern moon, swaying in the wind . . . forever . . . .*

1

Situation Critical

IN THE LAST QUARTER OF THE TWENTIETH CENTURY, INTER-
national political processes have, apparently, become increasingly concerned with a wide range of environmental problems. A common argument can now be heard from the politicians' offices as well as from
within the walls of academe and even corporate boardrooms: the previously unchallenged notion of state sovereignty has given way to new and
better forms of international cooperation in the face of environmental
problems. Few, if any, of the exponents of this view would argue that the
management of this acknowledged interdependence has been straightforward, but hope is continually held out that increased awareness of the
fragility of the natural environment has necessitated greater effort on collective measures to halt destructive practices.

The governing arrangements established in this more rational system, we are frequently told by international relations scholars, demonstrate a new reality in interstate relations—one in which state power has
been diminished and restructured along more cooperative lines to meet
the obviously transnational dimensions of the crisis. If we move carefully and base our arguments on solid knowledge, it is argued, we will
continue to take steady steps toward a more ecologically sound world
order. Incremental change may not be dramatic, but it is, these scholars
reassure, having the inevitable effect of shaping the freedom of maneuverability of both states and institutions. From this perspective we can
clearly see the dawn of a new, norm-rich world order from which we
will all benefit.

In the view of the defenders of incremental change and international
"regime formation,"[1] we are encouraged to believe in the persuasive

ability of scientific knowledge about both the causes and the cures of environmental degradation to lead even the most recalcitrant of polluters into agreements that will limit their actions. We are reassured that, when faced with domestic pressure and scientific evidence, state leaders will make concessions that are in the greater interests of the natural world rather than in their narrower national interest. Furthermore, we are asked to be optimistic about scientific research itself: in its ability to provide us with a neutral, value-free picture of the state of the world's environment and to point to the specific action necessary to turn the corner toward environmental sustainability. And finally, we are asked to celebrate the new forms of technology that are held out as the savior of our currently destructive practices: technology transfers to the developing world will assist with pollution reduction, and our own continuing efforts will guarantee that we will find solutions to ongoing problems.

The way forward, argues the incrementalist, is to focus on one limited and therefore manageable problem at a time. Let us not take on too much at a time; let us take sure steps based on scientific fact and not bite off more than we can chew. Green diplomacy—by which I mean the process of ordering the international governance issues dealing with the natural world and its myriad problems and challenges—is now a regular part of the international scene, and as long as we do not push too hard or too fast we can make steady progress. By focusing on one specific and limited issue at a time we will triumph. Small steps are needed to establish a body of law to guarantee environmental standards. It may not be a perfect scenario but we are told to be realistic about the international system and the very obvious difficulties in attempting to negotiate instruments of governance when states define their national interests judiciously while guarding their sovereignty jealously. Machiavelli—taken as shorthand for the brute reality of state power—may be greener now,[2] but cooperative interdependence has its limits and sovereignty must be protected. If we set our sights too high and attempt to link issues, we will achieve little, if anything, of substance.

Not only is the state presented as being increasingly imbued with this new, Green Enlightenment, but corporations have also, so we are told, turned the same hue, a claim reinforced by their bombardment of consumers with advertisements and merchandise designed and labeled as ecologically sound. Now, if governments and business leaders are indeed serious converts to the cause of saving the environment, what need is there for alternatives, in thought or deed, to incrementalist green diplomacy? We are told that not only are such alternatives superfluous, they are at best naïve and at worst counterproductive. This is not the terrain for grassroots movements or small-scale projects; these are huge problems demanding overarching, intergovernmental activity. We are directed to "leave it to the specialists"—those with the oversight of the whole issue—and we need not worry, because we can relax in the knowledge that an agreed framework has been found: that of sustainable development.

REFRAMING THE ISSUE

Not everyone, of course, is happy with this presentation of the necessary rules of engagement. Increasingly, we see the claims of the international institutions—especially, but not exclusively, those of the economic variety—being contradicted by the results of their policies. As a result, students, farmers, industrial workers, and others from around the world are meeting up: they meet on the streets to protest, at international conferences to think through strategies, and over the Internet to share ideas about tactics. The claims of the international incrementalists ring hollow in these ears, and the responses of the state leaders in their own locale when challenged by the protesters display remarkable similarities: send in the riot police wearing what appears to be standard-issue crowd control gear (the globalization of riot fashion?) and carrying a hefty supply of pepper spray.

What sense are we to make of this? Which claims are correct and what is the appropriate approach to adopt to deal with the myriad environmental problems that we collectively face? Can we not just adopt the methods that have apparently been used so successfully to gain multilateral agreements on ways to deal with serious problems such as global warming and ozone depletion and turn our attention to the other severe tasks at hand? What need is there for a fundamental rethink or critique?

The beginning point to answering all of these questions is of necessity a consideration of whether the promised transformation of the international rules has indeed occurred. Calling into question the reality of this supposed transformation is the topic of this inquiry. My inquisition stems from a belief that the presentation of such optimism—which is based on the supposedly scientific answers to so-called rational problems—is not only misleading but is actually blinding us to the radical transformation in our thinking and subsequently to the prevalent forms of social organization that must take place before any qualitative improvement in the condition of the natural world can result. Such radical thinking, I argue, is not to be limited only to specific technical issues of separate environmental problems but rather must be more wide-ranging and more integrated into a consideration of the social context within which these problems exist.

Drawing on the insights of Critical Theory,[3] I seek to highlight the way in which the framing of the environmental issue can be seen as both a product and a way of perpetuating a form of societal organization that represses the real possibilities that exist to liberate individuals and establish the preconditions for ecologically sound existence. The argument that will be presented in this book is that the optimism demonstrated by the supporters of green diplomacy is misguided and serves only to maintain environmentally destructive political, economic, and social structures. The very way in which we regard the world has led to—and continues to deepen—the destruction of the environment. The existing social structures, based as they are on the perpetuation of the growth model and continual profit seeking, are connected to, embedded in, and act as a reaffirmation of this worldview. Many of the advocates of the incrementalist approach are well intentioned and believe wholeheartedly that we must work within the limitations as we find them; others have a vested interest in ensuring that the questions and issues are not framed in such a manner that they call into question the status quo view of markets, science, and progress.

The argument used by those academics who support and encourage the regime formation approach to environmental politics is that we must work toward the goals that can be "realistically" achieved within the boundaries of the current international system. It has been acknowledged by at least one scholar of regime formation that "an emphasis on regimes can be criticized by those for whom anything other than clearly transformatory agendas are inadequate."[4] Instead of then looking closely at what such a critique would lead to, it is inevitably dismissed because "the scope of such agendas soon extends far beyond specifically environmental issues."[5] This inquiry into international environmental problems, which extends beyond the specifics of the individual problems, is in fact the point of such critiques, and this book will argue that it is the green diplomats and their champions who are on the wrong track, a road to environmental hell paved with their overly limited intentions. We need to stop looking at the "new" Machiavelli—the modern state and its business friends—through green-tinted spectacles. The reality is far uglier and the situation far worse than presented.

THE NATURAL WORLD AND INTERNATIONAL RELATIONS

The treatment of the global environmental crisis in the field of international relations is limited by the weakness of the theories that have generally been used to guide both its scholarship as well as the practical construction of international agreements. It can alas be said with certainty that reflexivity—an essential self-consciousness about the process of theorizing itself—has not traditionally been greatly valued within the field, and although there have been theoretical battles between those holding different perspectives for as long as the discipline has existed, until relatively recently there has been a decided lack of recognition of the role of knowledge claims and the power inherent in the framing of the questions for study. Needless to say, outside academe in the "real world" of international relations, the movement has been even slower.

Before turning our attention to the impact that such reflexivity might have on the problem at hand, let us consider the mainstream thinking of the discipline as it pertains to the natural world. The exploitation of natural resources has long played a central part in the musings on interstate power struggles. The dominance of the realist school of thought in the aftermath of World War II echoed the widely held belief that the natural world could be considered as nothing more than stocks of resources that could be brought under control in the interests of industrial production (including war-fighting capability) and therefore as an important element in the calculation of power. Hans Morgenthau—widely regarded as the grand master of realist thinking—argued (correctly) that "as the absolute importance of the control of raw materials for natural power has increased in proportion to the mechanisation of warfare, so certain raw materials have gained importance over others."[6] The objective then was to ensure the national interest of the state by protecting the existing resources and ensuring access to those that were not plentiful within a state's boundaries.

The recognition of the changing need for raw materials did not, needless to say, lead realist international relations scholars to a discussion of the environmental costs of militarism precisely because the major tenet of this theory is that we must take the world as we find it;

normative wishes to change the natural order of interstate relations merely cloud issues with potentially disastrous effects. Realism recognized, as Morgenthau informed us, that "politics, like society in general, is governed by objective laws that have their roots in human nature. . . . The operation of these laws being impervious to our preferences, men will change them only at the risk of failure."[7] Much of the literature that now exists on the security costs of environmental degradation reproduces this logic when it refers to water or other resource shortages in terms only of struggles and potential war.[8]

By the 1970s, a challenge was being mounted against the perceived limitations of the realist model of power politics. Framed originally in terms of *complex interdependence,*[9] this revision of the realist model was inspired by the inability of scholars and practitioners alike to deal with a world order that no longer seemed to fit into the easy patterns of prediction offered by the preeminent international relations theory. The debacle in Vietnam, the influence of the Organization of Petroleum-Exporting Countries (OPEC), transborder environmental problems, and a range of other issues seemed to beg fundamental questions about the ordering of the international system and the relationship between military might and international influence and the calculation of power. The critics of realism challenged the orthodoxy of the state-centric model and demanded that to be understood properly, power in international relations would have to be conceived in broader terms and consideration would have to be given to the relative roles of a range of actors (including multinational corporations and other nonstate actors) and an increasingly complex web of interrelationships between (and even within) states. This newer school of thought entered into the discipline determined to be taken seriously as a theory to guide action at the practical level of engagement—they were keen to stress that they were not *idealists* merely presenting a picture of the world that they wished existed.

It was out of this challenge and in the space created by the early critics that the focus landed on *regime* formation as a fresh approach to institutional management. The debates in the journals soon became fixed on the ways and means to conceptualize institution building with a view to understanding the relations of power at the international level. What had begun as complex interdependence developed further in these debates and has been variously referred to as neoliberalism, neoliberal internationalism, and neoliberal institutionalism, and although there are subtle differences in the various approaches collected under these labels, it is fair to say that an important aspect of the work was directed to understanding the extent to which coordinated effort comes about and the impact that such action has on the international system.[10] Realists were also part of the debates, and although a different picture emerged about the ways and means of institution building, a newer approach to the older theory took on some of the challenges and engaged fully in the discussions. Indeed, by the early 1990s, some scholars were arguing that there was a growing together of perspectives and despite some lingering areas of emphasis a shared research project should be encouraged.[11]

But why mention these abstract debates in such detail? As we shall see throughout this book, the concept of management is extraordinarily important and it is at the level of institutional management that the green diplomat is so eagerly engaged. The advent of the language of regime building led to the easier acceptance, on the part of practitioners, of the feasibility of the international activity that has become central to the issues of concern here.

In terms of the depiction of the natural world, however, little had changed. Regardless of whether the realist was considering the power behind building institutions and considering the means to utilize such activity to the full benefit of maximizing power, or whether the liberal institutionalist was promoting the benefits of cooperation and articulating the promise of legal norms and regulations, the underlying thinking about the natural world was one of management and control. That world remained a storehouse of resources and commodities around which conflict or cooperation revolves. There was, for realist and institutionalist alike, a clear separation between the external controllable world and the rational political world of hard decisionmaking: a view of the *use* of nature based on instrumental reason was the order of the day.[12] Later chapters will consider at length the basis, evolution, and implications of this view. Here, it is crucial to recognize that the differences between these two theoretical models are primarily concerned with the institutional mechanisms that can be established to "deal with" the natural world. These mechanisms could consist of collective arrangements (e.g., to protect the ozone layer), the joint protection of a natural resource (e.g., the Antarctic), or rules and regulations with regard to scientific breakthroughs (e.g., genetic modification). Each school of thought believes itself to be presenting the tools with which the policymaker can deal with the actually existing world. Institutionalists are merely attempting to provide a more accurate and subtler picture on the basis of which to evaluate policy options: to refine rather than redefine realism. In neither school of thought is there a basic awareness of the constitutive nature of knowledge, despite a recognition of the role of ideas in the formulation of policies.

We have had decades of institution building, however, and the environment has continued to deteriorate. Those articulating the incrementalist management solution will respond that, while we have not gone far enough fast enough, we must work within the boundaries as they exist in the messy world of interstate competition. The activity around regime formation continues to be examined by international relations experts in the hope that the existing case studies will help us to better understand the institutional mechanisms and thereby lead us to more effective and efficient institution building.[13] Research priorities are determined accordingly, and the resulting application of such research allows for the strengthening and deepening of the arrangements. The legal norms become more rigorous and the codification of common standards continues apace. At the same time we lose biodiversity, the hole in the ozone layer grows, the ocean continues to be polluted, and a whole host of other environmental problems make themselves known to us. Crucially, there are additional issues—such as genetic modification and gene mapping—that demand a level of moral and critical reflection extraordinarily difficult to achieve when the guiding theories are merely providing tools for dealing with "reality." Perhaps there is indeed more to the world's environmental problems than merely the intransigence of a few state leaders or the ill-informed actions of a few transnational capitalists. Could there be something fundamentally wrong with the way in which the questions are being posed and the problems are being answered?

This reflection returns us to the point made earlier that international relations theory has not been terribly good at reflecting upon the process of theorizing itself. If theories are seen as merely maps of existing reality, the framing of the issues is limited at the outset. A different type of theory is perhaps necessary.

Inspired by Critical Theory, some international relations scholars have in recent years attempted to broaden the discussion of the interstate system so that it becomes more than merely a picture of reality. By drawing on Max Horkheimer's insights into the nature of knowledge, Robert Cox has been most articulate in describing the various roles of theory:

> Beginning with its problematic, theory can serve two distinct purposes. One is a simple, direct response: to be a guide to help solve the problems posed within the terms of the particular perspective which was the point of departure. The other is more reflective upon the process of theorizing itself: to become clearly aware of the perspective

which gives rise to theorizing, and its relation to other perspectives (to achieve a perspective on perspectives); and to open up the possibility of choosing a different valid perspective from which the problematic becomes one of creating an alternative world. Each of these purposes gives rise to a different kind of theory.

The first purpose gives rise to *problem-solving theory*. It takes the world as it finds it, with the prevailing social and power relationships and the institutions into which they are organized, as the given framework for action. The general aim of problem-solving is to make these relationships and institutions work smoothly by dealing effectively with particular sources of trouble. Since the general pattern of institutions and relationships is not called into question, particular problems can be considered in relation to the specialized areas of activity in which they arise. . . .

The second purpose leads to *critical theory*. It is critical in the sense that it stands apart from the prevailing order of the world and asks how that order came about. Critical theory, unlike problem-solving theory, does not take institutions and social and power relations for granted but calls them into question by concerning itself with their origins and how and whether they might be in the process of changing. It is directed toward an appraisal of the very framework for action, or problematic, which problem-solving theory accepts as its parameters. Critical theory is directed to the social and political complex as a whole rather than to the separate parts.[14]

By adopting a methodology and epistemology that accepts the existing world order as a given and that seeks merely to solve problems within it, the realists and the neoliberal institutionalists—be they academics, activists, diplomats, or state leaders—are thus fulfilling a conservative agenda, for it is no less ideological to seek the maintenance of a system than it is to seek to change it. Cox is correct to argue that the assumption of an unchangeable structure is more than a methodological convenience and indeed extends to an ideological bias. Indeed, it should be clear that such theories serve the interests of those who are comfortable with the given order.[15] If the incremental environmental action advocated by the problem-solvers is seen as a demonstrable failure, the case is more easily made for a critical approach.

CRITICAL THEORY AND THE NATURAL WORLD

Reflexivity has increased within the discipline of international relations. Not surprisingly, the theoretical input from feminist, postmodern, and neo-Gramscian perspectives (to name but three) has greatly improved the state of the discipline generally: the "restructuring of international relations theory" has, it would appear, begun in earnest.[16] Many scholars interested in international environmental issues have begun to critique what can safely be called the status quo presentation of the international environmental agenda, and their works will be drawn on throughout this book. This book, however, is not intended as an examination of a particular theoretical model. Nor does it limit its consideration to theories of international relations. I believe that in order to offer a comprehensive critique of the issues included in the presentation of green diplomacy, it is fruitful to draw on a range of insights made initially by certain members of the Institute for Social Research (commonly referred to as the Frankfurt School) and their own (albeit not uniform) brand of Critical Theory. Many of these insights have indeed already helped to direct the turn to greater reflexivity within the academic discipline of international relations.

Established in 1923, the Frankfurt School emerged as a dynamic and influential center of scholarship under the leadership of its third director, Max Horkheimer, appointed in 1930. By drawing on a wide range of disciplines, the school attempted to transcend the normally accepted disciplinary divisions of those seeking an understanding of the operation of modern society. Insights from philosophy, sociology, social psychology, political science, economics, and cultural studies were all brought to bear on the relationship between theory and practice with the express desire to explore the potential for political, social, and economic transformation of modern societies.[17]

To undertake this critique of green diplomacy, I want to draw mainly on the writings of Max Horkheimer, Theodor Adorno, and, perhaps especially, Herbert Marcuse. Together, their writings offer insights into a range of areas impacting dramatically on the operation of power relations within society and, by extension, to problems of social organization and environmental destruction. The thoughtful considerations presented by these writers on science, technology, language, aesthetics, capitalism, and perhaps especially on the modern bureaucratic state's ability to absorb and diffuse dissent, are of import for today's consideration of global environmental problems.[18]

Some may consider the application of such concepts and tools to the international realm a slightly dubious exercise given the fact that these writers, concerned as they were with the fate of the individual in advanced industrial societies, had little explicit to say about the realm of political activity known as international relations. They did, however, have much to say about the linkages between knowledge and power, the impact of instrumental rationality, and the destructive practices (in human psychological, environmental, and economic terms) of capitalism. In attempting to understand social processes, and possibilities for transformation, we should surely remain open to useful maps wherever we might find them. More specifically, however, aside from the generally useful conceptual tools they offered, the efficacy of these critiques stems from the fact that the global order is currently in a period of flux not dissimilar to that which prompted the Frankfurt School into action in the first instance. Many of the ideological, cultural, and technical mechanisms of domination that were of interest then have strong and increasing relevance for those seeking a deeper understanding of international political relations now.

These writers were inspired to work across disciplinary boundaries—to *reintegrate* them—in an attempt to understand the changing configurations of economy, society, and culture that they saw developing within capitalism. They believed that orthodox Marxism needed reinvigorating, not rejecting, in order to truly comprehend the modern world and the transition to the new stage of capitalist development that they were witnessing. Attempting to understand the apparent failure of the socialist project to materialize as expected (and predicted) by Marxian orthodoxy, they drew on Marx's early work and on the writings—in particular—of Freud, Weber, Hegel, and Lukács in an attempt to understand prevalent techniques and structures of domination.[19] Equipped with a multidisciplinary understanding of the role of culture, science, technology, and capital in the reproduction and transformation of society, the brand of Critical Theory developed by the Frankfurt School offered insight into the very different forms of social control and exploitation utilized in different stages of capitalist development. Douglas Kellner has argued persuasively that it is precisely Critical Theory's interest in responding to succeeding crises of capitalism and Marxism that should be of special interest today as we attempt to understand the dramatic changes from state capitalism to what he refers to as "Techno-Capitalism"[20] and what I will refer to as transnational or global capitalism, which results, I argue, from the currently fashionable and dramatically preponderant policies of neoliberal economics.

The discourse of globalization, with its air of inevitability—President Clinton's "great tide, inexorably wearing away at the established order of things"[21]—serves to mystify the fact that state structures have long served the interests of capital. While its internationalization may be a qualitatively new phase, the power of the state to control and influence developments—in addition to its role as a facilitator and defender of the free flow of capital, a glorified transmission belt for capital mobility—is both ever-changing and ever-present.[22] Although my focus is on the environment, and my critique will be confined to those aspects of modern society (state and global) that impact on that issue, the general mystique surrounding globalization itself constitutes such an impact. The failure of both realist and neoliberal institutionalist theory to demystify and critique the myriad and interlinked processes that have been collected under the buzzword *globalization* translates directly into inadequate prescriptions for saving the natural environment threatened *by* the form of international capital exchange that constitutes neoliberal orthodoxy. The realists argue that states compete, as they always have, to protect their national interest. The addition of so-called environmental security issues (by which they really mean nothing more than an old-fashioned competition for scarce natural resources) does not fundamentally change their calculation of power in the international realm.[23] The institutionalists seek to impress on us their belief in the efficiency of rules-based economic and environmental regimes as a protection of our interests; they accept the myth of the demise of state sovereignty and see in it an opportunity to limit the more environmentally destructive practices of previous eras. There is, in fact, as we shall explore, the development of the most intriguing argument at the basis of the incrementalists' views that economic regimes to establish rules for trade are in and of themselves "green."

The belief that economics plays a central role in all social processes is the thread that ties together the attempts of the Critical Theorists to illustrate and understand new and evolving forms of domination and destruction. It is, I believe, essential that we continue to seek deeper understandings of attempts to make existing market logic appear inevitable and beyond contestation and also that we maintain a critical interest in the role of science, technology, language, and technical rationality, in order to properly understand the contradictions and containments in modern forms of capitalism and state/interstate organization. It is not within the scope of this work to undertake a comprehensive critique of the current shape of so-called international society.[24] It is my belief, however, that a consideration of global politics with a focus on green diplomacy and with these issues in mind will assist us in our efforts to critique the failed promise of the incrementalist in addition to seeing the possibilities inherent in the system that, if released, would lead to a greener future. The variety of ways in which the tools offered by the Critical Theorists will be used are set out below.

There are a number of interesting works available that draw on the insights of the Frankfurt School to consider environmental degradation specifically, pointing to the broader political, social, economic, and indeed theoretical roots of the problem.[25] At the level of global political relations, however, this analysis is not as well developed as it could be, especially given the nature of today's global environmental problems and the proposed interstate solutions. Indeed, the protesters against globalization make the links, but the academic community has thus far largely failed to present a sustained multidimensional analysis of the modern way of thinking and its international manifestations vis-à-vis the environment.[26] My intent is to offer such a critique of status quo international relations and to destabilize the rationale presented by those writers on global environmental problems who defend an incrementalist approach toward sustainability and seek to work within existing structures for change.

TOOLS FOR THE CRITIQUE

The early Frankfurt School theorists offered a rich and complex set of tools with which they sought to understand and critique the society in which they lived. There are inevitable problems in attempting to apply their ideas to the international level, but they are certainly not insurmountable.

The most important contribution these writers made was to rethink the roots of our technical-rational way of viewing the world—both natural and social. Although they did not have their critique focused specifically on the environmental impact of the modern way of thinking, it certainly pointed to the myriad problems that its adoption has led to. Developed in relation to this central problematic, the Frankfurt School writers also considered the role of language, capitalism, and forces for stabilizing dissent. Marcuse added to this critique by looking for the possible sources of resistance to the status quo forces. Each of these areas of critique are considered briefly below and will be developed throughout the following chapters.

Modernity and Ways of Thinking About the Natural World

The body of ideas identified as the Enlightenment—which took as its core concepts science, rationality, and progress—had become firmly established by the eighteenth century. Central to its powerful worldview was a belief in the need to dominate nature. Stemming from a radical critique of the power of superstition and myth, and building on latent socioeconomic tendencies within Western civilization, Enlightenment thinkers presented the exhilarating possibility of knowledge being used to free human beings from the limitations of an unreasonable social order. The application of science to this project was expected to be completely objective and, as such, able to answer effectively questions of import for sustaining and improving the human condition.

The promise of liberation inherent in these ideas was a powerful one and its impact profound. One of the most influential advocates of the Enlightenment worldview was the seventeenth-century British scientist, philosopher, and politician Francis Bacon. Bacon argued that there could be a progressive march toward certain knowledge and that each generation would build on the findings of the previous one. Central to his belief of scientific progress was a view of the importance of dominating and molding nature, wresting from it the secrets of the working of the universe. Bacon was clear that the benefits of scientific knowledge would be extended to the entire human race. Through its scientific endeavors, "the human race [could] recover that right over nature which belongs to it by divine bequest."[27] Humankind could return to the Garden of Eden through the power of knowledge; this was to be the goal. Bacon was not the only—or even the most scientifically proficient—advocate of the new rationality; his significance rests upon his ability to popularize the main ideas.

This radically revised view of science was further transformed when linked to a mechanistic view of nature and Cartesian rationality. Descartes's dictum "I think, therefore I am" succinctly sums up the central concept of the separation of humans from their natural surroundings, a split widely regarded as a major source of the modern understanding of our place in nature and our resulting, widespread alienation from the natural world.[28]

By the twentieth century, it was apparent to some that the emancipatory promise of the Enlightenment had not only not been fulfilled, but also was leading to a new level of human captivity and barbarism. It was to this issue that the Critical Theorists directed their attention. In their pathbreaking *Dialectic of Enlightenment* (1944), Adorno and Horkheimer provided a sustained and intelligent critique of science, technology, and instrumental reason.[29] Beginning their inquiry with the ancient world and its myths, they presented a nuanced understanding of the development of objectification and the inevitable domination of the natural world that results. Adorno and Horkheimer argued that the form of knowledge and its attendant methodology cannot be considered separately from social and political structures. The uses to which the exercise of knowledge are put are more likely to serve the interests of the few, with the application of science to find new and better ways to exploit natural resources or to improve industrial technologies a more likely outcome than a better existence for all. Despite its failure to fulfill its promise of liberation, however, the privileging of this form of instrumental rationality had become pervasive and deeply embedded. The dominance of this way of seeing the world, and the corresponding elimination of all forms of thought that ran counter to it, had serious repercussions for the natural environment. The role of science and technology in society became, as a result of the supremacy of instrumental reason, a method establishing domination as both norm and goal. "What men want to learn from nature is how to use it in order to dominate it and other men. That is the only aim. Ruthlessly, in despite of itself, the Enlightenment has extinguished any trace of its own self-consciousness."[30]

Once embedded, the technical control of all aspects of human existence became accepted: a new myth was inevitable. In Douglas Kellner's words: "All other modes of thought, ranging from myth and religion to critical and speculative philosophy, were deemed by enlightenment rationality as inferior and ineffective in the struggle to dominate nature. Against this position . . . Horkheimer and Adorno argue that, while enlightenment is often posed against myth, enlightenment itself becomes myth, and myth is itself permeated with enlightenment rationality."[31]

This critique of the modern form of rationality was not intended to lead to a glorification of a supposedly simpler past—the call of Critical Theory is explicitly *not* for a return to a romantic prehistory: "we are the heirs, for better or worse, of the Enlightenment and technological progress. To oppose these by regressing to more primitive stages does not alleviate the permanent crisis they have brought about. On the contrary, such expedients lead from historically reasonable to utterly barbaric forms of social domination. The sole way of assisting nature is to unshackle its seeming opposite, independent thought."[32] I cite this appeal to be clear about the intention of my critique of green diplomacy.

This book does not offer a solution based on green romanticism. Rather, it suggests that the answers lie not so much in the past as in the liberating of possibilities masked by existing social relations.

The status quo theories of realism and neoliberal institutionalism, each deeply imbued with the ethos and assumptions of instrumental rationality, accept unquestioningly Enlightenment logic and method and seek to frame environmental issues solely in terms of problems to be solved or managed separately from a consideration of social and economic processes. Both schools believe there is a world of knowable facts and that normative values cannot—indeed must not—enter into the consideration of politically possible options. In international relations—as in other disciplines—the existing mainstream approaches serve to maintain the system, never to liberate the potential existing within it. It is, as a result, doomed from the start in its quest to deal successfully with the fundamental causes, or even consequences, of environmental destruction.

A critical theory approach takes us beyond the false fact-value split of Enlightenment thought. From the beginning of his time as director of the Institute for Social Research, Horkheimer sought to make clear the high costs of the disciplinary divisions so commonly accepted in the social sciences. In calling for the reintegration of the disciplines, the institute's program then became one of attempting to think about specific problems in more complex and holistic ways. In the case of environmental politics, I will demonstrate that not only do artificial intellectual divisions continue, but also that the continual carving up of specific problems serves to obfuscate the linkages that must be recognized. We need to evaluate the human, ecological, economic, and psychological costs of current environmental problems; this is extraordinarily difficult given the continued supremacy of instrumental reason. The solutions put forward by regime theorists and advocates of liberal economic relations will be treated as an example of the limited way of thinking hindering efforts at restoring ecological health.

Herbert Marcuse's work reaffirmed the broad lines of his colleagues' conclusions while helping to bring the repressive social institutions that go hand in hand with the objectification of external nature into sharper focus. Marcuse clarified the ways in which the dominant scientific method operates in the service of the prevailing interests of a society, and how problems solved through this method thus stemmed from and reinforced those interests. His writings point to the way in which the individual rationality that triumphed over forms of myth and superstition—and thereby placed the individual in a critical stance outside social organization—during the Enlightenment period was subsequently undermined by the basis of instrumental rationality itself. Furthermore, Marcuse argued, the application of scientific thought is prevalent in everyday discourse and behavior, leading irrevocably to the same logic and rationality of domination.[33] In this way Marcuse's interest in the costs of technical rationality are directly applied to the practices of modern society—including those of ecological destruction. For this reason, Marcuse's understanding of the irrationality of seeking scientific-technical solutions to society's problems will be of great import to my critique of green diplomacy.

It is the preeminence of the scientific method, privileged as it is in all areas of inquiry, that has the inevitable effect of pushing any consideration outside the realm of problem solving and into the world of values, the very concept of which then takes on a pejorative connotation. Subjectivity may be provided for in a metaphysical manner but, as such, it cannot be proven rationally, and cannot therefore rise to equal standing with objective findings. Any attempt to raise moral or ethical justifications for doing—or not doing—something becomes caught in this logic. Increasingly, then, values—however morally pressing they might be seen to be—became secondary to the *real business of life*.[34] Inevitably, any idea that raised questions about the rational project for societal organization—or sought to suggest that there might be a moral, divine, or merely humane reason for pausing for reflection that could not be verified by scientific method—became suspect, perceived as an attempt to distract attention from the "guaranteed" progress of modern society, or dismissed as a mask for a hidden agenda. In terms of green diplomacy, as we shall see, even a supposedly value-laden concept such as sustainable development is dramatically undermined by the reliance on scientific answers and the quest for technological solutions.

Again, it is wrong to consider these early members of the Frankfurt School as anti-science or anti-technology—their insights were into the social uses of each via the mode of rationality. The domination of nature is not a foregone conclusion of science; what we need to concentrate on is the structure of knowledge, which, given its technical rationalist formulation, is indeed destructive. The structure of science is socially bound and a change in social relations could lead to a different kind of science.[35] Marcuse has been criticized for not taking his ideas about new science far enough, and while it may be true that he did not provide the specifics of what such a framework might look like, the arguments he presents most certainly offer a fruitful vein of inquiry. Marcuse's arguments about science and technology can most usefully be considered alongside the arguments of those scientists who have taken issue with the prevailing hegemony of instrumental methodologies.[36] I will return to Marcuse's writings on science in Chapter 5 to demonstrate the importance of new thinking within scientific method itself in any quest for an environmentally sound path of development.

In sum, it is the unquestioned acceptance of the use of instrumental reason as a means for dealing with serious ecological problems that is the problem—not science or technology itself. The reason why most current efforts to resolve serious environmental problems are gravely limited before they even begin is precisely because of their inability to move beyond damaging and unreflexive forms of rationality. The rules and regulations (the regimes) with which the state system is content are, in fact, mere applications of a science and technology deliberately and artificially delinked from social and political considerations. This should not be seen as a conspiracy—it is merely the acceptance of a form of rationality that is so deeply embedded in our society as to make a challenge to it very difficult without recourse to the tools and ideas presented by these critical theorists.

Language of Total Administration

In addition to recognizing the extent of the domination of technical rationality, it is also important to consider the way in which the very language we speak serves to reinforce the status quo by becoming closed to the potential dynamic inherent in discourse. The language of fact and description, Marcuse argues, leaves no space for a discussion of potentially disruptive alternatives. Marcuse examines in illuminating detail the ability of the closed language of the type of discourse so often seen in modern societies to unify opposites and to assimilate potentially critical terms in a manner that deprives them of any critical intent.[37] Language, Marcuse argues, reflects the technical and rational, but it also becomes an instrument of control precisely because it reduces activity and relationships to operational terms. Acronyms take on loaded and fixed meaning, and concepts sanctioned by intellectuals shape the discourse in predetermined ways that "govern the analysis of human reality."[38] Language can become a key means of silencing critical dissent when concepts are deployed to reduce the tension between the existing reality and radical challenges to it. The operational treatment of the concept of sustainable development will be shown to assume such a political function and will be analyzed as an example of a "therapeutic and operational concept" designed to pacify protest and absorb critical thinking.[39]

Economics and the Environment

Although the manner in which the environmental crisis is considered vis-à-vis instrumental logic is of crucial import, so too is the reality of the capitalist system. Here the early Frankfurt School writers can assist with a consideration of the economic roots of environmentally destructive practices. The ecological impact of capitalist logic, with its inbuilt celebration of consumption and waste, was of major interest to the Critical Theorists. It is, however, a concern almost entirely absent from mainstream green diplomacy. Indeed, the focus of the green incrementalist demonstrably fails to theorize the true interconnections of capital, science, and technology. The hope held out for collaborative arrangements—regimes—is telling indeed; the theory of regime formation contains within it no clear conceptualization of the state or any special interest in the role of capital exchange. Perhaps of even greater import, due to its carefully partitioned realm of study (the impact of disciplinary limits among other things), regime theory absolves itself of responsibility to consider—to any extent—the global restructuring of capital and the possible ramifications this might have for the environmental health and well-being of the planet. Indeed, the only time the economic relations between states is considered in terms of environmental issues is when multilateral economic institutions (such as the World Trade Organization, the Organization for Economic Cooperation and Development, and the like) posit the claim that the "freeing of trade" will undoubtedly result in higher environmental standards around the world.

As mentioned above, we are living in an age of contradiction comparable to that of the early Frankfurt School writers. Whereas they attempted to come to terms with a dramatic shift in the nature of production in the movement toward monopoly capitalism, we are witnessing a profound shift toward the transnationalization of capital. A constant factor in the two situations is the ecological cost involved. As Marcuse argued three decades ago: "The process by which nature is subjected to the violence of exploitation and pollution is first of all an economic one (an aspect of the mode of production), but it is a political process as well."[40] The success of the cheerleaders for "free" trade in convincing us that more trade and economic growth necessarily equals a cleaner environment—the irrational presented as rational—means that this debate must be revisited in both its economic and its political contexts.

Containment

Critical Theory also provides the necessary tools for examining the many ways in which the prevailing order maintains its control of the debate by masking dangerous practices and packaging the debate in ways that obscure the destructive forces at work in the system; by containing, in short, the impact and radicalism of critiques aimed at it. As mentioned above, economics is considered only to the extent that its relations are seen to be beneficial to the environment. In addition to a critique of the dubious logic utilized to make that claim, it is also important to destabilize the popular concept of sustainable development so favored by the advocates of green diplomacy. It is with the widespread acceptance of this concept that the status quo has had the most success in containing and stabilizing earlier green critiques of society and in supporting and reaffirming existing structures and power relations—both at the state level as well as at the level of global relations. Indeed, the response to mass protest movements in a number of (mostly western) states in the 1960s and 1970s, movements that examined the environmental costs of economic growth, was the suggestion that the way to avoid ecological destruction was to trade more and ensure the continued economic growth patterns of the world system. Thus defined, sustainable development is an interesting concept and has been adopted by international organizations, multilateral economic bodies, governments, and even many environmental organizations. It bears a staggering resemblance (as I shall demonstrate in greater detail in Chapter 2) to Herbert Marcuse's concept of *one-dimensional thought*.

Resistance

In addition to a careful examination of the strategies of containment, a critical theory of international environmental relations must consider as well the areas of contestation and struggle. Where there are attempts to stabilize and unify, so too are there underlying struggles and challenges to the existing social order. On the one hand, international and domestic institutions possess the determination and resources to contain and absorb demands for a qualitative change to both the way we perceive the natural world and the demands for changes to social structures that necessarily stem from such altered worldviews. But on the other hand, we can clearly see the tendencies that threaten to break through the containment and look at the potential masked by the presented logic of the status quo. To argue that the two tendencies exist is not a contradiction, and this is most obvious in the debates surrounding the direction of international economic relations.

It seems clear that the current attempts to contain the contradictions of transnationalized capital are being challenged by forceful movements (the plural is deliberate and accurate) seeking to make links about the social, economic, and political costs of the supposedly inevitable and desirable process of globalization. Not finding it to be such a desirable set of policies, protesters take to the streets around the world and are a force of contradiction to—and negation of—the promises of the international institutions with the power to make macropolicies and dictate micropolicies for the states that make up the neoliberal community. Of course the power to contain is tremendous, but we must look at the resistance to it as well. Liberating potential exists within the system and, by drawing on the insights of critical social theory, we can seek to understand the potential for the existing struggles in addition to where/when and in what fashion they could be strengthened. Marcuse's concept of the "Great Refusal" will be used to draw out the "protest against that which is" vis-à-vis the environmental crisis, and this will, of necessity, take us to the anti-globalization debates.[41]

Long before the advent of postmodern critiques of the severe limitations of language and presentations of reality, the early writings of the Frankfurt School sought to remind us that there are levels of domination and exploitation that run much deeper than those of economic and/or political control. In an age of the celebration of the globalized marketplace and its reification as an inevitable, desirable outcome of human progress, the Frankfurt School's reminder of the price we pay for an acceptance of instrumental reason is worth returning to as its celebration and affirmation finds its way into the governance literature of international relations writers and practitioners.[42]

While it remains the case that the bulk of regulation and control that individuals face continues to be within the state, protest groups are focusing more and more on the impact of regulations and control exerted by institutions of international governance. The exposure of the limits of green diplomacy *should* allow for the illumination of some serious flaws within the international governance literature. The extent to which the global system has become administered along the lines of those presented by the Critical Theorists is a necessary component of this critique.

It is also important to recognize the contradictions within the very logic presented by green diplomacy, and this is an interesting prospect if we undertake an "immanent critique" of the promises of it. The method, as defined by David Held,

> starts with the conceptual principles and standards of an object, and unfolds their implications and consequences. Then it re-examines and reassesses the object . . . in light of these implications and consequences. Critique proceeds, so to speak, "from within" and hopes to avoid, thereby, the charge that its concepts impose irrelevant criteria of evaluation on the object. As a result, a new understanding of the object is generated—a new comprehension of contradictions and possibilities. The original image of the object is transcended and the object itself is brought partly into flux.[43]

This form of critique will be undertaken throughout the book, and the promises and concepts of the status quo approach to environmental degradation will be examined with a view to revealing the contradictions and tensions inherent in them. It is a result of these contradictions—experienced at a commonsense level by the anti-globalization protesters—that an important element of destabilization of status quo logic can be clearly witnessed. It is the unkeepable promises (the so obviously *unsustainable* sustainable development of international growth patterns) and the irrationality of the supposedly logical and reasonable responses of the incrementalists and fixers (new chemicals to deal with destruction wrought by old chemicals originally introduced for exactly the same purpose)[44] that can both feed the existing protest movements and demonstrate what is necessary for the promises to be fulfilled.

Resistance comes from and informs the structures of the system and the force of ideas. We need to be concerned with what Marcuse referred to as the "historical alternatives which haunt the established society as subversive tendencies and forces."[45] Neither the forces of stabilization nor those of destabilization—or negation, to use Marcuse's concept— are predetermined but rather play themselves out in opposition to each other. The struggle of those against the status quo view of international environmental issues will be viewed in this light.

CONCLUSION

This book is not an in-depth examination of Critical Theory, but it does seek to put the tools and ideas presented by its early articulators to work in order to destabilize the standard presentation of the incrementalist approach to global ecological health. Supported by many academics, governments, international organizations, and business elites, the mainstream route for dealing with shared environmental crises is based on a number of assumptions: (1) the role of instrumental logic will provide answers to scientific and technological questions, ensuring that ecological balance is sustained; (2) market structures—if properly managed—can respond to such problems that present themselves as ecological externalities; (3) the concept of sustainable development provides us with the framework within which the market can develop along ecologically sound lines; and (4) green diplomacy—that is, the multilateral efforts at finding collaborative agreements (regimes) to place effective limits on human action—will succeed in establishing the necessary bureaucratic mechanisms to ensure environmental protection.

Each of these assumptions will be examined in relation to one another, in the following pages. All are consequences, in fact, of the same unreflexive rationality—a fundamentally unenlightened worldview—that Horkheimer, Adorno, Marcuse, and others saw as leading the modern world to disaster. For exponents and practitioners of this unreflexive rationality—such as the status quo international relations theorists—there is a basic assumption that we already know how to think clearly and effectively about the problems facing us: the assumption, in other words, that *how* we think is *not* one of those problems. For Critical Theory, however, it is the core of the problematic: existing ways of thinking are indeed a major obstacle blocking our escape route. How can we begin to find the best way out if we do not even know we are trapped? Understanding—demystifying—the given situation is the essential first step, but it must go further. A critical theory of international environmental relations should also make clear the contradictions and failures of green diplomacy and, perhaps most important of all, move beyond the critique to point in the direction of alternatives. And finally, we should keep remembering that "what is denounced as 'utopian' is no longer that which has 'no place' and cannot have any place in the historical universe, but rather that which is blocked from coming about by the power of the established societies."[46]

NOTES

1. The concept of *regime* is complex and will be explored in great depth in Chapter 4. In basic terms, regimes are the institutionalized agreements that

provide the rules and norms governing state behavior in a specific issue area. In international legal terms, they are held to be binding. For a good introduction to the concept, see Little, "International Regimes," pp. 231–247. See also Vogler, *The Global Commons.*

2. I borrow this concept from Brenton, *The Greening of Machiavelli.*

3. I use capital letters here to distinguish the Frankfurt School theory from other theories that are referred to as critical theories in a more generic sense (e.g., postmodernism and feminist theories).

4. Greene, "Environmental Issues," p. 324.

5. Ibid.

6. Morgenthau, *Politics Among Nations,* p. 111.

7. Ibid., p. 4. There are tensions within Morgenthau's work, however, about the scientific nature of realism. Subsequent realist theorists—most notably Kenneth N. Waltz—attempted to rid the theory of its ambiguities and make it more "scientific." See Waltz, *Theory of International Politics.*

8. For a critique of this literature, see Barnett, "Destabilizing the Environment-Conflict Thesis."

9. Keohane and Nye, *Power and Interdependence.*

10. I will adopt the title of neoliberal institutionalist at this point, but the variations within the broadly defined liberal school of international relations will become more important in later chapters. The internationalists, for example, believe more strongly in the potential of international trade to deliver global peace and prosperity. The institutionalists, however, believe that although a free trade regime will provide incentives for environmental improvement, they are skeptical about the claims. See Little, "International Regimes." The views on free trade and the environment have come to the fore in the international monetary institutions and in the declaratory policies of government leaders and therefore become very important in Chapter 3, where I discuss the claims made about the "green benefits" of global trade relations.

11. Baldwin, ed., *Neorealism and Neoliberalism.*

12. For a fulsome critique of the limitations of these theories from an ecological perspective, see Laferriere, "Emancipating International Relations Theory." Doran, "Earth, Power, Knowledge," offers an introduction to the subfield of international relations referred to as global environmental politics and the development of a critical dimension to it. Saurin, "Global Environmental Degradation, Modernity, and Environmental Knowledge," looks at global environmental degradation and its relationship to modernization.

13. For an excellent example of looking at case studies to learn how better to formulate policies, see Young and Osherenko, eds., *Polar Politics.*

14. Cox, "Social Forces, States, and World Orders," pp. 207–208. For Horkheimer's distinction between traditional and critical theory, see his *Critical Theory,* pp. 188–243.

15. Ibid., p. 209.

16. For a clear and interesting presentation of the attempts in this direction, see Neufeld, *The Restructuring of International Relations Theory;* and George, *Discourses of Global Politics.*

17. The key participants in these early years included Max Horkheimer, Theodor Adorno, Herbert Marcuse, Erich Fromm (until his later break with the

school), Franz Neuman, Leo Lowenthal, Friedrich Pollock, and Walter Benjamin (until his untimely death in 1940). Jürgen Habermas is the major figure in this tradition today. For an excellent collection of essays, see Bronner and Kellner, *Critical Theory and Society.* For useful introductions to the project of developing a critical theory of society, see Held, *Introduction to Critical Theory;* and Kellner, *Critical Theory, Marxism, and Modernity.*

18. There are problems, however, with some of the arguments and views of these writers. The sharpness of Horkheimer's critique dulled in later years, and Adorno's pessimism got the best of him. Although Marcuse continued to modify his views and deal with changing circumstances throughout his life (i.e., he continued to *apply* critical theory to his own work), there are several aspects of his work with which I disagree. This being said, it is important to reclaim some of the critiques and demonstrate their validity to today's issues.

19. For discussion of the influences on the early members of the Frankfurt School, see Kellner, *Critical Theory, Marxism, and Modernity;* and Held, *Introduction to Critical Theory.* For the debates within Marxism about its usefulness in understanding the ecological consequences of capitalism, see, for example, Benton, "Marxism and Natural Limits"; Foster, "Marx and the Environment"; Grundman, "The Ecological Challenge to Marxism"; and Leiss, *The Domination of Nature.*

20. See Kellner, *Critical Theory, Marxism, and Modernity,* especially chap. 7. Kellner, writing in 1989, speaks of technocapitalism as a means of identifying new configurations of capitalism, but he does not see a shift to a different stage of capitalism. While I, too, am not convinced of the argument that we have moved to a new stage, it does seem that the increasingly global nature of capital formation, witnessed in the decade since Kellner conceived of the idea of technocapitalism, justifies the use of a concept that points to its essential quality—that is, its transnationalization.

21. Clinton, "Remarks by the President to the Fifty-second Session of the United Nations General Assembly," p. 2.

22. For an excellent consideration of the role of the state in the globalized economy, see Panitch, "Globalisation and the State." I do not wish to enter the debates over the meaning of *globalization* in detail. Suffice it to say that for the purposes of the argument presented in this book, *globalization* can be used as a shorthand way of referring to a transnationalization of capitalism that is presented as inevitable but that is, in fact, the result of specific policy directions and is driven by international institutions with market liberalization as their objective.

23. Scholte, "Beyond the Buzzword." Scholte provides an interesting introduction into the ways in which a variety of international relations theories conceptualize the "phenomenon" of globalization.

24. The concept of "international society" is in itself dubious. In my opinion, the current neoliberal institutionalist uses this concept as part of its obfuscation of transnational capitalism. The concept of "global civil society" is interesting to consider in this context. See, for example, Colas, "The Promises of International Civil Society."

25. See, for example, Merchant, *Ecology;* Leiss, *The Domination of Nature;* and Luke, *Ecocritique* (especially chap. 7). For a critique of the Frankfurt

School's engagement with environmental issues, see Eckersley, *Environmentalism and Political Theory.*

26. An exception to this is Paterson, *Understanding Global Environmental Politics.*

27. Bacon, as quoted in Merchant, *The Death of Nature,* p. 172. See also Bacon, *The New Organon and Related Writings.*

28. For a discussion of the way in which Descartes's failings have been discussed without shaking our view in the basic split, see Evernden, *The Natural Alien.*

29. Resistance to the dualism that Enlightenment thought advocates has existed throughout the period. For a consideration of the response of the Romantic movement and the way it "nourishes ecocentrism," see Pepper, *Modern Environmentalism,* pp. 188–205. See also the interesting discussion of the Romantics in Bate, *The Song of the Earth.* For an explicit view of one Romantic writer's rejection of the Baconian view of mastering nature, see Mary Shelley's *Frankenstein.* Shelley's Dr. Frankenstein proclaims: "So much has been done, exclaimed the soul of Frankenstein—more, far more, will I achieve; treading in the steps already marked, I will pioneer a new way, explore unknown powers, and unfold to the world the deepest mysteries of creation" (p. 33). Shelley points to the costs of a scientific view that proclaims nature the mere subject of inquiry. For further consideration of Shelley and a critique of Enlightenment science, see Mellor, "A Feminist Critique of Science."

30. Adorno and Horkheimer, *Dialectic of Enlightenment,* p. 4. For another critique of this way of thinking and its implicit responsibility for the Holocaust, see Bauman, *Modernity and the Holocaust.* Bauman sums up the argument thus: "from the Enlightenment on, the modern world was distinguished by its activist, engineering attitude toward nature and toward itself. Science was not to be conducted for its own sake; it was seen as, first and foremost, an instrument of awesome power allowing its holder to improve on reality, to re-shape it according to human plans and designs, and to assist it in its drive to self-perfection" (p. 70). Note that Bauman's argument is that the Nazi project was a product of our commonplace way of seeing the world—not something separate and opposed to it.

31. Kellner, *Critical Theory, Marxism, and Modernity,* p. 90.

32. Horkheimer, *Eclipse of Reason,* p. 127.

33. Marcuse, *One Dimensional Man,* especially pp. 154–166. See also his much earlier explication of the issue in "Some Social Implications of Modern Technology."

34. Ibid., p. 149.

35. I am not using Jürgen Habermas's critique precisely, because he attempts to rehabilitate Enlightenment rationality in such a way as to deny the possibility of a different kind of science. Habermas's view is that instrumental reason is essential in the human treatment of the natural world; it is misapplied when it is used in the sphere of human communication. This, it seems to me, is a retreat from the important critique offered by the first generation of Frankfurt School members and does not offer us sufficient insight either into the roots of the environmental problem or, indeed, for possible ways forward. For

Habermas's critique of Marcuse as a "romantic hangover of German Idealism," see his *Toward a Rational Society,* chap. 6. For a full and interesting discussion of the comparison between Habermas and Marcuse in this regard, see Alford, *Science and the Revenge of Nature.* And see also H. T. Wilson, "Science, Critique, and Criticism." Wilson offers interesting insights into the debate between Habermas and Marcuse and considers this debate in relation to Habermas's ideas in relation to Popper. For a straightforward presentation of the central arguments of the first-generation Frankfurt School, see Agger, "On Science as Domination."

36. See, for example, Bohm, *Wholeness and the Implicate Order,* and Lewontin, *Biology as Ideology.*

37. Marcuse, *One Dimensional Man,* pp. 90–104.

38. Ibid., p. 106.

39. For a further discussion of the so-called therapeutic concept, see ibid., pp. 107–108.

40. Marcuse, "Ecology and Revolution," p. 52.

41. Marcuse, *One Dimensional Man,* p. 63. In this passage, Marcuse is referring to art and its "rationality of negation." The aesthetic dimension that was of great import to Marcuse will also be examined with reference to the current protest movements, but the concept of the "Great Refusal" will be used in a more general sense to draw out the broad-based forces of negation.

42. See, for example, Commission on Global Governance, *Our Global Neighbourhood.*

43. Held, *Introduction to Critical Theory,* p. 184.

44. The efforts to deal with the problems of ozone depletion are startling in their contradictions and the blind spots they display. For example, the chemical compound chiefly responsible for the problem—chlorofluorocarbons (CFCs)—were developed by General Motors in 1931 as an answer to toxic chemicals in the atmosphere. CFCs were seen to be inert and nontoxic in the lower atmosphere. Now we are asked to "celebrate the progress" of the institutional arrangement to phase out the use of these chemicals, which have been replaced by hydrochlorofluorocarbons (HCFCs), which are only 1–10 percent as destructive of the ozone layer and will be phased out themselves as we approach the middle of the twenty-first century! We are, in the meantime, awaiting the development of new chemicals to fulfill the same functions, which science will assure us are not harmful to the stratosphere. For the origins of CFCs, see Haas, "Banning Chlorofluorocarbons," and Vogler, *The Global Commons,* pp. 124–126. For a discussion of the destructiveness of HCFCs, see Porter and Brown, *Global Environmental Politics,* p. 66. The case of ozone depletion will be dealt with comprehensively in Chapter 4.

45. Marcuse, *One Dimensional Man,* pp. xi–xii.

46. Marcuse, *An Essay on Liberation,* pp. 3–4.

2

From Protest to Sustainable Development: The Advent of Green Diplomacy

THE ISSUE OF A DEGRADING ENVIRONMENT WAS THRUST ONTO the political agendas of most Western industrialized states in the 1960s by environmental activists determined to force politicians to respond to the myriad problems facing local communities. Armed with evidence of increased cancer rates, species extinction, overdevelopment, and careless (sometimes criminal) corporate behavior, these early green activists sought to make links between economic decisionmaking, environmental degradation, and corporate greed. While many scientists backed a traditional and cautious line of inquiry into the causes of the evident deterioration, others—most notably Rachel Carson[1]—were producing the kinds of works that not only provided ammunition to the protesters but also inspired generations of concerned citizens to look beyond the rhetoric of their governments and the various scientific and corporate interests intent on maintaining support for a "business-as-usual" mind-set. Likewise in the realm of economics one could witness the powerful logic of those rogue economists—such as E. F. Schumacher[2]—who argued for so-called conserver societies and sought to make transparent the environmental costs of industrial society. There were even some governments (such as Sweden) that believed it to be in their national interest to take an early lead in attempting to deal with the sources of environmental destruction, and with the increasingly transboundary nature of problems such as air and water pollution, the issue was thereby pushed up the international political agenda as well.

This chapter tells the story of the international community's response to emerging environmental crisis. The development of green diplomacy has been slow but steady and has been frequently presented as a hopeful and realistic solution to shared problems. My argument quite clearly contrasts with the optimism displayed by the mainstream coverage of this issue and posits instead that the actions taken at the international diplomatic level over the past thirty years have led (in part unintentionally) to a repackaging of the environmental debate in such a way as to deny the credibility of the voices of those making connections between the impact of economic activity and environmental destruction. The displayed faith in the ability of science, technology, and market solutions to answer the world's problems—be they poverty, underdevelopment, or environmental destruction—serves to reaffirm the destructive ways of thinking about the natural world pointed to in Chapter 1. In addition, the reembedding of Enlightenment optimism has served to silence the critics and contain the dissent of those earlier protesters intent on getting to the roots of the problem. This reestablishment of the logic of "progress" will be demonstrated through a consideration of the articulation of the very important framing device of sustainable development and through a discussion of the attempts to carve out a space for nongovernmental organizations (NGOs) on the part of the green diplomats within the evolving international environmental and economic structures.

From the Stockholm Conference of 1972 through to the Rio Conference twenty years later and the preparation of its follow-up gathering, let us consider the greening of diplomacy and its effects on radical reconsiderations of the causes of environmental destruction. But first, let us consider the backdrop to the discussions—the protest movements and the challenges to orthodoxy that fueled them.

PRESSING FOR CHANGE:
THE PROTEST MOVEMENT OF THE 1960s

Looking back to the 1960s and 1970s from the early twenty-first century is a startling exercise. The protesters on the streets of virtually every major Western democratic society were making arguments broadly similar to those we hear today from the streets of Washington, D.C., Seattle, Prague, Davos, Quebec City, or any other city brave enough to host a meeting of representatives of the major international economic or regional organizations. Although often based on an articulation of local and community concerns—combined with a strong pacifist and particularly anti–Vietnam War emphasis—the protesters of thirty to thirty-five years ago were talking about the environmental costs of corporate development and the militarization of society, the environmental racism implicit in the location of toxic waste dumps, and the fallacy of the belief in the possibility of perpetual growth and materialism that was so evidently dominating capitalist societies. Given the widespread scale of the protests of those heady years we should feel compelled to examine why there continues to be a need for such opposition. What happened to the protests and the developing green consciousness that more than a quarter of a century later we can examine the record only to discover that the environment has deteriorated further, that there is greater disparity between rich and poor, that there is less local control over the immediate causes of pollution, that environmental racism is now more obvious in the international arena, and that the environmental costs of militarism continue to increase dramatically?

It is not surprising that the publication of Rachel Carson's *Silent Spring* in 1962 is often cited as a turning point in the environmental movement, but the reason is not as obvious as it might first appear. Many remember Carson's book because it gave specific examples of the toxic pollution that people could see around them. Carson tapped into a rising awareness on the part of average citizens, and the accessibility of her writing style and the passion with which she approached her topic guaranteed her a voice in the media. It is also true, however, that Carson's message about the dangers of chemical pesticides was in stark contrast to the widespread view of scientific progress and the human ability to triumph over nature to ensure continued economic growth. Scientists were not supposed to contradict the view that science was by its very nature a progressive activity leading to a bountiful and more leisurely future for all, and Carson was attacked by other scientists for her pessimism and her "purple prose."[3]

The debates that raged around Carson's book point to a more important debate, however, than the arguments about the "safe" levels of pesticide and chemical use or the effects of such use on other species. Perhaps even more unsettling for many people was the shaking of their faith in science as a pure and honest pursuit—a pursuit that transcended political controversy. The Enlightenment view of scientific inquiry as a dispassionate quest for truth that could thereby lead to a better world for all had been accepted at an almost unconscious level and had been reaffirmed in the decades following World War II (especially in the West) as supposed technological advances made life simpler and apparently better for many people. But questions were beginning to be raised about the wisdom of such a view. As the scientists working on behalf of chemical manufacturers in the United States attempted to discredit Carson's academic credentials and even her mental stability, it became patently obvious to many that scientific evidence was contestable. At an intuitive level, then, many came to regard scientific claims with greater skepticism than they had previously. This skepticism necessarily had a spillover effect when government agencies claimed solid scientific evidence in defense of a chemical product or the placement of an industrial site or waste. The linkages between science, economics, and the deterioration of the environment became much tighter and more articulate once science was knocked off its pedestal.

Carson's exposé was merely the beginning. A large number of books were published throughout the 1960s and 1970s that set out in stark terms the terrible environmental crisis facing humankind.[4] Citizens groups were springing up around the world and the establishment of Earth Day in 1970 made clear to the politicians that the environment was a topic on the political agenda and they had better take note. Increasingly the concerned citizen was speaking in terms of *limits,* inspired by books such as *The Limits to Growth,*[5] *The Limits of Human Nature,*[6] and *The Limits to Satisfaction,*[7] to name but three. The language was subtly changing from the Enlightenment-directed sense of never-ending growth, prosperity, and inevitable human control of all nature to one of humility, preservation, and sustainability.

An essential part of the efforts toward a new worldview inevitably incorporated a new economic view. By the 1970s, the protest groups—at least in the West—were protesting against corporate greed and the New Left movement was framing the debate in terms of socialist and communitarian ideals. The protests also came from economists themselves, and E. F. Schumacher's *Small Is Beautiful* had an impact on the 1970s akin to Carson's book a decade earlier. Subtitled *A Study of Economics As If People Mattered,* Schumacher's book critiqued the environmental pollution and incredible inefficiency of capitalism and argued passionately that "in the excitement over the unfolding of his scientific and technical powers, modern man has built a system of production that ravishes nature and a type of society that mutilates man."[8] Schumacher's critique of materialism, growth, and Enlightenment thought combined for maximum impact and sold well—indeed, Schumacher's book is still selling well. Economics and the environmental crisis were thoroughly fused in his analysis, and the discussions and debates it generated were focused on steady-state economics and alternative economic structures. The way forward, it was increasingly argued, was to change the economic system that was strangling the planet.[9]

The impact of such perspectives on the international political community and its powerful vested economic interests was an essential step in the development of green diplomacy.

THE UN CONFERENCE ON THE HUMAN ENVIRONMENT

Those who would have us believe that steady progress has been made in the international realm toward environmental protection begin their story with the UN Conference on the Human Environment (better known as the Stockholm Conference), held in 1972. It is here, they argue, that we can witness the first step toward the type of diplomacy and cooperation that is necessary if we are to solve the world's environmental problems. Although certainly not inspired solely by the protesting environmentalists, the first big intergovernmental environmental conference was nonetheless held against a backdrop of an increasingly vocal movement. It is safe to assume that at least some state leaders agreed to support the Stockholm Conference in part to appease their own publics and to be able to demonstrate that they were indeed participating in activities designed to ease the problems.

The initiative for the conference came initially from Sweden and, in 1968, the UN General Assembly passed a resolution calling for a conference whose formal aim would be "to provide a framework for comprehensive consideration within the UN of the problems of the human environment in order to focus the attention of governments and public opinion on the importance and urgency of this question."[10] The conference was held in June 1972 with Canadian industrialist Maurice Strong in the chair. Representatives of 114 countries participated, but these were the early days of green diplomacy and only two heads of state were in attendance: Olaf Palme as host, and Indira Gandhi of India. The supposedly global nature of the conference was severely limited by the withdrawal of the Soviet Bloc countries when the Americans refused to allow East German participation.[11]

The story of the Stockholm Conference has been told a number of times,[12] but it is important to keep in mind the major issues of the day and the hope that was garnered by the self-proclaimed success of the meeting. The conference concluded with the Stockholm Declaration, a statement of the twenty-six broad principles agreed to by the participants as the way forward in the shared management of the global environment. The declaration was never intended to be anything more than a foundation to build on and contained no promises of specific environmental improvements. It was seen, in a sense, as a starting point for the future cooperation of the international community, and although none of the participants claimed that improvement would be instantaneous, there was widespread enthusiasm at the prospect of cooperation on areas of shared concern. Article 21 is usually highlighted for the very good reason that it contains the guarantee protecting "the sovereign rights of states to exploit their own resources in line with their own environmental policies, [provided they] ensure that activities in their control do not damage the environment of other states."[13] In short, the participating states agreed to cooperate, but they also wanted it to be made absolutely clear that this was not to infringe on any decisionmaking powers they held. It is also important to recognize the extent to which article 21 explicitly reaffirms resource exploitation as the basis for the economic growth of the state.

If the declaration can be seen to be lacking in concrete direction, the Action Plan agreed to at Stockholm is even more vague. Comprising a list of 109 recommendations, this plan lacks any requirement for formal commitment and ranges widely over a series of related issues—everything from atmospheric pollution to technology transfer and the impact of environmental deterioration on trade relations. The list is important as an indication of the range of issues discussed (and fought over) in Stockholm that summer, and presents a clear indication of the way in which the problems were to be thought about in the subsequent years. Maurice Strong recollects the "attentive faces of the multitudes" as he outlined the categories to be contained in the plan:

> Environmental Assessment . . . which was a co-operative approach to accumulating the necessary data and to providing objective assessments of potential problems or opportunities; the Environmental Management Activities, to provide support at the international level for good management initiatives; and the Supporting Measures, which would be education and training programs but also a way of putting money where our mouths were, a way of backing each agreed-on action with financial and organizational support.[14]

Assessment, management, and support were indeed the key concepts arising from the Stockholm Conference.

Aside from the documents that are presented as evidence of an emerging green diplomacy, the Stockholm Conference is remembered as well for the establishment of the UN Environment Programme (UNEP), and it is here that the beginnings of an institutional approach to common environmental problems can be seen. I shall consider the extent of

UNEP's success in Chapter 4; for now, suffice it to say that despite a relatively small budget, UNEP has managed at times to live up to its mandate of facilitating environmental activities through the United Nations.[15]

This depiction of the UN Conference on the Human Environment mirrors the standard presentation of what happened in Stockholm in the summer of 1972. Differences of opinion of course abound as to the relative successes and failures of that early attempt on the part of states to come together with a common environmental purpose. But much more happened at the conference than this presentation would suggest. There was not just one conference but three, and any accurate history of green diplomacy should reflect on the two unofficial conferences. Taken together, all three conferences shared the battleground for the framing of the debate over the global environment.

The Alternative Conferences

Leaving aside (for now) the possible reasons for the near complete absence of discussion on the part of international relations experts of the range of arguments presented at the forums outside the official meeting hall at the Stockholm Conference, it is essential to clarify the sentiments that drove a wide range of people to make their way to Sweden that summer. It was outside the conference halls and away from Maurice Strong's strict control of the official agenda that connections were being made in a way that, had they been acted upon, could have prevented the serious environmental deterioration that followed the purported breakthrough of the official gathering.[16]

International conferences of the type epitomized by the UN conference in Stockholm have come to see an unofficial parallel meeting of citizens groups as a standard—and indeed desirable—feature of the event. The Stockholm Conference was the first international conference that celebrated—at least publicly—the participation of nongovernmental organizations. Strong himself sees this conference as marking the entry of environmentalists into international politics and was aware of the increased relationship between what went on at international meetings and what subsequently occurred in domestic settings.[17]

The group of environmentalists that together made up the Environment Forum were primarily (but not exclusively) from the developed world and included a wide variety of nongovernmental organizations, which created inevitable difficulties in speaking with one voice. Nonetheless, this group succeeded in gaining limited access to the decisionmakers at the official conference through their protests, through their news-paper, and through a formal statement to the conference. Many of the is-sues that bedeviled the official conference also cut lines through this forum, most notably the issue of population control. As with any such group drawn together with a shared interest, there were bound to be di-visions, and certainly some groups within the forum were more intent on uncovering the economic roots of the environmental problem while others were interested in more concrete social alternatives (e.g., farm-ing, marketing, etc.). Despite the differences, however, the forum con-tinuously articulated the need to consider redistributive issues as a start-ing point. This was not a business-as-usual approach, and its sometimes raucous protests often left Strong on the defensive. The presentation of the activist involvement has subsequently been heralded as a great step forward in openness and accountability, but it is highly questionable that this energetic but fragmented forum achieved much of substance at the conference.[18] What will become clear, however, is the degree to which Maurice Strong himself learned from this experience. He would be more than willing to be seen to encourage NGO participation at the next UN conference, but he would take measures to ensure that such participation would be on his terms and that arguments would be held within strictly controlled limits. The need for a framing device was ev-ident if green diplomacy was to reaffirm the role of the state and the market—especially the market!

The NGO forum has been given scant attention aside from the op-timistic view that it ushered in a new era of participant involvement in international diplomacy. But there was another conference held in Stockholm in June 1972 that has been almost written out of the history of environmentalism: the Dai Dong Independent Conference on the En-vironment. The silence on the part of those recounting the story of inter-national action on the environment is telling, for it was at this confer-ence (which met from June 1 to June 6—ending one day after the official UN conference began its proceedings) that a concerted effort was made to shape the discourse of the problem in a manner that went to the root causes.[19]

The Dai Dong Conference was put together by the International Fellowship of Reconciliation (IFOR), a group that had been inspired by a message presented to UN Secretary-General U Thant in May 1971 by a group of scientists representing more than 2,000 signatories.[20] While accepting many of the issues that would be accepted by Maurice Strong and the UN conference, the scientists had shifted the ground of debate by adding to the consideration of population, pollution control, and so on, the decidedly hot issues of war, disarmament, and a politicized notion of technology. The IFOR raised funds to hold a conference presumably knowing full well that their contribution could—if it was given a voice—call into question the manner in which the official conference would deal with the issues at hand. Fred Knelman tells us that the Dai Dong Conference sought to link social, political, economic, and cultural structures with the myriad problems facing the world (nuclear war, population growth, environment, and resource and power maldistribution). And while the official conference was marred by the absence of the East Bloc countries, the Dai Dong meeting did not suffer the same fate.[21]

Of course it is quite easy to reject the arguments put forward at the Dai Dong Conference as being of minimal import due to the unofficial status of the meeting. The participants at the official conference would doubtless argue that they did not have the freedom to debate and discuss the issues in the manner in which they were undertaken at either of the unofficial conferences because they were there to represent states and, in the nitty-gritty of interstate negotiations, such luxuries as intellectual engagement with the broader nature of the problem are both naïve and dangerous. The realpolitik of the situation calls for, such participants insist, the cool and collected bargaining of those who really understand the difficulties of diplomatic maneuvering. The defenders of the incrementalist approach are correct about the slow and steady movement of the international process, but their depiction of reality serves to amplify the critique being offered at the Dai Dong Conference about the limitations of state interests and actions. For those signing on to the Dai Dong vision, the point was precisely the indivisibility of ecology and economics and the recognition that any sincere attempt to achieve long-term solutions would necessarily entail integrative and holistic solutions—not a patchwork of interstate bargains. Subjects such as war, nuclear testing, and the ecological catastrophe the world was then witnessing in Vietnam—which were not seen as suitable topics at the official conference—were debated and brought into the frame of reference at the Dai Dong meeting.

In short, this alternative conference sought to place the environmental crisis facing the international community in its broad context with a view to getting to the roots of the problem. To accept, as the official conference so clearly did, that the existing structures and ways of thinking could go unchallenged while searching for answers to the crisis was nonsensical. The Dai Dong Conference was a serious forum for debate and discussion; the UN conference by contrast was stage-managed and severely limited. Neither meeting was harmonious and many of the same issues were contentious. At the Dai Dong Conference, however, the question of economic structures and the status quo mind-set was brought to the fore. Instead of continually seeking to articulate a strategy for economic growth that would prove to be environmentally friendly (a strategy that has come, over the years, to look depressingly like rearranging the deck chairs on the *Titanic*), the Dai Dong Conference challenged both the economic logic as well as the faith in science and technology. It placed into sharp relief the failure of the Stockholm Conference to deal with the illogic of Enlightenment thought and pointed to the inability of the international community to develop a sense of humility in the face of disaster. This makes its subsequent virtual erasure from histories of the time all the more damaging and disturbing.

It seems clear that the official conference was convinced from the outset that no deep or critical thinking needed to be undertaken in order to deal with the environmental problems facing the world. The issue was framed as one of incremental change and interstate cooperation and, of course, as one of economic and technological adaptation. The participants at the Dai Dong Conference were just as sure of their position:

> The Dai Dong declaration rejected traditional economic growth and development, with its uncontrolled "hard" technologies and its new imperialism—the multinational corporation—as incompatible with environmental protection, the just distribution of resources, and the protection of differing cultures. The United Nations conference implicitly and explicitly expressed its faith in traditional economic growth and technology, using the time-worn and now historically invalidated argument that this was the only path to the equalization of development.[22]

The Official Assessment

The assessment of the official conference in the months and years following the Stockholm Conference varied. In his memoirs Maurice Strong places himself at the cutting edge of the environmental movement and paints the Stockholm Conference as "a major landmark launching a new era of international environmental diplomacy."[23] Caroline Thomas concurs with Strong's assessment when she presents Stockholm as "a milestone in the recognition of environmental issues in international relations,"[24] as does John McCormick when he describes it as a "landmark event in the growth of international environmentalism."[25]

This is, in fact, the standard and oft-repeated refrain from scholars of international environmental politics.

The conference was indeed a first step—but a first step toward what? While many observers see the conference as an essential beginning in terms of international diplomacy and the presentation of a blueprint for action, it can also be argued that what happened in Stockholm was the start of the absorption of the critical thinking that was attempting to call into question the basic assumptions of modernity that can be seen as the root of the problem. The divisions that existed at Stockholm are often presented in terms of the developing South in opposition to the developed North and/or the communist East versus the capitalist West (or democratic West, depending on whom you read). There was, however, much more happening in the world than this simplistic description would indicate.

In the late 1960s and early 1970s there existed a powerful critique of the status quo. It was arguably the protest and the "negative" (i.e., critical) thinking that forced a consideration of these issues onto the agenda and into the corridors of diplomatic power. The first step, then, from the perspective of those who sought to maintain the existing structures, was one of absorption of dissent. This is not to say that those individuals gathered together at the official conference in Stockholm were not sincere in their desire to improve the state of the world's environment. It is to argue, however, that through acceptance of the status quo, thinking about solutions is inevitably limited to tinkering rather than any kind of fundamental reevaluation.

STOCKHOLM TO THE BRUNDTLAND COMMISSION

Taken on its own terms the green diplomacy initiated at the Stockholm Conference had some notable successes in the subsequent years. The Convention on International Trade in Endangered Species (1973) was hailed as a success for its efforts to internationalize wildlife conservation (despite the loopholes it contains), and the Convention on Long-Range Transboundary Air Pollution (1979) was seen as an important first step in reducing dangerous chemical emissions. This was the beginning of regime formation—international agreements designed to pool energies and resources in the common fight against environmental degradation. It was accepted that the progress would be slow: what was important at this point in the history of green diplomacy was that the negotiating and the talking had begun.[26] The multilateral practices undertaken by the state participants were increasingly heralded as the way forward, and the previously strong and vocal critique about the relationship between economics and pollution was being marginalized. The deeply embedded myths of science, progress, growth, and freedom allowed the easy absorption of critique. If an environmental problem could be articulated, then technology and cooperation would find the answer. UN officials and government representatives alike were convinced that the way forward was through incremental steps to redress the evident problems. Needless to say, the environment continued to deteriorate and the international community continued to look for ways to move the process along more effectively.

By the time of the ten-year review gathering of the Stockholm Conference, it was clear that little action had been taken to achieve the goals set out at that grand event. Shortly thereafter the World Commission on Environment and Development (WCED, most commonly known as the Brundtland Commission in honor of its chair, former Norwegian prime minister Gro Harlem Brundtland) was convened to look at possible ways for the international community to take bigger steps toward environmental cleanup. Much has been written about this commission for the very good reason that it was with the activities and report of this group—with its central concept of sustainable development—that the international environmental issue has been framed for all subsequent discussions. This commission has had an impact on political discourse and popular consciousness far beyond its more specific recommendations to the United Nations.

The commission was established in 1983 by the UN General Assembly. With Brundtland in the chair and an assembled team of twenty-three prominent members drawn from twenty-two countries,[27] the commission established a Secretariat in Geneva, constituted three Advisory Panels (Energy, Industry, and Food Security), and, perhaps of greatest import, held public hearings in all regions of the world from March 1985 through February 1987. It published its report, *Our Common Future*, later in 1987.[28]

The mandate from the United Nations was clear:

1. to re-examine the critical issues of environment and development and to formulate innovative, concrete and realistic action proposals to deal with them;
2. to strengthen international co-operation on environment and development and to assess and propose new forms of co-operation that

      can break out of existing patterns and influence policies and events
      in the direction of needed change; and

3. to raise the level of understanding and commitment to action on the
   part of individuals, voluntary organizations, businesses, institutes
   and governments.[29]

    The report published by the WCED is perhaps one of the most important documents concerning international environmental issues yet published. The publicity it received and the success it has had in tightly framing the issue are extraordinary. From the perspective of the advocates of green diplomacy, it has been a dramatic success: the language of sustainable development has become firmly embedded in the lexicon of state leaders, corporate heads, and environmental movements alike. Defined as "development that meets the needs of the present without compromising the ability of future generations to meet their own needs,"[30] sustainable development has become a rallying cry for people the world round, and any attempt to call into question the concept itself is seen as virtually sacrilegious. From the celebrations at its launch through to the incorporation of the concept of sustainable development into domestic, international, and corporate policy formulation, the framing of the issue is firmly controlled and limited, and the negating propositions are successfully sidelined.

    The commission uses the language, sentiment, and passion of the environmental movement to reestablish the viability of a continuation of the economic growth ethic and to reaffirm the Enlightenment views of science, technology, and the inevitability of progress. The report is an ideal example of Orwellian doublespeak. Recognizing that increased levels of pollutants are caused by increased industrialization, the commission argues in a convincing fashion that the eradication of poverty through industrial growth will lead to a cleaner environment. This was clearly *not* done as a deliberate conspiracy to wrest the debate away from those engaged in deep critical thinking about the issue but rather as a result of the failure on the part of the participants to see beyond the ways of thinking so embedded in the structures around them. The members of the commission and, indeed, the vast majority of governmental, business, and social leaders are unable and/or unwilling to deal with such issues in anything other than a one-dimensional manner. Society's problems are conceived of as nothing more than glitches in the progressive march toward an ideal future.

    The commission posits that the pursuit of sustainable development requires a number of things to occur, and the list below makes clear the fact that the recommendations would be problem-solving within the terms of reference of the existing system rather than any fundamental (critical) thinking on the structures themselves. Sustainable development requires, argues the commission:

- a political system that secures effective citizen participation in decision making,
- an economic system that is able to generate surpluses and technical knowledge on a self-reliant and sustained basis,
- a social system that provides for solutions for the tensions arising from disharmonious development,
- a production system that respects the obligation to preserve the ecological base for development,
- a technological system that can search continuously for new solutions,
- an international system that fosters sustainable patterns of trade and finance, and,
- an administrative system that is flexible and has the capacity for self-correction.[31]

In order that the goal of sustainable development be achieved, the commission then focuses on the institutional and legal changes necessary. Through a detailed examination of the UN system (seen as essential to guide the global agenda), the commission seeks to establish new norms of state/interstate behavior, to strengthen and extend the existing laws and international agreements, and to develop procedures for avoiding and resolving environmental disputes. Its call for a universal declaration on environmental protection is precisely what Maurice Strong had sought in Stockholm, and the advocacy of better use of multilateral agreements was designed to strengthen the ability of the United Nations to contribute to international governance.

The report is a testament to the power of positive thinking. On the first page, the commission's optimism is palpable:

This Commission believes that people can build a future that is more prosperous, more just, and more secure. Our report, *Our Common Future,* is not a prediction of ever increasing environmental decay, poverty, and hardship in an ever more polluted world among ever decreasing resources. We see instead the possibility for a new era of economic growth, one that must be based on policies that sustain and expand the environmental resource base. And we believe such growth to be absolutely essential to relieve the great poverty that is deepening in much of the developing world.

But the Commission's hope for the future is conditional on decisive political action now to begin managing environmental resources to ensure both sustainable human progress and human survival. We are not forecasting a future; we are serving a notice—an urgent notice based on the latest and best scientific evidence—that the time has come to take decisions needed to secure the resources to sustain this and coming generations. We do not offer a detailed blueprint for action, but instead a pathway by which the peoples of the world may enlarge their spheres of co-operation.[32]

The report has come to be seen as a defining moment in the international community's willingness and ability to face the environmental crisis head-on. The concept of sustainable development has been described as revolutionary because it "subtly challenges so many presumptions, philosophical, political and religious."[33] But does it? The optimism and the reliance on trade, economics, and technological solutions to existing problems can—and should—be seen as a replaying of a very old song.

The Brundtland Commission managed to take environmental problems stemming from overdevelopment and make a case that they are, in fact, the result of underdevelopment. It looked at the problem of the misapplication of scientific knowledge and reassures us that it is the *correct* application of scientific knowledge that will inevitably lead us to Eden. The report speaks the language of Francis Bacon and René Descartes more surely than it speaks of the language of true environmental awareness. The recipe is obvious: take a political system that encourages citizen participation (but controlled participation, as we shall see), add capitalism (in domestic economies as well as internationally through free trade and global trade patterns), employ science and the search for technological fixes for any apparent problem, throw in institutions for ensuring multilateral agreements, and the answer will be *sustainable development*. By pointing to the fragmented nature of our knowledge and the Enlightenment-inspired inability to see the wholeness of any situation, the Brundtland Commission adopts the language of the radical environmentalist while ensuring that the solutions for our environmental problems are seen as being within the existing political, economic, and social structures—structures that have been responsible for the very problems they are being asked to consider. There is, of course, a way of making the connection between economics and ecological awareness, but here it is merely within the exigencies of economic rationality—a form of eco-nomics—and we are, as a result, left stranded with the perpetuation of what Marcuse refers to as "one-dimensional thought," in which there is little attempt to transcend the existing structures or practices of the given society.

In an age when the vast majority of the people who use the concept of sustainable development and set about incorporating its basic premises into their own specific agendas have never in fact read the report or, indeed, thought very deeply about its underlying assumptions, the intention of the crafters of the report is not of substantial import. It is essential to realize, however, the practical consequences of the commission's work: the environmental agenda became framed in such a way that deep critique was much more difficult—although not impossible—to articulate. It is very hard to contradict the concept of sustainable development precisely because the term *sustainable development* itself manages to unify the opposites and make itself immune to any expression of protest and refusal. Who can possibly go against a plan that offers the world both environmental improvement as well as a continuation of development with the promise of wealth for all? It is posed as unquestionable: both within reach and beyond doubt. It is seemingly above reproach in both its intent and its content. Marcuse points out the way in which language can "speak in constructions which impose upon the recipient the slanted and abridged meaning, the blocked development of content, the acceptance of that which is offered in the form in which it is offered."[34] The concept of sustainable development is a supreme example of this. By taking the language of ecology and diversity and marrying it to the economic exploitation and growth that led to environmental deterioration in the first instance, the Brundtland report can be seen to be responsible for the construction of a limited and limiting concept—one that defuses the critique by reconciling the inherent tension in the logic of growth and development. "What is needed now," the report suggests, "is a new era of economic growth—growth that is forceful and at the same time socially and environmentally sustainable."[35]

In what is perhaps the single most eloquent attack on the Brundtland report, Shiv Visvanathan challenges its authors and its audience to look at the way in which it has created "grammars that decide which sentence can be spoken and which cannot" and suggests that the import of the report is precisely in terms of the "logic of the world it seeks to create and impose."[36] Visvanathan sees the report as a well-intentioned attempt to deal with the situation, but nonetheless as an example of an attempt to control history along the desired Enlightenment route—a route that has been destructive all along. The concept of sustainable development is central to this:

> Every contemporary report needs a key word or slogan to keep it alive long after the report itself gathers dust. The key words of the Brundtland

Report are sustainable *development*. There is no greater contradiction in terms. Sustainability and development belong to different, almost incommensurable worlds. . . .

Sustainability is about care and concern; it speaks the ethics of self-restraint. It exudes the warmth of locality, of the Earth as home. Development is a genocidal act of control. It represents a contract between two major agents, between the modern nation-state and modern Western science. The first is deemed to be the privileged form of politics, the second claims to be the universal form of knowledge.[37]

Visvanathan strips bare the claims of the Brundtland report and makes clear the historical tendency from which it has emerged—the European Enlightenment notions of growth, science, and technology. Indeed, Visvanathan mocks the argument that growth and consumption can continue unchecked and depicts the Brundtland Commission's "ideal citizen" as a "consumer with the big mouth and a faith in science."[38] Cartesian rationality reigns supreme in the commission's report and Visvanathan is surely correct when he argues that "[d]eep down, the Brundtland Report still believes that the expert and the World Bank can save the world. All it needs is the application of better technology and management."[39] In pointing to the contradiction inherent in the chosen slogan, Visvanathan seeks to unblock the development of content in it so as to amplify the possibility for its own negation. However, the concept became accepted almost immediately and without much serious consideration of the underlying logic. For most people it was comforting to hear that we could have it all: growth and environmental protection, development and sustainability.

If the concept of sustainable development was comforting to the average individual, it must have come as a major relief to state leaders and to the corporate elite of the world. Having been forced to deal with a degree of critical thinking about the causes of environmental deterioration, the ball was once again back in their court thanks to the logic of the commission. It allowed them to appear green and progressive while continuing along the same path they had always traveled.

Sustainable development, as articulated by the commission, demonstrates the consolidation of power in terms of administration and domination. By portraying the myriad and complex problems of the natural environment as ones in need of scientific and technological solutions, the discourse around them becomes one of administrative power. In addition to this administrative function, the concept itself contains within it the necessary authority to preempt challenges from "below." After its initial articulation—which advertised to the world that the international community was taking the environmental crisis seriously and was committed to undertaking a radical plan of action to deal with it—the concept became used by state leaders the world round to diffuse criticism of environmentally damaging practices. Many states inaugurated a range of programs to ensure that the concept was given a place in discussions within local communities, and there is no question that many people took it seriously enough to use it to ensure change at the local level. Nonetheless, despite the use of the concept for gaining local support, the construction of the issue was such that the answer to this "big" problem of environmental deterioration would by necessity be dealt with by strong central administrations. Rather than weakening state leaders' power in the face of environmental problems of a transboundary nature, the concept became one that allowed the strengthening of governments vis-à-vis their own populations. The bottom-up protests against big government and big business had been neatly turned around: these were big problems needing big solutions, and these solutions could only be organized top-down. It was an amazingly efficient absorption of critique.

THE BRUNDTLAND COMMISSION
AND ENLIGHTENMENT THOUGHT

The way of thinking that the modern scientific method engenders allows for an operational rationality that leads to the use of technology as a form of social control and domination. I am not speaking here of the use of technology as the specific instrument of control (which is, of course, frequently the case), but rather of technology as the source of legitimation for expanding political power. Technology and the technological fix provide necessary legitimation of expanding political power. Let me take an example of this.

As previously mentioned, the 1960s and 1970s saw a large-scale protest movement that sought to articulate a broader critique of society; at least part of this critique took shape in the form of the environmental movement. Many writers, activists, and groups attempted to depict a society that had eliminated any fundamental consideration of the impact of its practices. Greed and profit margins were called into question, as was the use of dangerous technologies. There were subsequently two ways to engage with the issue as posed by protesters: in terms of social, political, and economic change, which went to the root of the problem, or in terms of the Enlightenment tradition of finding the supposedly rational and technological answer to any crisis that might present itself.

The response of the Brundtland Commission demonstrates both how deeply the Enlightenment current of thought runs and its practical effects. The fact that a commission charged with the task of examining the global environmental crisis can, after five years of investigation, return with a plan that is so thoroughly embedded in the same way of thinking is a testament to the power of the operational function of scientific rationality. The result has been extraordinary. Any voices raised in an effort to call into question this very way of thinking are silenced by the apparent logic of the Brundtland approach. Technology cannot be perceived as part of the problem; it *must* be part of the solution. Centuries of the scientific method tell us so.

Marcuse, in discussing the way in which technology provides the great rationalization of domination, wrote that "this unfreedom appears neither as irrational nor as political, but rather as submission to the technical apparatus which enlarges the comforts of life and increases the productivity of labor."[40] The same quote can be applied to the Brundtland report. The suggestions in the report present a view of the problem that determines the outcome. Technological rationality has once again been used to protect the tendency to dominate—which itself becomes internationalized.

It can reasonably be asked at this point, how does such an outcome occur? Why, for instance, does a report containing a celebration of human-environmental harmony come to be used as justification for continuing on with a business-as-usual approach to economic growth? Such an apparent misuse of the commission's intent is built into the report's own language. It is essential to consider the concept with a critical eye on the language used to express it. To do this, we need only examine Marcuse's consideration of the technical language of modern society. Language becomes closed to critical movement when it seeks to present reality in a technical and descriptive manner. Marcuse believed that such closed language "does not demonstrate and explain—it communicates decision, dictum, command."[41] Meanings and concepts become fixed and point to a concreteness that does not in fact exist but is presented as the only possible "reality." Such meanings, as pervasive as they are deceptive, stand in the way of a vocabulary that would seek to unravel contradictions and release critical energy and intent.

Sustainable development does not have the appearance of a descriptive—and thereby merely operational—concept. It can be seen as a concept designed to point to the environmental problems caused by modern industrial, postindustrial, and developing societies alike. On the face of it, then, one might well expect the concept of sustainable development to contain a critical meaning allowing for the tension/discrepancy between the concept and the immediate situation to become clear. Such a meaning would allow a vision of the ways in which the institutional organization and social, political, and economic structures of both individual societies as well as the international sphere as a whole were leading to the problem that needed to be dealt with. Given the way in which the concept was framed—from the Brundtland report onward—within the framework of existing social conditions and institutions, this critical aspect of the concept has been submerged and denied, although, crucially, never eradicated. Sustainable development was given a concrete meaning at the outset that served to limit the terms of the debate: no room was left for a conceptual critique of the facts of the existing order of things. Indeed, the concept was carefully positioned so that it would be of the utmost service in maintaining—albeit with some improvements—the existing arrangements.[42] This, as I shall demonstrate in the next chapter, becomes even more powerfully limiting when the neoliberal economic order adopts the concept and utilizes it to full effect in the advancement of deregulation of international capital. Despite this successful framing of the concept, it is nonetheless an attempt to retrieve the critical tension within the concept that is fueling many environmental and anti-globalization movements around the world. These efforts to put the critical content of sustainable development to work by making demands for a radical revision of the relationship between environmental and economic issues are central to any truly sustainable environmental future and will be considered in Chapter 5.

THE ROAD TO RIO: MANAGING THE MESSAGE

The Brundtland Commission's work played a central role in the direction of green diplomatic efforts even after its official work had ended. The central import of the concept of sustainable development to the overall management of the international process was recognized and, as a result, the Center for Our Common Future (COCF) was established in 1988 to harness an international community of supporters for the concept of sustainable development.

The primary function of the center at its inception was to spread the message of sustainable development to as many people as possible. The framing of the debate cannot be left to chance and in this case the spreading of the gospel necessitated translating the reports, sending out educational materials, and establishing partners around the world (intergovernmental organizations, financial organizations, youth groups, etc.) to ensure public commitment to the concept.[43] Once the decision had been made by the United Nations to organize another global conference on the environment, the focus of the center shifted to that of ensuring that the so-called Brundtland constituency was fed into the organizing process of the 1992 UN Conference on Environment and Development (UNCED)—often referred to as the Rio Conference.

While Tommy Koh of Singapore was chosen as the chair of the Preparatory Committee (known as PrepCom in international diplomatic terms), Maurice Strong was once again regarded favorably by the United Nations and was chosen as the Secretary-General of the upcoming international conference. Establishing a Secretariat in Geneva, Strong's position ensured that the structure of Rio would be similar to that of the Stockholm agenda and process from two decades earlier.[44] One of the lessons Strong learned from his experience nearly twenty years earlier, however, was the extent to which political protest could serve to disrupt the smooth operation of the conference proceedings. The story of Strong's handling of the NGO input into the preparatory process is an interesting one and not frequently told. Matthias Finger argues convincingly that, "[t]raumatized as he had been by heavy social movement protest in Stockholm in 1972, Strong was determined from the very beginning to pre-empt any opposition to UNCED."[45] Indeed, one of the enduring images of the Stockholm Conference is a bewildered Maurice Strong facing protesters—bewildered precisely because he thought they were on the same "side." The continued lack of understanding of his critics' position and their charge that his methods of dealing with the issue effectively serve to turn the problem into the solution runs throughout his memoir: he depicts those seeking to transform social, economic, and political relations as naïve children, while his own approach is repeatedly presented as rational, pragmatic, and manageable. He thereby demonstrates the limited nature of his understanding of the fundamentals of the issue.

The language being used throughout both the Brundtland and the PrepCom process was one of citizen participation and the importance of including diverse opinions and expertise. Indeed, the General Assembly Resolution that established the UNCED process requested NGO participation "as appropriate." The reality was quite different, as Finger points out. Strong and his colleagues very clearly wanted NGO participation insofar as it would contribute information and expertise, but there the participation would end. Strong had promised support for the principle of broad representation and participation within the official process. When it came to the crunch, however, he did not believe that it was practicable to go this route and instead looked for ways to encourage the various independent sectors to speak with one voice.[46] While the Secretariat was maneuvering to limit the participation of citizens groups, Strong was busily working with business leaders. With a group called the Business Council for Sustainable Development, which had in fact been set up at Strong's request, corporate executives discussed ways to ensure that their interests were adequately reflected in the UNCED process.[47]

THE RIO CONFERENCE

The political setting of the Rio Conference was markedly different from that of its predecessor. While Stockholm was held in the tense times of the Cold War, UNCED was clearly seen by many as a possible step into the potentially cooperative "new world order" that was so frequently discussed in the early 1990s. Add to the optimism of the international community the fact that the environment was increasingly seen as a topic of concern and the hopes were great that green diplomacy would score a significant victory. Over one hundred heads of state attended the proceedings, compared to two at the Stockholm Conference. The lengthy lead-up to the conference, the popularity of the Brundtland Commission, the massive media coverage, and NGO participation combined to guarantee that the world's attention would be focused on Rio de Janeiro for the proceedings.

In the lead-up to the conference, there was much concern that one very important head of state—then U.S. president George Bush—would not attend. The aspirations for a new form of international politics were quite clearly mingled with fears that the single most powerful (and polluting) country would fail to ensure the credibility of green diplomacy. In the end Bush got on the plane and headed off to Rio while stating forthrightly that the American way of life was not up for negotiation; in short, there would be no discussion of fundamental changes to consumption patterns while he was there. Although Bush was heavily criticized around the world for his apparently unyielding attitude, it should have come as little surprise. The fact that Bush apparently felt threatened by the language of sustainable development is a great deal more surprising.

As with any such international diplomatic effort, the conference in Rio did not mark the start of arguments and discussions. The PrepCom process had facilitated consultation between the states, and the participants had spent months drafting and planning the documents that would, it was hoped, be the formal conclusions of the conference. An attempt had been made to draft the basic principles of international cooperation on the environment as well as a document to establish some concrete measures for realizing these principles. In addition to this, there were two conventions being negotiated separately—the UN Framework Convention on Climate Change and the Convention on Biological Diversity. In addition to the documentation that was to be tabled at Rio, there was also an agenda including technology transfer, institutional adjustment, and financing plans.

The story of the outcome of the Rio Conference has been told from a variety of perspectives,[48] but it is important to set out the list of achievements—as claimed by the participants—reached that summer. The major documents agreed to were the Rio Declaration—a list of twenty-seven principles—and the 800-page program *Agenda 21*.[49] The declaration does what one would expect: it reaffirms the sovereign rights of states (as did its predecessor at the Stockholm Conference two decades earlier) and places the objective of sustainable development front and center. As with any international attempt to list principles, the declaration is a vague and general document that does not provide much of substance. It is difficult to see how this statement could ever be translated into meaningful action; it must rely on its moral authority to have any impact at all. The *Agenda 21*, however, was intended to be the basis of international action and the fruition of the efforts at green diplomacy. It takes the Brundtland Commission's ideas and attempts to give them a more practical intent. There is much that is admirable in the agenda in terms of a recognition of the serious problems facing the international community, but once again we are left with the international economic system being presented as the solution to the world's woes. The next chapter will address the issue of economics in more detail, but suffice it to say at this point that the framing of the debate in the interests of the status quo was further assisted by this document. This is precisely the reason that so many business leaders could sign on to the Rio process and support its findings.

Aside from these two main documents, there were three other documents up for discussion. The Statement on Forest Principles demonstrates the difficulties of transcending state economic interests. This document was intended to be a convention but was downgraded to a declaration because of the contentious nature of its content; there was no way to convince the countries intent on wood exports that they were engaged in an environmentally destructive practice. The Convention on Biodiversity had been negotiated under the auspices of the UNEP and was opened for signature at Rio, but the United States was not pleased with the results and held a hard line vis-à-vis intellectual property rights, an issue about which I will speak more in the next chapter. The Framework Convention on Climate Change was likewise opened for signature, having been prepared by the Intergovernmental Negotiating Committee under the auspices of the UN General Assembly. Again the United States was the spoiler—refusing to accept greenhouse gas targets—leaving the text with little more than vague statements regarding the "moral commitment" of states to stabilize their emissions. And again, this was merely a sign of things to come as green diplomacy set to work to demonstrate that the incrementalist approach is the way forward.

In terms of institutional arrangements, *Agenda 21* called for the establishment of a Commission for Sustainable Development—a high-level group to coordinate the programs and organization of the UN and international financial institutions.[50] It is here that we can see the institutional marriage of economic and environmental concerns—the Brundtland concept given realization by the Rio Conference. Other institutional mechanisms, such as the Global Environment Facility (GEF), although negotiated separately outside the UNCED process, figured prominently in the discussions in the run-up to the conference. Developing countries were wary of this economic mechanism designed to help tackle specific environmental problems (ozone in the first instance, with climate change and biodiversity being added) precisely because of its placement in the larger international institutional structures. The GEF was designed to be controlled by the World Bank and in a compromise was set to be jointly administered by that body in conjunction with the UNEP and the UN Development Programme (UNDP).[51] As we shall see, the dispute over the World Bank continues.

ASSESSING THE RIO CONFERENCE

A New Role for NGOs?

For all the talk of the increase in NGO participation, it is important that we not confuse attendance with influence. While it is true that a massive number of people (reports range from 20,000 to 30,000) attended the parallel NGO conference, the Global Forum, the decision taken at the first PrepCom meeting to disallow the negotiating role of NGOs in their work meant that there was little opportunity for these actors to make any substantial impact on the negotiations throughout the UNCED process.

Despite the officially limited role for NGOs, however, a change was clearly occurring. A small number of countries included NGO representatives on their delegations, while others gave their own NGO constituency a voice through their own domestic processes.[52] The promise of input was not to be denied and, for many environmentalists and social activists, the important task of articulating a more progressive alternative agenda continued to be uppermost in their activities. The "People's Earth Declaration: A Proactive Agenda for the Future," issued by the International NGO Forum, is an excellent example of reviving a critical meaning of the conceptual framework. By speaking of the tendency to engage in fine-tuning the destructive economic system, this forum pointed to the fact that the economic logic that was presented as the answer to the problem was in fact its source.[53] As shall be explored further, the reclaiming of the concept of sustainable development had begun. The challenge would be to articulate it in such a way that those in the corridors of economic, political, and diplomatic power would have little choice but to heed the call.

We need, as well, to consider the role of NGOs in a broader conceptual context. While the number of NGOs engaged in environmental advocacy work has certainly grown, we should not merely celebrate numbers but focus instead on the degree to which these activists think beyond the limited way encouraged by the green diplomats. If the reductionist way of thinking that lies at the root of the modern industrial and postindustrial societies is merely reproduced in the proposals of these actors, then the pressure is not for radical change but rather on a quicker pace of incremental reform. In short, these actors need to be considered vis-à-vis either their role in the perpetuation of the existing practices or their tendency to transcend them by reasserting the power of critique. Both tendencies exist and it is important to understand the tension within the situation both historically and currently to examine the possible outcome of the struggle. In a different context, Marcuse considered the tendency toward repression when reason itself is denied its negative power. If what is described as reasonable is merely the statement of existing reality, then it serves to pacify, coordinate, or liquidate opposition.[54] It is this denial of critique that can be seen so clearly in Maurice Strong's dismissal of radical alternatives. To counteract such powerful efforts to co-opt critique or deny alternative possibilities, the environmental NGOs that are dedicated to substantial change of a fundamental nature must unleash the dialectical process within reason itself. To do this they must begin with a subversion of the dominant mode of seeing the world as a storehouse of goods that merely need control and manipulation in order that the industrial project can continue unabated everywhere in the world.

There are those, of course, who look at the increase in nongovernmental organizations and their related activities and see a new politics emerging. However, there is nothing automatic about such a transformation. A look at the lack of lasting political impact from the movements of the 1960s and 1970s should teach us to be wary of such claims. Nonetheless, there are indications that the vast increase in grassroots movements has led, at least to some degree, to a change in the assumptions about sites of power and resistance.[55] Whatever the changing role of the NGO, the state has surely not disappeared, and we must consider the manner in which NGOs are presented as new actors when they are in many instances being brought to the negotiation table to serve the purposes and agendas of other actors—that is, states and businesses. There is very clear evidence that groups that are outside the mainstream thinking of environmental incrementalism are regarded with great suspicion and even disdain by those in control of the negotiations. The very existence of these groups, however, demonstrates the possibility that a critical spirit can shake the established discourse and open up the possibility of alternatives denied by the presentation of an immutable reality.

A New Phase in Green Diplomacy?

The big question at this point is whether or not the incrementalist approach of green diplomacy has worked. There are a number of quite obvious issues that must be pointed to if we are to understand the continuing deterioration of the environment.

First and foremost, of course, is the unwillingness of state actors to relinquish any substantial degree of sovereign power in the interests of the environment. The Stockholm-to-Rio time period demonstrates quite clearly that there is a near complete lack of willingness to tackle the tough problems. State leaders, of course, face elections and are concerned almost solely with presenting growth figures to their constituents in an effort to demonstrate that the economy is best served under their administration. The rhetoric of interdependence and cooperation is a mask that covers serious obstacles to achieving even the most limited of goals.

Maurice Strong himself reflects on the striking relevance of the comments made in his speech in Stockholm to the international environmental agenda as presented in Rio. Despite the efforts of the green diplomats, the supportive NGOs, the now enthusiastic corporate leaders, and the end of the Cold War, little had changed. "It was disappointing," Strong says, "to realize how little progress we had made in twenty years."[56] If it is disappointing to Strong, it is doubly disappointing to those who see serious limitations with the incrementalist approach.

AFTER RIO

The lack of commitment to concrete targets at the Rio Conference was a serious hindrance to the green diplomats, but they continued along with the same format nonetheless. Maurice Strong involved himself in a five-year review forum to consider ways of moving forward from the declaratory policy of the Rio Declaration to an action policy that would hope to realize the goals expressed therein. Some 500 participants from around the world attended, drawn mostly from what Strong likes to call "civil society stakeholders."[57] Strong is referring, of course, to the grassroots organizations and nongovernmental organizations that are so central to the success of his vision. As Strong sees it, if the ideals of sustainable development as framed by the green diplomats (i.e., a commitment to growth as a way of dealing with limits) are accepted at a grassroots level, it makes the organization of the global system much more straightforward. The concept—the rhetoric—is essential to the success of green diplomacy, and this concept, as we have seen, is an incredibly powerful one for uniting opposites and defusing critique. One-dimensional thought at its most potent.

There is more, however, to Strong's commitment to his "civil society stakeholders." The concept of civil society—which is used increasingly by governments and business leaders in the Western world—is an interesting one that, if we delve deeper into its origins, can perhaps serve us well in our efforts to understand green diplomacy. This once critical concept has been absorbed into unreflective and widespread usage, and this fact alone demonstrates the desire of the status quo to minimize the contested nature of social, political, and economic life. The concept of civil society has been used, especially by the Italian Marxist Antonio Gramsci (and by those who look to his work for insight into the operation of power), to gain insight into the sphere of political engagement in which consent is sought by the dominant (i.e., hegemonic) class and where the political and ideological struggles are played out in all those bodies and organizations not directly under the auspices of state control. Dominance is exercised in this sphere by persuading the subordinate classes to accept the values and ideas that best serve the interests of the hegemonic class. Seen in this light, the concept of "civil society stakeholders" can be seen as an attempt to nullify the struggles for the shaping of the society; instead, it is merely assumed that the subordinate classes have a stake in the formation of the order and as a result share in the outcomes of the decisions.

In his reflections on the Stockholm Conference, Strong explicitly makes the link between green diplomacy and the co-option of dissent. He gives himself an enormous amount of credit for his ability to be diplomatic in the face of critique—in this case coming from the countries of the South, which were enraged by the suggestion that it was *their* population problems that were the source of environmental destruction. Strong speaks about his "evolving fund of experience in dealing with conflict and diplomatic processes" and says: "I had learned never to confront but to co-opt, never to bully but to equivocate, and never to yield. When I entered the world of diplomacy as an amateur, a seasoned professional advised me to learn how to say 'hmmm' in negotiating difficult issues and when I didn't agree but didn't want to be offensive. I understood now, as I could never have when I was younger, that the oblique approach can often be the most direct one."[58] Since his entry into the leading positions of global green diplomacy, Strong has never yielded in the face of opposition and has always found the "oblique approach" as a way of neutralizing the protest against his mission.

Strong's commitment to getting the message of sustainable development into the public domain in the years between the Stockholm and

Rio Conferences, to be used as a framing device, has had the consequence of limiting the terms of the discourse. This denial of the critical content is far more powerful than any government legislation or corporate advertising campaign could ever hope to be. Yet Strong should not be seen as a Machiavellian operator knowing full well that his actions are having the effect of minimizing protest in order that destructive practices can continue apace. Along with other green diplomats of the world, he is convinced that the logic of the chosen route is the best path to a sustainable and environmentally sound future.

The big set-piece conferences to mark the anniversaries of Stockholm and Rio will doubtless continue. At the time of writing, preparations are well under way for the next environmental conference extravaganza to be held in Johannesburg, South Africa, in late summer 2002. This World Summit on Sustainable Development is being promoted as the conference that will present the international community with the opportunity to adopt "concrete steps" and "quantifiable targets" for implementing the (nonbinding) Agenda 21 agreed at Rio.[59]

It remains to be seen, of course, whether this conference will be the one where the fallacies embedded in the official language of sustainable development are exposed and dealt with. Given the usual process of participant accreditation, it seems unlikely that any radical critiques of the concept as defined and solidified in green diplomacy will be made within the conference hall. It seems clear that green diplomacy will continue to accept the limitations of the state system and will seek, with that system's help, to solve the problems inevitably generated by its operation. Green diplomats are, alas, victims of the tendency to accept one-dimensional thought; their powerful position in the shaping of the discourse means that they also serve to institutionalize it.

CONCLUSION

From Stockholm to Rio and beyond, the green diplomats have been busy in their attempts to find solutions to the environmental problems facing the international community, and they have been doing so in good faith. As we approach the tenth anniversary of Rio, it seems that we can state with some degree of certainty that the deterioration of the natural world has continued and that the methods used by the green diplomats have indeed failed to rectify the situation to any fundamental degree. The orthodox telling of the Stockholm-to-Rio trail asks us to celebrate the increased awareness of green issues. International action through green diplomacy is, we are asked to believe, dealing with the crisis in the only suitable, *rational* manner. It may not be perfect, its defenders argue, but it is all we have. We will look closer, of course, at the technical operation of the chosen method of regime formation, but for now it is important to call into question the framing of the problem.

The international community has certainly taken steps in a number of limited issue areas, but the largest step taken in these years has been the successful framing of the issue in terms of sustainable development. Now, this concept means nothing in and of itself. Indeed, as has been argued above, the concept is a useful one because it can mean so many things to so many people. The framing of this concept has, however, quite successfully taken a vibrant and politicized international environmental movement that was gaining ground in the mainstream consciousness through its articulation of the necessary recognition of limits and has turned the issue into one of increased growth, the necessity of top-down approaches, and an increased role for both state and business leaders in the finding of solutions. The sources of the problem—as articulated by the green movement in the 1960s and 1970s—have been given new powers by the green diplomats as the issue has been reconstituted to ensure that those responsible for the decisions that have led to the problems are seen instead as the saviors of the environment. We in the so-called civil society now have a stake in the process, but our role is not to lead the reconceptualization of the problem but rather to receive the wisdom of the green diplomats and to advance and endorse the cause of international cooperation in issues of trade, growth, and economic interdependence. In numerous ways, green diplomacy has been directed specifically at containing the forces and tendencies that challenge the status quo view of economics and international politics. Again, this is not to suggest a conspiracy but rather that the tendency to accept the given structures without question (one-dimensional thought) leads inevitably to efforts to make life within these structures run a bit more smoothly. In doing so, the dangerous practices are both reinforced and even celebrated.

Through a presentation of the nature of power in this cooperative, consensual light, the green diplomats have had great success in recasting the issue of environmental destruction from one of protest and resistance (Marcuse's "Great Refusal") to one of support for the status quo. The coherent framing of the issues in terms of economic growth and international trade by the green diplomats in the years between Stockholm and Rio can now play itself out. The stage has been set to absorb and diminish the protests and articulate critiques that presented a clearer view of the sources of environmental deterioration. There is nothing more dangerous than a challenge we wrongly think we are adequately responding to.

NOTES

1. Carson, *Silent Spring.*

2. Schumacher, *Small Is Beautiful.*

3. Maddox, *The Doomsday Syndrome,* p. 96. Maddox was one of Carson's most influential critics in part due to his position as editor of *Nature.* Maddox believed that Carson's technique was one of "calculated overdramatisation" (p. 15) and was therefore to be disregarded.

4. It is important to keep in mind the wide array of books available to those who wanted to read more about the social role of science and the potential environmental problems stemming from government and corporate decisionmaking. Among the most popular were Commoner, *The Closing Circle;* Ehrlich, *The Population Bomb;* Dubos, *Reason Awake;* Ellul, *The Technological Society;* and Nicholson, *The Environmental Revolution.* A collection of articles was drawn together by Friends of the Earth in 1970 designed specifically for a teach-in; see de Bell, *The Environmental Handbook.* Another popular book was Ward and Dubos, *Only One Earth,* which was an "unofficial report" commissioned by Maurice Strong and which was seen to set out the issues confronting the world at the time of the Stockholm Conference in 1972.

5. Meadows et al., *The Limits to Growth.* This report by the Club of Rome—a self-described "invisible college"—made headlines due to the controversial findings predicting that time was running out for humans. The language of "limits" used within it became common currency among environmentalists.

6. Benthall, *The Limits of Human Nature.* This volume of essays based on a course of lectures given at the Institute of Contemporary Arts in London shifted the debate over limits into the realm of humanity itself. Examining human nature and the limits within which it develops, this volume posed some extraordinary questions and thought-provoking issues. See especially Bohm, "Human Nature as the Product of Our Mental Models," pp. 92–114.

7. Leiss, *The Limits to Satisfaction.* In this volume, Leiss takes the discussion of limits beyond the standard discussion of what we might be forced to do as a result of resource scarcity and into a discussion of needs versus wants. Society's manipulation of needs is brilliantly explored in this book.

8. Schumacher, *Small Is Beautiful,* p. 246.

9. See, for example, Valaskakis et al., *The Conserver Society;* Daly, *Toward a Steady-State Economy* [reprinted as *Economics, Ecology, Ethics: Essays Toward a Steady-State Economy*]; Henderson, *Creating Alternative Futures;* and Marcuse, *One Dimensional Man.*

10. UN resolution found in Brenton, *The Greening of Machiavelli,* p. 34.

11. For a flavor of the diversity of feeling about the conference written at the time, see Ward, "The End of an Epoch?"; Morgan, "Stockholm"; Ungeheuer,

"Woodstockholm"; Sullivan, "The Stockholm Conference"; Commoner, "Motherhood in Stockholm"; and Langway and Edgerton, "The U.S. at Stockholm."

12. See, for example, Brenton, *The Greening of Machiavelli;* Strong, *Where on Earth Are We Going?;* McCormick, *The Global Environmental Movement;* and Elliott, *The Global Politics of the Environment.*

13. For the text of the declaration, see Imber, *Environment, Security, and UN Reform,* annex 1. For an interesting and in-depth legal discussion of the declaration, article by article, see Sohn, "The Stockholm Declaration on the Human Environment."

14. Strong, *Where on Earth Are We Going?* p. 128. For Strong's thoughts on the need for "management," see his "One Year After Stockholm."

15. For a concise discussion of UNEP's role, see Imber, *Environment, Security, and UN Reform,* chap. 4; and McCormick, *The Global Environmental Movement,* chap. 6.

16. To give Maurice Strong credit, his memoirs do reflect (to a minimal degree) the participation of the various citizens groups that gathered for the Environment Forum—the unofficial parallel meeting that has come to be seen as something of a requirement in any major environmental conference. As we shall see, however, Strong subsequently found ways of dealing with the counter-messages presented at such events by working harder in the lead-up to control both the participation at such events and, more importantly, their messages.

17. Strong, *Where on Earth Are We Going?* p. 132.

18. I say this despite Brenton's argument that: "It is difficult to believe that this did not push Western governments further in the direction of incorporating environmentalism in the Stockholm texts [than] they might have been willing to go in a more conventional, and private, negotiating process." Brenton, *The Greening of Machiavelli,* p. 44.

19. Knelman, "What Happened at Stockholm?" It is from this article that the following account is drawn, as there is little published material available on the Dai Dong Conference.

20. The message was drafted at a meeting in Menton, France, and was subsequently circulated among biologists and environmental scientists around the world. For a complete text of the message, see "A Message to Our 3.5 Billion Neighbours on Planet Earth from 2,200 Environmental Scientists," *The UNESCO Courier.*

21. Poland and Czechoslovakia (which did attend the official conference) were joined by the USSR and Hungary. Ibid., p. 33.

22. Ibid., p. 34.

23. Strong, *Where on Earth Are We Going?* p. 131.

24. Thomas, *The Environment in International Relations,* p. 21.

25. McCormick, *The Global Environmental Movement,* p. 88.

26. International conferences began to be held with unprecedented frequency and with specific goals. As Marvin Soroos points out, the Stockholm Conference was followed by a conference on human settlements, water, desertification, new and renewable sources of energy, and outer space, and two conferences on population. See Soroos, "The Tragedy of the Commons in Global Perspective," p. 346.

27. In addition to Brundtland, the commission included: Mansour Khalid, Susanna Agnelli, Saleh Abdulrahman Al-Athel, Pablo Gonzalez Casanova, Bernard T. G. Chidzero, Lamine Mohamed Fadika, Volker Hauff, Istvan Lang, Ma Shijun, Margarita Marino de Botero, Nagendra Singh, Paulo Nogueira-Neto, Saburo Okita, Shridrath S. Ramphal, William Doyle Ruckelshaus, Mohamed Sahnoun, Emil Salim, Bukar Shaib, Vladimir Sokolov, Janez Stanovnik, Maurice Strong, and Jim MacNeill (Secretary-General of the commission and ex-officio member).

28. World Commission on Environment and Development (WCED), *Our Common Future*. See annex 2 for a detailed description of the commission and its work.

29. Ibid., pp. 356–357.

30. Ibid., p. 43.

31. Ibid., p. 65.

32. Ibid., pp. 1–2.

33. Cook, ed., *Pears Cyclopaedia*, Y3.

34. Marcuse, *One Dimensional Man*, pp. 90–91.

35. WCED, *Our Common Future*, p. xii.

36. Visvanathan, "Mrs. Brundtland's Disenchanted Cosmos," p. 378. Visvanathan's article was published initially in the superb Indian journal *Lokayan Bulletin* under the title "Brundtland's Non-Magical Cosmos." For other critiques of the Brundtland report, see Clow, "Sustainable Development"; Williams, "Aid, Sustainable Development, and the Environmental Crisis"; Luke, "Sustainable Development as a Power/Knowledge System"; and Chatterjee and Finger, *The Earth Brokers*, chap. 3.

37. Visvanathan, "Mrs. Brundtland's Disenchanted Cosmos," p. 378.

38. Ibid., p. 383.

39. Ibid., p. 384.

40. Marcuse, *One Dimensional Man*, p. 158.

41. Ibid., p. 101.

42. For an intriguing and comprehensive examination of the transitive versus operational meanings of concepts, see Marcuse, *One Dimensional Man*, chap. 4.

43. Finger, "Environmental NGOs in the UNCED Process," pp. 191–192.

44. Ibid., pp. 194–196. Finger clearly demonstrates the degree to which the Rio process would mirror the Stockholm process in terms of working structures, the same intellectual categories for negotiations, similar dates and places for PrepCom meetings, and a similar output in terms of the documentation.

45. Ibid., p. 195.

46. Ibid., pp. 198–201.

47. Ibid., pp. 201–202. See also Greer and Bruno, *Greenwash*, pp. 28–29.

48. For an excellent critique of the Rio Conference from the perspective of the developing worlds, see Middleton, O'Keefe, and Moyo, *Tears of the Crocodile*. For a positive presentation of the objectives and outcomes, see Strong, *Where on Earth Are We Going?*; and Roche, *A Bargain for Humanity*. For basic presentations of the issues discussed, see Elliott, *The Global Politics of the Environment;* and Brenton, *The Greening of Machiavelli;* and for a critique of the

conference that fits into the themes developed in this book, see Chatterjee and Finger, *The Earth Brokers,* chap. 4.

49. A more manageable version of this was published two years later by Daniel Sitarz: *Agenda 21: The Earth Summit Strategy to Save Our Planet.*

50. Ibid., pp. 312–313.

51. Brenton, *The Greening of Machiavelli,* pp. 208–210.

52. Finger, "Environmental NGOs in the UNCED Process."

53. International NGO Forum, "People's Earth Declaration."

54. Marcuse, *Reason and Revolution,* p. 434. In his epilogue to the book, Marcuse considers the tension within the modern concept of reason and considers Hegel's "power of negativity" and its decline in late industrial society. Marcuse's point is that once reason is denied its oppositional negative power, it unfolds its repressive force. These ideas were played out in greater detail in *One Dimensional Man* many years later.

55. For discussions of the role of a so-called transnational civil society, see Ruggie, "Territoriality and Beyond"; Ekins, *A New World Order;* Lipschutz, "Reconstructing World Politics"; Finger, "NGOs and Transformation"; Willetts, "From Stockholm to Rio and Beyond"; Clark et al., "The Sovereign Limits of Global Civil Society"; Pasha and Blaney, "Ellusive Paradise"; and Williams and Ford, "The World Trade Organisation, Social Movements, and Global Environmental Management."

56. Strong, *Where on Earth Are We Going?* p. 223.

57. Ibid., p. 283.

58. Ibid., p. 123.

59. The documentation surrounding its organization reiterates once again the central precepts of the Brundtland Commission and does not appear to take on the important root causes of environmental destruction. See United Nations, *Johannesburg Summit 2002: World Summit on Sustainable Development,* available at www.johannesburgsummit.org.

3

Globalizing Unsustainability

IN THE LAST CHAPTER, I FOCUSED ON THE ADVENT OF GREEN diplomacy and its success in developing a framing device for the issue of global environmental destruction. I offered a critique of the operational treatment of the concept of sustainable development and the political function that it has taken on. Although the possibility of the concept having a transitive meaning cannot be denied, the way in which the international environmental debate has been framed through the use of this concept has served to limit the development of a dialectical movement within the concept at a popular level. Indeed, the concept has been used as a technique to undermine critique and to gain support for the expansion of global capital. The orthodoxy of current international economic structures is celebrated—with its façade of greater democratic accountability—and as a result we are faced with the further deepening of the destructive environmental consequences of the economic system.

The concept of sustainable development has successfully turned the problematic around in the mainstream consciousness and taken it from a discussion that recognizes necessary limits to one of a merely technical problem of finding the right strategy for limitless growth. The advocates of green diplomacy have worked diligently for more than thirty years to find solutions to specific problems, but the lack of critical reflection on the broader context in which they work means that the solutions they seek are within a system of increasingly internationalized trade. Top-down management, technical rationality, and the institutionalization of free trade and global economic relations are now the order of the day. The challenge to think about the relationship between economics and environmental destruction has been largely resisted, and the marriage of economics to environment has taken on a form that celebrates economic growth and an increase in the power vested in international capital institutions and businesses.

The acceptance (sometimes celebration) by today's incrementalist green diplomat of the confines of the logic of economic "globalization" is disturbing and counterproductive on a number of counts. First of all, the language used by the cheerleaders of neoliberal economic policy serves to mystify the operation of global capitalism and to present it as an inevitable phenomenon whose consequences will be of benefit to the citizens of the world. For this mystification to take hold in the popular imagination, the concept of globalization has been linked to that of sustainable development in an attempt to present the workings of the liberal international economic system as inherently green. With this rearticulation of the growth ethic and all the environmentally damaging repercussions that stem from it, the irrational is presented as rational: the opposites are wedded. Both the language of globalization and the neoliberal practices that give the concept its practical intent are used as instruments of control, and the problems faced are dealt with in technical and operational terms. The "inexorable tide" of the globalizing marketplace serves to present the phenomenon as outside the realm of human control, and alternative economic models—many of which *are* environmentally sound—are silenced and pushed to the margins, as are those who advocate them in numerous locales around the globe.

In this chapter I will examine the environmental implications of the practical workings of the concept of sustainable development as it is linked to economic globalization. I will consider the role of international economic institutions and the way in which the concept has helped to further deepen the destructive environmental practices that the Frankfurt School writers and those who utilize their insights have pointed to over the decades. I will consider the origins of the discourse of economic development and will argue that today's green diplomats are—wittingly or unwittingly—supportive of a status quo system that reembeds the dangerous and environmentally destructive practices they claim to be dealing with.

THE ENLIGHTENMENT AND THE
ECONOMIC MODEL OF PROGRESS

The most logical point of entry into a discussion about the current linkage between trade and environmental protection is a consideration of the linkage historically. It is no coincidence that the rise of markets and the advent of the Enlightenment thought discussed in Chapter 1 occurred simultaneously. Indeed, the shift toward a mechanized view of nature in the sixteenth century assisted with the development of markets and states. The rhetorical promise of the Enlightenment was for a better life for all, with answers to problems facing humankind in the development of an easier life. The questions for which answers were sought, however, were inevitably those of import to the nascent capitalist society. Adrian Atkinson makes this point when he demonstrates the efforts of the scientists of the sixteenth century: investigating problems of pumping and ventilation to help increase mining production, investigating mathematics and astronomy to improve navigational skills, and looking for information about ballistics to increase military efficiency.[1] Bacon's promise of a return to the Garden of Eden certainly resulted in higher profits and an easier lifestyle for some, but it was at great cost to the majority of the population and certainly at an enormous cost to the natural world.

There were other serious ramifications of the way of thinking brought into the mainstream by the Enlightenment thinkers. As the view that the natural world required human intervention and transformation took hold, it became a convenient justification for imperial activity. The need for an expanded resource base was undeniable and, as William Leiss has argued, the idea of human intervention "was used to justify the conquest and resettlement of so-called backward areas . . . where it was claimed the native populations were not improving sufficiently the regime of nature."[2] As J. Ann Tickner has pointed out in a concise presentation of these issues, "the expansion of the European state system meant that the scientific revolution's mechanistic attitude toward nature began to take on global dimensions with far-reaching implications for non-western ecological traditions which were not able to withstand assimilation by the global economy."[3] This process of the expansion of the state system through colonialism—with its Enlightenment ideology underpinning it—has had dire consequences for the state of the world's environment. As Leiss has argued, the "doctrine of continuous progress became widely accepted. . . . 'Development' became a fundamental category of social thought."[4] It is extraordinary that the ideas so central to the Enlightenment project continue to dominate the thinking of the twenty-first century. The language surrounding the globalization debates of today are similar and depend on the same categories of thought.

The international organizations established at the end of World War II—the so-called Bretton Woods institutions—have created the momentum for the further development of the world's economy and, based as it is on the same ideas of progress, domination, and economic growth, the ecological costs are as great as (if not greater than) those of the age of empire. As with the attempts to resist colonial control, there are many localities today fighting to preserve an economic system and a view of nature that contradict and resist the dominant worldview. The organization of the international marketplace and its structures makes resistance extraordinarily difficult. Add to this a form of green diplomacy that accepts the destructive principles, and the chances for a fundamental shift to a more ecologically sustainable international economic system appear difficult in the extreme. The current linking of economics and the environment through the Brundtland process has become so successful precisely because it does not challenge us to think beyond the orthodoxy. Indeed, as argued in the last chapter, the linkage is of precisely the same logic as the Enlightenment discourse.

A close examination of the rationale of our international economic system must be undertaken in order to expose the logical inconsistency inherent in it. The orthodox argument, which abounds today under the broad category of sustainable development as presented by the green diplomats, is that the answer to current environmental problems lies in increased growth, better international institutions for regulating and overseeing free trade, and a greater role for the market. When Maurice Strong speaks of "eco-nomics,"[5] he is indeed linking economics to ecology, but in a destructive manner reminiscent of the development logic of the sixteenth and seventeenth centuries.

The task before us is to articulate the need for a revolution of thought as powerful as that seen during the Age of Enlightenment. A prerequisite of this challenge is to destabilize the message of top-down management and corporate solutions to environmental problems. These ideas are extended and reproduced through the latest form of imperialism—the globalizing marketplace.

THE LIBERAL INTERNATIONAL ECONOMIC ORDER

When the framers of the Liberal International Economic Order (LIEO) got together at Bretton Woods toward the end of World War II, environmental issues were not on their mind. The shaping of the postwar peace was focused on preventing the economic competition that was seen as destructive to interstate relations. The institutionalization of liberal trading practices and indeed liberal ideology was seen as the key to future stability and security. However, the framework for international order that was established in that small New Hampshire town in 1944 has become the focus for the current debate about global environmental problems.

The creation of the International Monetary Fund (IMF), the World Bank, and the General Agreement on Tariffs and Trade (GATT) established the foundations for the organization of a liberal trading order that has expanded massively since the end of the war. These separate but interlinked institutions guaranteed not only economic prosperity but also the state-sponsored dedication to markets. The United States was the strongest country after the war, and as a result the peace could be shaped largely in its interest. Support for the system from its allies was, if not inevitable, highly likely given the shared system of beliefs and aspirations. Limiting exchange-rate fluctuations (so damaging in the interwar period), ensuring money for the rebuilding of economies, and guaranteeing an open and fair trading system were to be the cornerstones of the international order.

The point of this chapter is not to chronicle in detail the transnationalization of the economy,[6] but rather to point out that the various commissions and conferences dedicated to demonstrating the potential for multilateral cooperation in the interests of the environment do not take place in a vacuum. The backdrop to the green diplomacy is, in fact, composed of a set of social, political, and economic relations that are framed in a very specific way, serving to limit the potential for substantial alteration of the destructive environmental practices embedded within them. Economic multilateral activities create the structures and limit the thought processes of those engaged in pursuing environmental solutions.

A tension existed within the logic underwriting the creation of these postwar economic structures. Market efficiency and liberal trading arrangements were seen as the necessary components to unlock the potential for social, political, and economic progress. Governments would, it was widely believed, act as mediators between the market and the public with the provision of social programs. A contradiction emerged, however, and governments repeatedly *chose* the path of efficiency in a rush to embrace the "rational" and integrated international marketplace. The freeing of capital from domestic constraints, the valorization of the free market, and the extension of the liberal trading order far beyond that envisioned by the framers of the Bretton Woods institutions soon took precedence over the provision of social progress. We were left with the hollow promise that efficiency in and of itself would produce environmental, social, and political progress. The extension of this logic is the backdrop to today's green diplomacy.

Despite calls for modifications to the Bretton Woods system, the Brundtland Commission accepts the basic working premise of free and open trade guaranteed by multilateral economic structures and seeks to operate within them. The logical contradictions of the claims made are not, as we have seen, dealt with in any substantive manner. The solidification of the notion that deregulated international trade leads inexorably to higher environmental standards is at the root of the claims of the green diplomats and has led to a degree of enthusiasm on the part of state and corporate leaders. Viewing the way these arguments are made and the dangers contained within them for true environmental sustainability is a crucial step along the path to considering alternatives.

SUSTAINABLE DEVELOPMENT AND TRADE

The Case for Free Trade

A straightforwardly optimistic case is often made concerning the benefits presumed to flow from an increase in international trade governed by free market institutions. Economist Jagdish Bhagwati argues, for instance, that free trade encourages growth, which in turn allows for an increase in tax resources: "without such revenues," he argues, "little can be achieved, no matter how pure one's motives may be."[7] The argument is presented as self-evident: pollution-fighting techniques will be more freely available to the industrializing countries as a result of such cooperative policies; free trade leads inevitably to efficiency and it will therefore, by its very nature, generally help the environmental situation; a global marketplace makes it easier for the consumer to exert pressure on governments and businesses to raise standards. There can be no doubt, Bhagwati argues, that there will be a leveling upward of standards as a result of free trade initiatives.[8] In rejecting what he speaks of as the "moral militancy of environmentalists," Bhagwati describes the quest for environmental standards as a form of imperialism—eco-imperialism.[9]

For those supporting the idea that globalizing trade relations leads inexorably to environmental stability, there is almost a sense of bewilderment at the attacks from environmental activists, organizations, and, indeed, some economists. *The Economist,* that venerable and reliable magazine of the status quo, has repeatedly made the case for free trade. The "fact" that trade benefits the environment is so clear to the editors that it can be succinctly summarized: "The reason is that it boosts economic growth. As people get richer, they want a cleaner environment—and they acquire the means to pay for it."[10] *The Economist* denies that there will be a so-called "race to the bottom" merely because some countries have lower standards; in fact, such a differential in standards is an important part of the logic of comparative advantage and is thus a "valuable principle" to be protected. This is competition, and the marketplace (the consumers) will subsequently decide which products they will choose.[11]

The Case Against Free Trade

There are a range of arguments that can be marshaled against the presentation of the orthodox liberal view vis-à-vis the environment and economic structures. The fact that a concept such as sustainable development can be adopted so readily by so many people with such varying agendas demonstrates the power of the underlying conceptions that shape and guide our environmental concerns.

Most straightforward, of course, is the critique offered by many economists that so-called free trade is not at all what it appears. Former World Bank economist Herman Daly argues that what is commonly referred to as free trade should in fact be called deregulated international commerce. The original articulation of comparative advantage—by British economist David Ricardo (1772–1823)—was based on the belief that a country's production is limited by its own capital and resources; some products are comparatively less expensive to produce than others. With a system of free trade a country is able to concentrate on the area where it has a comparative advantage and trade with another country to ensure that a range of goods and produce are available to the citizens of both countries. What is assumed in this view, is that capital is immobile—that it cannot cross borders. In the present era, however, free trade is not based on comparative advantage at all, but rather on the interests and profit margins of large transnational corporations. Capital is mobile and the quest of corporate executives is to move operations to the locations where there are lower trade and environmental standards and thereby maximize profit.[12] As Daly points out, it is illogical in the extreme to appeal to a principle that is based on a premise of capital *immobility* in order to support a system in favor of capital *mobility*.[13] Once again, the irrational presented as the rational.

The fallacious argument that consumer choice and the free operation of the market will lead to an increase in environmental standards is underpinned by a faith that markets are, in fact, neutral and self-regulating institutions. The belief that an increased standard of living will lead to demands for environmental protection successfully masks the reality of the manipulation of the market through advertising, with a prime example being the increased campaigns to present a variety of goods, services, and resources as green. The demands, in short, might be made by the consumer, but we have more than enough evidence that they are often shaped and sometimes even created.

The reality of this deregulated international commerce is a lowering rather than the claimed raising of environmental standards. The elites in countries deemed to be undeveloped in the current system (as defined by conventional growth-model indicators) are often desperate to encourage inward investment. The rules and dictates of the international financial organizations add to the environmental problems by establishing targets that are impossible to meet without instituting environmentally destructive policies and practices.

In the context of the broader critique offered here, it is important to recognize that there is another important component of the trade-environment linkage made by the advocates of eco-nomics. The way of perceiving the world in terms of inevitable progress based on rationally—and quantifiably—defined ends has led to a highly technocratic calculation of progress. Economics as a discipline fits soundly into these Enlightenment ideals. The reduction of life to models for calculation offers us a very skewed sense of well-being, development, and progress. Rationality must be seen to be objective and there must, as a result, be scientific ways to demonstrate success and failure and measure progress and decline. This key task is performed in the modern "science" of economics by the concepts of gross national product (GNP) and gross domestic product (GDP).[14]

The ability to devise a number that can be seen to represent the growth of a country's economy and, furthermore, be accepted without question as a measure of progress is stunningly effective. The presentation of GNP as a rationally calculated figure leads to a widespread acceptance of the idea that never-ending growth of production and consumption is not only important, it is the only meaningful indicator of a society's progress. The application of instrumental reason in this case assists—indeed, is essential to—the building of a mass consensus behind the need for economic growth. But there are two aspects of the calculation that are not commonly known by the people who absorb the annual statements and accept the supposedly objective picture thus presented.

First, the calculation of GNP does not include any unpaid service or activity, an omission that not only masks the contribution of unpaid workers (usually women), but serves also to celebrate economies fully integrated into a cash economy while indicating that societies that continue to celebrate sustainable living through small-scale exchange and barter are somehow backward. The GNP is not, in short, an accurate indicator of a country's economic activity, despite claims to the contrary. Of great import, however, is the reinforcement of the logic of the Western development model and the inevitably widespread view of the lack of "progress" and "development" elsewhere. Second, and also of import to our consideration of environmental issues, is the fact that the figure calculated does not take into consideration the deterioration of physical resources. In fact, the increase in the exploitation of resource extraction is a positive gain for the figure of GNP, and this rational calculation thus celebrates consumption and waste. A country that ensures that environmental considerations take precedence over economic projects will have to suffer the consequence: so-called sluggish growth of GNP, which will be seen as an indication of inept management quite possibly requiring tough medicine from the international economic organizations that administer the multilateral arrangements. This is the irrational once again presented as rational.

The widespread faith in objective and rational indicators of growth has led to a situation where such an environmentally destructive calculation of progress can be seen as the answer to environmental deterioration. Following Joseph Schumpeter, Herman Daly refers to "pre-analytic visions" and points out that the assumptions built into the current system have the effect of reinforcing the problem.[15] For example, if we accept the argument that growth inevitably decreases poverty, then the question is framed in such a way as to increase growth. No challenge can be presented because decreasing poverty is an obviously impressive goal. If our assumption, however, comes to be that an increase in growth leads to an increase in the exploitation of natural resources and therefore to environmental degradation, the problematic is shifted from its axis. As matters stand, however, the linkage between growth and environmental sustainability is presented as being an obvious and unquestionable truth and, in the age of global capital mobility, the logic is internationalized: "if trade is made freer, the world will get richer—and that is the surest way to make it cleaner too."[16] Such a claim serves effectively as a simplification to undermine any possible critique.

THE INSTITUTIONALIZATION OF FREE TRADE

While the debate surrounding free trade is ongoing, the institutionalization of its mechanisms continues apace. Through bilateral and multilateral agreements, the logic of "free" trade and growth is instituted. The proponents of the various agreements—the North American Free Trade Agreement (NAFTA) and the World Trade Organization (WTO) being two major examples—continue to couch the debate in terms of sustainable development, and posit the inherently green credentials of such trading arrangements. The liberal institutionalist is in full flow here with the arguments that a rules-based international economy guarantees the conditions for the realization of environmental standards. The transnationalization of capital is presented as the only logical course of action: the technical rationality of the quantifiably defined economic indicators of GNP and GDP tell us so. Economics is presented as scientifically quantifiable and arguments to the contrary are said to be emotional, illogical, or utopian.

The unquestioned nature of these concepts is a direct result of the technical rationality embedded in the organizational structure of international society more generally. We see quite clearly the application of instrumental reason through the major economic indicators, and the unquestioned nature of this activity serves to make the current structure of economic and social relations appear to be the inevitable—and optimum—outcome of rationally chosen priorities and policies. Such are the arguments presented by supporters of international free trade agreements. But does the reality match the promise of environmental sustainability?

The North American Free Trade Agreement

Nowhere are the inherent dangers of free trade, or rather, deregulated international commerce, more evident than in the trade agreement brought into being by the United States, Canada, and Mexico. The push toward liberalized trade markets in North America reflects the trend toward corporate freedom of maneuverability more clearly than in any other trade agreement. Despite claims that potential impacts on the environment will be guarded against by a so-called side agreement and its creation of the North American Commission for Environmental Co-operation, a number of lawsuits are providing evidence to the contrary.

NAFTA came into effect on January 1, 1994, after lengthy and often acrimonious negotiations. Many citizens of Canada and the United States, the two original participants of the Free Trade Area, which was to be extended, were unsure as to the effects the agreement would have on a range of issues, and high on the list of concerns was the environment. A range of public interest groups in both countries sounded the alarm to warn fellow citizens about the potentially destructive environmental impact hidden in the arrangements being negotiated. In the United States a coalition of interest groups—among them Ralph Nader's Public Citizen—filed a court petition to require NAFTA to undertake an environmental impact statement prior to final approval. Although a federal judge initially ruled in the interests of the petitioners, President George Bush's fast-track legislation won the day and the ruling was overturned by a higher court. Derek Churchill and Richard Worthington are correct to point to the "remarkable consensus on the primacy of brute GNP growth as the goal of development" that lay behind these "polarized" debates.[17] Nonetheless, those protesting the NAFTA agreement had legitimate environmental concerns as well.

A major source of problems for the participating states regards three clauses contained within chapter 11 of the agreement, which allows a corporation to sue a government if it believes that its export opportunities are being hindered by laws enacted in the government of the country. It is unlikely that the signatories realized what they were letting themselves in for with this clause, but it is clear that the results have had a devastating effect on the natural environment. It is doubtful that even the most adamant opponent of the trade deal realized the full extent of the damage or the impact that chapter 11 would have on the ability of the participating countries to enact environmental laws and regulations in accordance with their own standards. The fact that many corporate and governmental leaders seek the institutionalization of corporate rights in this manner through broader international trade agreements makes an examination of the NAFTA process of special relevance.

The stated intention of chapter 11 has nothing whatsoever to do with environmental legislation but was rather intended to prevent governments from treating foreign investors differently than the corporations operating domestically and to prevent the nationalization or expropriation of foreign investment. On the face of it, these provisions seem to fit in with established trade deals, which is why it is somewhat surprising that they have been used in a blatant manner to challenge domestic governmental legislation. The examination of two cases—one taken by a U.S. corporation against the Canadian government and one taken by a Canadian corporation against the U.S. government, both about gasoline additives—will serve to highlight the important points of the issue.

Ethyl Oil v. the Canadian government. The case of Ethyl Oil has been widely cited to demonstrate the fact that free trade hinders rather than assists the realization of environmental standards. The facts of the case are more complex than are often presented by those arguing that corporations can force governments to rescind environmental legislation: this does not diminish the charge against NAFTA's chapter 11, but we should be clear about the details surrounding the legal case against the Canadian government.[18]

Ethyl Corporation's claim against Canada came after the government passed the Manganese-Based Fuel Additives Act following a legislative debate in 1997. The arguments were not about methylcyclopentadienyl manganese tricarbonyl (MMT), Ethyl Corporation's product, but rather about the use of manganese as a gasoline additive. The concerns stemmed from two quite separate environmental claims: first from car manufacturers, representatives of which claimed that the additive was causing emission control devices to fail in cars and resulting in higher levels of pollutants; and second from some scientific quarters, where the argument was being made that MMT was potentially dangerous to the human brain.[19] The Canadian government did not ban MMT outright, in part because of the difficulty in having a chemical categorized as unsafe under its own regulatory procedures, a situation that in itself begs a number of questions. Instead, the government banned the "importation and interprovincial transportation" of the fuel additive, which was only found in Ethyl Corporation's product. The Canadian government was certainly not the first site of resistance to MMT; it has been banned in many parts of the world, including several U.S. states. Ethyl Corporation saw a way of challenging the Canadian legislation through the use of the so-called investor-to-state mechanism of NAFTA and was determined to restore the reputation of its chemical additive.

Ethyl Corporation invoked three articles of chapter 11 to bring its claim. First, Ethyl argued that the government was breaking regulations that provided for the equal treatment of foreign and domestic corporations (article 1102) because it knew that MMT was made only by Ethyl and that such a ban would favor Canadian investors. Second, and obviously related, was Ethyl's argument that if MMT were removed from the Canadian market, competition would be eliminated and Canadian-made gasoline additives (such as ethanol) would be unfairly favored (article 1106). Finally, Ethyl argued that the action amounted to the expropriation of Ethyl Corporation's Canadian operations (article 1110) because the decision would effectively put Ethyl's Canadian subsidiary out of business. In addition to these claims, Ethyl argued that Canada's actions would do harm to the firm's ability to market MMT elsewhere. By the time the costs were added up, the corporation was seeking over U.S.$250 million in damages, but the Canadian government settled in 1998 before it ever got to a NAFTA tribunal hearing. Canada paid the corporation an estimated U.S.$13 million in damages plus legal costs and, in addition, issued a public statement declaring MMT safe.

Methanex Corp. v. the U.S. government. In a case almost mirroring that of *Ethyl Oil,* Methanex Corp., a Canadian business, launched a suit in 1999 to force a change in California's decision to ban a gasoline additive—methyl tertiary butyl ether (MTBE)—a move taken as a result of strong evidence that MTBE is contaminating water supplies throughout the state. Methanex is arguing that California's actions are unfairly affecting its ability to sell methanol, a key ingredient in MTBE, and is seeking damages of U.S.$970 million. The same logic as the *Ethyl* case applied: a very broad definition of expropriation. Methanex is arguing that its subsidiary in Texas and its production facility in Louisiana will be gravely affected by California's decision. The added twist to this case is that although the state government took the action, the NAFTA provisions allow only for the corporation to bring a suit against the federal government. A range of domestic political issues—including the right of a state legislature to consider and act on its own environmental, health, and safety standards—are now in question.

* * *

These two cases could put the participating NAFTA states in an interesting position: the United States being forced to allow the use of an environmentally dangerous chemical produced by a Canadian corporation and Canada being forced to allow the use of an environmentally dangerous chemical produced by a U.S. corporation. A very strange kind of equality indeed. The only sure thing about this trend is that corporate rights are being enshrined in trade deals while the onus is placed on legislative bodies to struggle to find ways to maintain environmental, health, and safety standards.

Even if the actions taken by Canada or California violate, in some way, the letter of NAFTA, this is surely not the point. The *Ethyl* and *Methanex* cases demonstrate quite clearly the ways in which the agreement can be used by corporations seeking to protect their own profit margin and thus cash in on a discourse in which their presumed rights put the health and environmental rights of citizens very much in second place. As mentioned above, the traditional role of the state as mediator of the worst excesses of capitalism (and not very successfully at that) has been largely removed by the supposed logic of globalization, and this type of investor-to-state dispute resolution mechanism is precisely the technique by which it is being undermined. Negotiated by those with corporate interests in mind, NAFTA celebrates deregulated trade and ensures that the private sector does not suffer as a result of public interest, and that it further benefits from a transfer of authority from the participating governments to unaccountable trade tribunals that certainly do not have within their remit the consideration of issues from a broad social or environmental perspective. There is no space here for reflection—only administrative, managerial, and legal detail. Can this possibly be seen as environmentally sound, even in the frame of reference of the green diplomat?

Cases such as these, however, will never get a full public hearing: the negotiations for settlements as well as the NAFTA tribunal hearings themselves go on behind closed doors. The three-member tribunal panel is picked by the two sides (one each and one jointly agreed upon), and it meets in private with no provision whatsoever for public involvement in the process. Issues of public policy are increasingly presented as technical and legal matters to be decided in terms of calculable interests and not as matters suitable for public (or even legislative) debate and input. This has, indeed, been happening at the domestic level for decades, and the added interstate level merely deepens and extends a process that has been widely accepted by most people as the logical way to conduct politics—even in democracies.

Although a number of these cases have come to light, it seems likely that fewer and fewer cases will do so in the future. My argument here is clearly not that corporations will begin to act within a more environmental framework but rather that governments will seek to ensure that their legislation does not put them into the position of such legal challenges. It is already the case in Canada that proposed environmental legislation—emanating from both federal and provincial governments—must be submitted to the Department of Foreign Affairs and International Trade Canada before it can be passed. The result is obvious: any legislation that risks the invocation of chapter 11 will not be allowed through the democratic processes.[20]

There is a deeper critique that is absent from the hue and cry raised about corporate power. In terms of the broader critique of green diplomacy it is an essential one to make. In both the *Ethyl* and *Methanex* cases, the gasoline additive in question was developed as a technological fix for an existing environmental problem. Ethyl Corporation developed MMT when the Canadian government prohibited the use of lead as an additive, and marketed it as a product designed to enhance fuel efficiency. Methanex Corp. developed MTBE in an effort to cut tailpipe emissions and thereby make gasoline "greener" by reducing air pollution. The fact that both of these solutions—provided by technological ingenuity—have led to further environmental problems *should* be leading us to consider the deeper issues at hand. The lack of such critique demonstrates, alas, how deeply embedded the logic of technological progress is.

The North American Agreement on Environmental Cooperation

But what of the famous environmental side agreement—formally called the North American Agreement on Environmental Cooperation (NAAEC)—that was designed to protect the participating countries against any diminishment of their environmental standards? Held up by the participating states as a pathbreaking mechanism to ensure that the environment is given due consideration in relation to trade, the NAAEC in fact does little to change the predominance of commercial interests in the relationships between Canada, the United States, and Mexico.

The Commission for Environmental Cooperation (CEC) was established by the NAAEC, but this watchdog is extraordinarily tame. Headquartered in Montreal, the CEC is at best an institution for preventing countries from using lax environmental standards to gain a trade advantage.[21] Although its provisions allow for citizens and nongovernmental organizations to complain if a government fails to enforce its own laws, it is quite clear that the lack of enforcement authority undermines its worthy declaratory purposes. The participating governments have all been criticized for attempting to keep the CEC toothless and indeed for working hard to ensure that the CEC is brought more carefully into line with the intentions of the economic interests of the participating states.

The existence of the CEC seems little more than a cosmetic alteration designed to absorb critique from the respective publics; as long as there is an environmental agreement to hold up, the majority of the North American population is not aware of its severe limitations and the CEC is therefore quite successful in absorbing critique. George Crowell is not overstating the case when he argues that "[r]ather than serving to limit the potential damage, the [environmental side agreement] appears to be designed to avoid interference with the freedoms that NAFTA grants to corporations to disregard or to exploit the environment."[22]

INTERNATIONAL ORGANIZATIONS AND SUSTAINABLE DEVELOPMENT: BEYOND BRETTON WOODS

The World Trade Organization

The development of support for the liberalization of trade through the creation of trade rules was deepened at Bretton Woods through the creation of the General Agreement on Tarrifs and Trade. In the early years no concern existed about the environmental consequences of the free trade rationale, but as the topic became more popular, those who advocated expanding the range of goods and services covered by the GATT held firmly to the position that trade and environmental protection could be mutually reinforcing goals. The Brundtland report assisted the GATT with its green image by marrying the issues together in a manner that was consistent with the goals of economic growth, free trade, and capital mobility—the cornerstones of the GATT process. Sustainable development was incorporated into GATT documents and the lip service paid to environmental considerations began.[23] Contradictions between the declaratory policy and the reality of GATT dispute resolution, however, quickly became apparent.

Perhaps the most famous case is the so-called *Dolphin-Tuna* case. Simply stated, this legal action was concerned with U.S. regulations that banned imports of Mexican tuna because the nets used by tuna fishers in Mexico were designed in such a way that they caught and drowned dolphins. In 1992 the GATT Dispute Settlement Panel ruled in favor of

Mexico and argued that the United States was not entitled to block imports for environmental reasons and that the attempt to do so was breaking the sacred principle of *comparative advantage*. Free trade rules are specific: a country may have its own environmental standards but it must not unilaterally impose these standards on others by preventing access to their markets.[24] Defenders of the ruling argue that the principle must be kept in place and that the way to deal with the issue necessarily involves appropriate labeling so that the decision is left to the consumer.[25] This, however, is a disingenuous argument given the resistance to labeling from many businesses—including (perhaps especially) U.S. businesses. As with the NAFTA rulings discussed above, the discrepancy between the liberalization of trade and the protection of the environment is vast.

The discussions in the Uruguay Round of GATT talks further extended the rationale of liberalization of trade and continued to play on the theme of sustainable development. By the end of the process, a new organization—the World Trade Organization—was established to take over where the GATT left off. On January 1, 1995, the WTO came into being with the declared goal of

> raising standards of living, ensuring full employment and a large and steadily growing volume of real income and effective demand, and expanding the production of and trade in goods and services, while allowing for the optimal use of the world's resources in accordance with the objective of sustainable development, seeking both to protect and preserve the environment and to enhance the means for doing so in a manner consistent with their respective needs and concerns at different levels of development.[26]

Once again, however, the language of eco-nomics fails to live up to its promise. Despite its claims that environmental protection could be easily integrated into the considerations of liberalized trade, the rules of the game demonstrate the contrary. As within the rules of NAFTA, it is the mobility of capital that is of greatest import in the WTO regime. The resulting impact on health and safety standards, environmental regulation, and labor rights has been profound as the competition for the cheapest production costs spins out of control, leaving capital free to roam wherever it can find—or create through hard-bargaining with state leaders—a marginal advantage.

The WTO goes far beyond the transparent reduction of tariffs that the GATT promised as the mostly likely way to avoid international trade conflict and the resulting tendency toward wars. The WTO opens virtually every aspect of life up to the market and to the logic of growth and profit. Services (including healthcare), intellectual property (i.e., patents and copyrights), and investments have all been added. The bottom line is of sole concern, and attempts to develop minimum standards to protect environmental or labor rights or, indeed, state-sponsored social programs are seen as inherently uncalculable and therefore to be considered suspiciously as attempts to gain economic advantage. This way of conceiving of reality allows for no moves into the realm of values or of public goods defined as anything other than an increasing ability to consume. This is, then, demonstrably and inherently anti-ecological.

The institutional mechanisms of the World Trade Organization take the decisionmaking out of the realm of public debate and place it in the hands of the so-called trade experts. There is no place here for any consideration of "externalities" (i.e., environmental costs) or even for experts in areas of environmental deterioration: the emphasis, rather, is solidly directed to reducing all decisions to the sterile language of trade advantages and calculations of predictable outcomes. These outcomes are certainly what they claim to be: the rulings of the dispute resolution tribunals (which meet in closed sessions) *predictably* rule against any claimant making a broader environmental or public interest case.[27] While the World Trade Organization is certainly finding success with its cherished goal of harmonizing standards, it is, alas, indisputable that the shift is toward the lowest—not the highest—common denominator.

The World Bank and the International Monetary Fund

The other two pillars of the Bretton Woods system—the World Bank and the International Monetary Fund (IMF)—have also come under attack in recent years for their apparent unwillingness to take environmental issues seriously. Although the World Bank has in fact attempted to make some changes in recent years to incorporate environmental awareness into its projects, albeit within a solid commitment to the techniques of eco-nomics, the IMF has proven itself to be steadfastly resistant to the cries of the protesters on the streets.

The World Bank began its engagement with demands of environmentalists as early as the 1970s. Successive Bank leaders have sought to incorporate an environmental component into the growth model favored by the institution and by 1987 a coherent environmental policy was devised through which economic decisions would be taken.[28] It is quite clear that the Bank believes that it has taken a great step forward by incorporating environmental assessment requirements and establishing environmental divisions for their various regions of activity. Although criticism remains—and it comes sometimes from Bank-commissioned experts[29]—the institution is seen as moving in the right direction. It was rewarded by the international community with the central role in the administration of the Global Environment Facility (GEF)—originally designed as the mechanism for funding technical assistance in areas of energy efficiency and projects designed to assist with the protection of the ozone layer and increasingly used as the funding mechanism for a range of international environmental regimes.[30]

Herman Daly, one of the world's better-known ecological economists and himself once an employee of the Bank, gave the institution a bit of advice when he left, thereby demonstrating that the attempt to co-opt him had failed miserably:

> Move away from the ideology of global economic integration by free trade, free capital mobility, and export-led growth—and toward a more nationalist orientation that seeks to develop domestic production for internal markets as the first option, having recourse to international trade only when clearly much more efficient. . . . "Global competitiveness" (frequently a thought-substituting slogan) usually reflects not so much a real increase in resource productivity as a standards-lowering competition to reduce wages, externalize environmental and social costs, and export natural capital at low prices while calling it income.[31]

Aside from the critique of the Bank's apparent lack of ability to live up to the promise of its own environmental agenda, we can once again see more profound failure just below the surface. For, despite the rhetoric of reducing environmental risks and enhancing the livelihoods of the world's poor, the World Bank is solidly locked into the Enlightenment worldview of progress through growth and consumption—not to mention an unquestioned view of the role of capitalism in modern international society.

While the Bank's president, James Wolfensohn, positions himself as a defender of the poor and marginalized, he continues to see the goal of trade and financial liberalization as a vital piece of the puzzle; we merely need to "use the energy and technology driving globalization to help the poor."[32] This depiction of technology as a neutral force outside the realm of politics and manipulation, and of economic growth (as defined, once again, by GNP growth indicators) as a self-evidently positive and irresistible process, demonstrates clearly that the equally prevalent discussions within Bank jargon of "stimulating private sector growth," "leveraging investment," and "promoting economic reform" are if anything more important to its worldview than true ecological sustainability. Indeed, Wolfensohn is an articulate cheerleader for the school of thought that holds economic globalization to be an unstoppable force when he argues that "this is something which is happening as a result of technology,"[33] thereby denying that deliberate action has been taken on the part of the individuals representing national interests and acting as facilitators of capital interests. In reality, the most substantial change being witnessed here involves the myriad ways in which technology is being utilized by powerful interests and the transnationalization of capitalist logic.

While the World Bank attempts to put a green face to its operations, the International Monetary Fund has made little effort to respond to the critics of globalization and its environmental costs. The concept of sustainable development has, however, been useful to this financial institute, which was established alongside the World Bank in order to facilitate the expansion and growth of trade by ensuring exchange-rate stability. Perhaps more honest than most of the international agencies that bring the rhetoric of sustainability into their verbal toolbox to aid in the fight against those seeking alternative economic structures for society, the IMF is explicit about the way in which a definition can be found to give credibility to its policies. The IMF will only utilize the concept in a way the institution feels "comfortable with," that is to say, a definition that makes explicit the necessity of economic growth:

> This definition fits nicely with the IMF's concept of "high quality growth," which we believe is central to sustainable development. . . . At the time of the Rio Earth Summit, the link between macroeconomics and the environment was largely unexplored. But since then, a lot of research has been carried out, and we now know, without doubt, that macroeconomics and the environment are inextricably linked. The old concept of environment as a constraint to development has given way to one of environment as a partner in growth and development.[34]

Aside from attempts to paint the policies of the institution a shade of green, however, the IMF has done little. Indeed, the logic of capital transfer and exchange stability that underwrites the policies of the IMF has acted instead to guarantee that the strict dictates to borrowing countries (the famed Structural Adjustment Policies) lead inevitably to the recipient country's undermining of its own social, environmental, and health standards.[35]

The Organization for
Economic Cooperation and Development

International organizations with a more limited mandate than that of the World Trade Organization also find the concept of sustainable development of import in their articulation of the way forward for global economics. The Organization for Economic Cooperation and Development (OECD) has, perhaps unwittingly, played a significant role in the increase in public awareness and debate over the supposed inherent value of trade.[36] While echoing the standard line about the value of economic globalization for the opening up of opportunities for "structural and/or technological changes that could help in the search for solutions over the longer term,"[37] the OECD hit the public radar screen as a result of its attempt to develop and negotiate a code of conduct and guidelines for multilateral investment issues, which was perceived by many as a bill of rights for transnational corporations.

The OECD is firmly embedded in the logic of global competitiveness and liberalization and uses the cold and calculating technospeak so prevalent in the language of transnational capital. The OECD speaks of "dematerialization" (i.e., each unit of GDP is produced with fewer inputs of environmental resources) and of "depollution" (i.e., pollution being "decoupled" from economic production) without a hint of irony.[38] This is the presentation of the self-evident reality with its declaration that liberalization of trade "will have a generally positive effect on the environment, by improving the efficient allocation of resources, and thus promoting economic growth and increasing general welfare."[39]

As part of its offerings, the OECD is proud of its work toward the negotiation of the Multilateral Agreement on Investment (MAI), an international agreement dedicated to investor rights that, had it not been blocked by the widespread opposition within the populations of the negotiating countries, would have served to extend the rights enjoyed by multinational corporations within NAFTA to all OECD countries.[40] Although the plans were dropped, there can be no doubt that the attempt to institutionalize these rules is ongoing through the World Trade Organization. Corporate rights to sue governments are clearly not about raising environmental standards but rather about freeing corporations from any annoying national barriers to their free rein.

Undermining Culture and Biodiversity

An important aspect of the deregulation of trade as it impacts relations between the under- and overdeveloped worlds is the rapid transition to the total commodification of agriculture. With potentially dramatic results not only for the safety of the food we consume but also for biodiversity, the issue of biotechnology places in stark relief the power of multinational corporations to shape the international agenda. Although the scope does not exist here for an extended consideration of the many ways in which the practices of multinational corporations undermine culture and biodiversity, it is nonetheless essential to point to the power being wielded in defense of environmentally dangerous practices.

There are at least three critical issues involved in the current enthusiasm for the genetic engineering of nature: first, the hollowness of the promise that the purpose of undertaking research to technologically "enhance" food is being undertaken for altruistic purposes to feed the poor; second, the approach to nature implicit in this attempt to control and commodify its every aspect; and third, the power of the multinational corporations driving the process.

Genetic modification is presented by its advocates as a leap forward in attaining high-yield crops with which to "feed the world." The ideas and language put forward by its supporters are very similar to those of Francis Bacon. But is the claim true? As Vandana Shiva has demonstrated, the picture of the helpful transnational corporation spending its money in order that the world can be fed is pure fantasy.[41]

The high yield promised by the genetically altered seed is a fallacy when the calculations are undertaken with biodiversity in mind. The conventional biotech calculation is carried out in such a way that it disallows the high productivity of diversity by figuring the yield in terms of production per unit area of a single crop. Planting a single crop in an entire field will indeed increase the yield, but the picture is more complex than this. Planting multiple crops in a mixture will lead to smaller individual yields but also to an overall increase in yield.[42] Thus, an essentially artificial idea of progress is constantly being broadcast by major seed manufacturers in their quest for markets: small-scale farmers are seen as being unable to make the most of their fields in a manner reminiscent of the arguments used in the age of imperialism to justify its "civilization" of "primitive" peoples.

We are witnessing two opposing views of the natural world. On the one hand we have small-scale farmers and their defenders who articulate the need for seeing the world as an ecosystem that is carefully balanced, while on the other hand we have technicians and corporate leaders who carve up the natural world and seek to manipulate, control, and market nature's component parts. Although there are myriad quotes to demonstrate this, consider the chief executive of Cargill: "We bring Indian farmers smart technologies which prevent bees from usurping the pollen." Similarly, biotech corporation Monsanto distributed literature to sell its herbicide-resistant crops by declaring that they prevent "weeds from stealing the sunshine."[43] As Shiva says,

> the imperative to stamp out the smallest insect, the smallest plant, the smallest peasant comes from a deep fear—the fear of everything that is alive and free. And this deep insecurity and fear is unleashing the violence against all people and all species. The global free trade economy has become a threat to sustainability and the very survival of the poor and other species is at stake not just as a side effect or as an exception but in a systemic way through a restructuring of our worldview at the most fundamental level. Sustainability, sharing and survival is being economically outlawed in the name of market competitiveness and market efficiency.[44]

Corporate needs are not—cannot be—the same as those of the average person. The struggle to define acceptable ways of living within an artificially constructed global structure that values profit and competitiveness above all else is one in which the odds are clearly stacked against those outside the meetings that establish the rules. The biotech corporations are fighting against demands that food be labeled, and against requests that countries be given the option not to import genetically modified foods: they have largely won the right to patent traditional seeds and medicines and sell them back to the farmers who have used and developed them naturally for generations. This really is "eco-piracy," legitimated by "rules" embedded in trade deals promising a harvest of "improved" foods made possible by superior, enlightened thinking.

There can be no doubting the determination of the biotech companies or their public relations machines to convince the public of the supposed benefits of genetically engineered foods. Leaked documents from the giant public relations firm Burson Marsteller demonstrate the biotech industry's plan for managing and manipulating the public debate in their favor. Faced with widespread European consumer resistance to the products, the biotechnology corporation EuropaBio sought help from this company. Burson Marsteller was the firm hired by the

Business Council for Sustainable Development (BCSD) to sell the council's message at the Rio Conference. It developed its expertise of dealing with the public "image" of corporations at Three Mile Island and Bhopal.[45] The strategy is chilling and displays just how powerful advertising can be.[46]

THE RESPONSE OF BIG BUSINESS

The concept of sustainable development, as has been noted, was taken on keenly by business leaders around the world. Chief executive officers of major multinational corporations were smart enough to realize that the future of the public relations battle lay within the terrain established by this concept. At last—they must have thought—a concept that has the blessing of the green diplomats that allows us to continue to articulate the need for increased trade, increased growth, and a continuation of the exploitation of natural resources in the name of profit. Linked to the institutionalization of the globalization of trade with state leaders increasingly seeing their role as one of facilitator of the needs of the market, this new relationship was celebrated by the business elites. Corporations proclaim their support for the supposedly progressive notion of sustainable development but continue to undertake environmentally damaging steps in the pursuit of better return on their share prices. The very nature of international trade, based as it is on a growth ethic and the utilization of ever larger stocks of natural resources, is itself environmentally damaging. Furthermore, corporations—again with the aid of state leaders—are engaged in the undermining of traditional cultures and numerous small-scale economic communities, and all the while they are eagerly engaged in anti-environmental lobbying in a variety of situations, most notably the international environmental conference circuit. And all of this is tied up in a neat package through the most extraordinary efforts at what has come to be known as *greenwash*—the tried and tested practice of selling a message along with a product.

It is within this context that Jim MacNeill can somehow express amazement at the support for the concept of sustainable development on the part of business leaders:

Who, in 1985, would have predicted that the concept of sustainable development would capture the imagination of people, politicians, industrialists and environmental leaders all over the world? Who would have predicted that leader after leader would undergo a public baptism as a born-again environmentalist? And who would have predicted that sustainable development would now be a regular feature of the debates of the UN system, the OECD, and the annual summits of the G7 groups of major industrial democracies—or that it would have become a daily concern of many companies in the Fortune 500?[47]

MacNeill believes that there has been a major breakthrough in the way in which the human relationship with the natural world is viewed, and that, given our realization that Earth's ecological system is "totally and irreversibly interlocked" with the economic system,[48] we can move forward with putting effective trade and trade-related policies in place. Although MacNeill recognizes that there are ways in which trade policies can contribute to patterns of production that are environmentally damaging, he believes that the damage occurs when governments intervene in (i.e., distort) trade flows by instituting subsidies to protect markets— particularly agriculture, energy, and natural resources. Because his assumptions are based on growth, progress, and the grammar of development, however, it is not surprising that this solution for environmentally destructive practices revolves around increased market liberalization. Why, then, is he surprised that the Fortune 500 companies support this particular version of eco-nomics?

Business Leaders Meet the Green Diplomats

As mentioned in Chapter 2, business leaders played a role at the Rio Conference with the blessing of Maurice Strong. Indeed, the Business Council for Sustainable Development, the major vehicle for the intervention of business interests into the environmental agenda at the UN conference, was itself the result of Maurice Strong's initiative to bring business leaders more closely into the process of green diplomacy. In 1990, Strong invited Swiss industrialist Stephan Schmidheiny to be his principal business adviser and asked him to "undertake the formidable task of mobilizing the participation and support of the business community."[49] Schmidheiny proceeded to bring together business leaders in an effort to articulate a business perspective of sustainable development and to feed their views into the UNCED process. The difficulties faced by the NGO community in its quest to have any substantial impact on the workings of green diplomacy at the Rio Conference stand in stark contrast to the easy access provided to the BCSD through Stephan

Schmidheiny. The reason is clear: generally, business leaders accept the underlying assumptions that Strong desired to see entrenched in the so-called pragmatic solutions that the green diplomats sought. There were no dissenters here, merely cheerleaders for the freedom of the market-place, for the perpetual growth of the economy, and for profit; the fact that the concept of sustainable development could so easily be mapped onto the needs of the business world speaks volumes.

As part of the effort, Schmidheiny and his Business Council for Sustainable Development released a book in 1992 titled *Changing Course: A Global Business Perspective on Development and the Environment,* which became a standard in the burgeoning literature on sustainable development. In it, the BCSD includes its declaration that "[b]usiness will play a vital role in the future health of this planet. As business leaders, we are committed to sustainable development, to meeting the needs of the present without compromising the welfare of future generations."[50] The BCSD restates the Brundtland principles and seeks to put flesh on their bones by considering the possible expansion of supplies of renewable resources, the substitution where necessary of limited ones, eco-efficiency, open and competitive markets, trade, technological advances, and so on. It is a corporate executive's dream: being feted by the green diplomats for speaking the language of growth, exploitation, and the importance of business leadership.

The BCSD has subsequently merged with the World Industry Council for the Environment (WICE), an initiative of the International Chamber of Commerce, to become the World Business Council for Sustainable Development (WBCSD). A coalition of well over 100 international companies that claim to share a commitment to the principles of sustainable development, the WBCSD aims to bring together interested parties (government, business, and other organizations) to seek high environmental standards.[51] It should come as no surprise that companies such as the Body Shop that can arguably be said to embrace an environmentally sound ethic are not members of these organizations. Instead, the chemical, oil, and industrial polluters of the world sign up and receive the stamp of approval and the benefits of a green marketing logo for their advertisements.

Greenwash

Although the conference in Rio initiated a new phase in the corporate world's attempt to present a green face to the public (BCSD hired the giant public relations firm of Burson Marsteller to assist with this project),[52] the public relations exercise had been ongoing for a number of years. It was essential that business leaders present themselves as being ahead of the game in terms of responding to environmental deterioration. They knew that it would be much easier to avoid government regulation if they could make a strong case for self-regulating practices that established environmental codes of practice. Of course the product labeling that goes on under the auspices of the various industry codes appears to be much more rigorous than it in fact is. There are two examples that should be singled out for special attention: the Responsible Care initiative taken by the chemical industry in 1984 and the Rotterdam Charter for Sustainable Development adopted by the International Chamber of Commerce in 1990.

Responsible Care. *Responsible Care* is a wonderfully warm name given to the framework for the chemical industry to improve its environmental standards by dedicating itself to annual self-evaluation and the acceptance of so-called guiding principles. Not surprisingly, the whole thrust of the initiative is the development of better products and standards with no self-examination of the inevitability of the chemical industry's toxic content. There are no criteria established about what constitutes an environmental danger, and indeed the chemicals that are produced (including those that are demonstrably harmful to the environment in general, and the ozone layer in particular) are presented as being safe.[53] The chemical industry really has not moved very far from the days of its attack on Rachel Carson.

Rotterdam Charter for Sustainable Development. The International Chamber of Commerce produced its principles for environmental management in 1991. The Business Charter for Sustainable Development (sometimes referred to as the Rotterdam Charter) spun off from the Brundtland Commission and draws heavily on the notion of sustainable development. As with the Brundtland report, the emphasis is on growth, as witnessed by the highly contestable notion that "[e]conomic growth provides the conditions in which protection of the environment can best be achieved, and environmental protection, in balance with other human goals, is necessary to achieve growth that is sustainable."[54]

Once signed on to these codes for corporate conduct, the transnational corporation has a ready advertising tool: the credibility of a green marketing campaign. The remaking of chemical, oil, industrial, and agricultural business companies in the image of environmentally friendly and responsible businesses has been a major boon to the public relations industry. Consumers attempting to choose between products are bombarded with a litany of claims about the safety and indeed positive environmental benefits of the products they are purchasing. The stamp of approval that these corporations get by suggesting adherence to environmentally sound principles both relaxes consumers wary of environmental problems and reinforces the idea that we can have it all—a better environment to live in while we continue to consume resources and mass-produced products. The corporations need these codes of conduct to sell their products; the consumer needs them in order to continue to feel that it is no longer necessary to speak that dreadful and constructing language of limits that was so prevalent just a few decades ago. Indeed, as Toby Smith has argued, green marketing has become central to the reinforcement of what she calls "productivism" or "an expansionist, growth-oriented ethic."[55]

The claim that corporate rethinking of previously destructive environmental practices has been undertaken is most certainly overstated. Environmental departments may have been created within most major corporations, but with little legislation being put in place by domestic or international authorities, they continue to be their own guardians in terms of environmental standards. Indeed, the fight is on to ensure that legally binding measures be kept out of the equation and the logic of free trade, and the promises of capital mobility have been utilized to herald the dawn of a newly efficient and green international economic scene. The UNCED process, with its apparent openness to debate, ensured that proposals to regulate or even monitor the practices of large corporations were mostly removed from UNCED's documentation at the behest of the business community.[56]

GREEN DIPLOMACY AND THE "RADICAL" CONSIDERATION OF INTERNATIONAL ECONOMIC RELATIONS

The Commission on Global Governance

At the end of the Cold War and at the impetus of former West German chancellor Willy Brandt, the Commission on Global Governance (CGG) was established. Although this commission was not concerned solely with environmental issues, its broad mandate to consider the directions for the international community necessarily meant that it was seen to be of import for the entire notion of green diplomacy. Its focus on the operation of the international economic system was considered in the context of so-called human security issues such as poverty, development, environmental sustainability, and so on. The ever present green diplomat Maurice Strong was on the CGG and has subsequently taken some of the suggestions made by the commission for UN reform into his positions as executive coordinator for UN reform (a rank of undersecretary-general) and chairman of the Steering Committee for Reform, which comprised senior UN officials.[57]

The CGG released its report—*Our Global Neighbourhood*—in 1995, and it can be argued that it was one of the first coherent and popularly read presentations of the necessity to ensure that the economic liberalization project launched at Bretton Woods would be extended into the post–Cold War era.[58] The commission recognized the many problems of the existing world order but sought nonetheless to look for solutions within the existing structures and to "humanize" rather than challenge the logic of globalized economic efficiency.

The report not only contains a vision for the future but presents a program of action as well. On offer, the CGG claims, is a reconceptualization of the international economic order designed to ensure that institutions overseeing economic globalization will be made accountable for their actions, thus guaranteeing the realization of social, political, and economic advances to be enjoyed by individuals the world round. With its claim to point the way into the twenty-first century by offering supposedly radical suggestions for the promotion of "security in its widest sense, including the security of people and the planet," the commission sets itself a formidable task. Believing that the post–Cold War world offers the opportunity for "global governance," "enlightened leadership," and a stronger role for an "international civil society," this is a report designed to offer hope for the citizens of the world.

An examination of the CGG's work is therefore useful because it provides insight into the way in which the globalized marketplace is being thought about by those well-intentioned world leaders who believe that their contribution can make for a more just and secure world order. The concept of sustainable development is celebrated and used as the central feature of the proposals for a more workable and cooperative international economic system through UN reform. With the ideological barriers removed, the commission argues, all shared international problems can be dealt with, and among these problems is, of course, the deterioration of the environment. The commission believes that "in the long run . . . there should be no conflict between free trade and the ambitions of sustainable development and improved social standards, since as countries develop they will naturally wish to adopt higher standards."[59] This view clearly fits with the optimism of green diplomacy and, furthermore, reestablishes the desirability of having top-down solutions directly linked to the current orthodoxy of trade and growth. The commission presents what it claims are radical ideas for dealing with the problems facing the international community—an important one of which is clearly environmental deterioration. The solutions could be summed up by suggesting that better economic management will lead to a cleaner environment. The freeing of trade will lead to a leveling of environmental standards, and the language of the report is, in places, reminiscent of the worst of Francis Bacon's consideration of the natural world as a mere storehouse of resources for exploitation: the commission speaks, for instance, of the "unrealized potential of tapping the energy of deep-sea currents, from aquaculture, and from space research and exploration."[60] Although the commission suggests that the UN's Trusteeship Council be reconfigured so as to administer environmental treaties and to oversee the so-called global commons, the suggestion not only presents the commons as a place for shared profits, but any positive environmental objectives here are more than offset by the language of economic growth and corporate control.

And what of the concept of global civil society, which is replayed once again in this report? Through the renewal in faith in the liberal ideology, the CGG aims to convince that the end of the Cold War has miraculously left the "citizens of the world" with the power to influence decisionmaking, with the likely result being a more enlightened, peaceful, and just international system. This power will only be realized, however, if these civil society organizations agree to work with international organizations and within the rule of law to achieve change. The much heralded international civil society subsequently becomes the target for institutionalization within existing structures. Through the reform of the United Nations, the commission envisages the establishment of an Annual Forum of Civil Society, which would allow this new and powerful actor (and the commission does speak of it as a singular force) an "entry point" for its views into the deliberation of the United Nations.[61] The goal of including nonstate actors would be further strengthened, the commission argues, through the addition of a "Right of Petition": this would be made available to international civil society to allow direct access to the UN Security Council to raise serious issues of concern. Of course, "the arrangements by which it can be exercised would have to be strictly circumscribed in scope for the facility to be manageable and effective. This could be achieved through the careful delineation of its parameters and the development of a screening process."[62]

The suggestion that civil society organizations must be institutionalized within the UN system is merely one part of the CGG's strategy for ensuring the smooth operation of the proposed international structures: so-called people power is acceptable so long as it is deployed in defense of, and operates in deference to, the commission's proposed world order. Vision and values are necessary to guide the world into the twenty-first century, and for an ethical dimension to be added to the proposed global governance, the commission urges the articulation and acceptance of a set of core values that can be used to unite people from different backgrounds. Despite the fact that such a universal ethic has long proven elusive, the commission implores us to recognize the need for rights and responsibilities to be expressed in an effort to strengthen individual commitment to the "global neighborhood." In other words, as long as we all believe in the same basic rules, progress can be made: "Without the objectives and limits that a global ethic would provide, however, global civil society would become unfocused and even unruly. That could make effective global governance difficult."[63] Civil society thus begins to appear more as a tame force intended to play a role in the maintenance of the system than as an authentic arena for the interplay of legitimate demands of interests groups, whether nationally or internationally constituted.[64]

The UN's Answer: The Global Compact

The Commission on Global Governance was not an official UN commission and therefore its findings and recommendations were not officially fed into the UN structure. Nonetheless, Secretary-General Kofi Annan has been keen to find institutional solutions to the social and environmental problems brought with the increasingly liberalized markets of global trade. In an address to the World Economic Forum in Davos, Switzerland, in January 1999—the annual gathering of journalists and corporate and political elites—Annan introduced his plan for developing a "creative partnership" between the United Nations and the private sector. Annan proposed the creation of what he called a "Global Compact" designed to establish the human face for the globalizing market.

Annan wanted, in short, to "find a way of embedding the global market in a network of shared values."[65] Here, Annan can be seen to be putting the institutional fine-tuning to the ideas expressed by the Commission on Global Governance regarding the necessity of developing a shared commitment to the world order structures.

Annan has long spoken about the need for finding a way to exercise control over the worst excesses of the free market, but his thinking is firmly embedded in the orthodoxy. His proposal that the goals of the United Nations and those of business are mutually supportive demonstrate his wholesale acceptance of the growth and development logic of Enlightenment thought. Annan speaks the language of progress admirably: "[L]et's choose to unite the powers of markets with the authority of universal ideals. Let us choose to reconcile the creative forces of private entrepreneurship with the needs of the disadvantaged and the requirements of the future generations."[66]

Annan's concerns have focused on the gap between the UN's institutional structures and the freewheeling globalization process. As with the Commission on Global Governance, Annan is seeking to establish the United Nations in some kind of authoritative role vis-à-vis the developing international order. Annan is clearly aware that the rule-making that has gone on in the past decade or so has been about ensuring the rights and freedoms of the corporate players in the international order; the social dimension is missing from these agreements, and Annan sees a role for the United Nations in ensuring that some semblance of balance is restored to the governance of the international system.

The Global Compact set out nine principles that Annan was eager for corporations to sign on to: two for human rights, four for labor issues, and three for environmental protection. Annan's invitation was successful, not least because of the increasingly vocal attacks on the free trade ethos by those looking closely at the human rights, labor, and environmental practices that many argue have been trampled under the stampede toward the free market goals. Annan offered legitimacy to corporations that were already busily claiming that their global practices were socially responsible. In return, and in addition to the obvious goal of improving the social conditions of people around the world, Annan sought to increase the role of the United Nations in defining the new corporate order. To do so, he was apparently happy to make the case for the opening of markets as the way to a more prosperous future.[67]

It is worth mentioning in passing that the United Nations had, prior to 1992, a division called the UN Center on Transnational Corporations, whose task was to monitor corporate activities. The center was essentially dismantled prior to the Rio Conference and was replaced with a new Division on Transnational Corporation and Investment with the remit of promoting foreign investment.[68] The Global Compact must be considered in the light of such decisions.

CONCLUSION: GLOBALIZING UNSUSTAINABILITY

The problem, of course, with the current discussions of how to ensure sustainable growth and development is that the circle cannot be squared. The heartfelt efforts by the green diplomats to bridge the gap between economics and environmental issues is doomed to fail because of their acceptance of the destructive practices inherent in the growth ethic. Economic growth and the organization of international society around the goals of efficient capital mobility and the profit margin its controllers seek are inherently anti-ecological. Any way it is looked at, the extraction of raw materials for the manufacture of goods—the demand for which in many cases has been artificially created—does not lead to an ecologically sound existence. No amount of masking the reality with talk of environmentally friendly technologies will offset the destructiveness of the growth ethic when the resounding failure of the technological fix is taken into consideration. The failure to see the world holistically and, instead, seeing ourselves as outside nature, with the promise of our own superiority to fix what goes wrong, are deeply embedded in the status quo approach that has led to the destruction it now seeks to confront.

The concept of globalization is difficult to define, but it is most certainly not an inevitable and irreversible phenomenon that we should be merely seeking to manage. It is—if it is anything at all definable—a set of multiple processes based on human decisions and priorities established by actors with power and influence. Jan Scholte is correct to acknowledge that the consequences of globalization "will be considerably influenced by the sorts of knowledge constructed about, and fed into, the process,"[69] and it is quite clear that the discourse of growth and market liberalization has the upper hand in the debate. The eagerness with which the multinational corporate elite and the international economic institutions have accepted, adopted, and co-opted the concept of sustainable development has merely served to deny the realization of alternative paths such as those that were being articulated at the dawn of the environmental movement, paths that would deny profit and growth as the sole legitimate way of organizing society—either domestically or internationally. The freeing of global markets and the articulation of the possibility of doing so in the interests of an "improved" world mask a set of social, economic, and political relations that are unjust and destructive of both human happiness as well as the natural environment.

The tinkering around the edges of the international economic governance mechanisms and institutions may have garnered the support of the green diplomats, but the reality is disturbing. Any presentation of so-called free trade and global markets as an acceptable framework within which to seek environmental solutions denies the reality of the "globalization of unsustainable production and consumption" and a "recolonization of the planet."[70] The naïve faith placed in the goodwill and intentions of the world's corporate elite to fulfill their promise of environmental sustainability by green diplomats is nothing short of staggering. The belief that the answers to the global community's myriad environmental problems lie in the free movement of capital and an increase in production of goods demonstrates the lack of critical thinking and the triumph of one-dimensional thought.

This is the backdrop against which the green diplomats look for incremental steps toward a more environmentally sustainable future, a background they find acceptable as a set of social relations within which to work. The articulate defender of the status quo approach, who charges that we will make no progress if we cast our net so wide as to include economic relations, is not being realistic as is claimed, but is rather the willing or accidental advocate of the social relations of domination and control.

NOTES

1. Atkinson, *Principles of Political Ecology,* p. 135.
2. Leiss, *The Domination of Nature,* p. 74.
3. Tickner, "An Ecofeminist Perspective on International Political Economy," p. 62. I should note here that I disagree with Tickner's belief that the Brundtland worldview would produce a "quite different interaction between states and markets." Clearly my own analysis is that the Brundtland report, although articulating the need for cooperative international arrangements, fails ultimately to provide anything other than a tinkering with the established order. See also Merchant, *The Death of Nature,* for further insight into the impact of Enlightenment thinking.

4. Leiss, *The Domination of Nature*, p. 185.

5. In his closing address to the Rio Conference, Strong said: "The President of one of the great corporations of our world told the Preparatory Committee . . . that the present economic system is simply not adequate. This doesn't mean it needs to be scrapped, but it needs to be radically revised to bring it into tune with eco-realities. We need to move to a real eco-nomic system." It is not clear who the president was, but it is certain that he was not talking about the elimination of growth, trade, exploitation, or profit. See Strong, "A Time of Transition," p. 3.

6. For one of the best critical accounts of the establishment of the postwar economic order, see Gill and Law, *The Global Political Economy*.

7. Bhagwati, "The Case for Free Trade," p. 19.

8. Ibid., pp. 18–23.

9. Ibid., p. 21. Bhagwati is borrowing this term from an Indian magazine that he says is "the most radical of today's proenvironmental magazines in India." He does not acknowledge the wide range of Indian environmental movements that are returning to the nonviolent tactics of *satyagraha* in order to challenge the Indian government's probusiness and development strategy. The politics of local resistance to global trade is evident across India from prawn fishers to anti-dam protesters.

10. "Why Greens Should Love Trade," *The Economist*, p. 17.

11. Ibid., p. 17.

12. Daly, *Beyond Growth*, pp. 152–154; Daly, "The Perils of Free Trade."

13. Daly, *Beyond Growth*, p. 153.

14. GNP measures the market value of goods and services produced by a country's industry both at home and abroad. GDP measures the value of goods and services (including savings and investment) within a country's borders including those produced by foreign investors. For a comprehensive examination of the origins and logic of the concept of GNP and the dangers of a growth-based economics (from the perspective of an economist), see Hodson, *The Diseconomics of Growth*. See also Henderson, *Creating Alternative Futures;* and Daly, *Beyond Growth*. For a consideration of the history of this type of measurement and an argument for the necessity of devising a better one, see Cobb, Halstead, and Rowe, "If the GDP Is Up, Why Is America Down?"

15. Daly, *Beyond Growth*.

16. "Why Greens Should Love Trade," *The Economist*, p. 18.

17. Churchill and Worthington, "The North American Free Trade Agreement and the Environment," p. 91.

18. For a comprehensive examination of the entire case, including a consideration of the competing industry (oil versus automobile manufacturing) and the challenge from a group of provinces to the Canadian government's efforts to ban the additive, see "The Clash Between Trade and Environment in Canada: Ethyl's NAFTA Chapter 11 Investor-to-State Challenge" of the Baker and McKenzie law firm, available at www.bakerinfor.com/publications/documents/771_tx.htm. This article maintains that the outcome of the challenge was legally just.

19. See Clarke and Barlow, *MAI*, pp. 90–91.

20. Barlow and Clarke, *Global Showdown*, p. 117.

21. The CEC comprises a Council (composed of environment ministers, or the equivalent, of each participating country), a Joint Public Advisory Committee (comprised of five members from each country appointed by their government, and designed to build consensus on issues of environmental concern), and a Secretariat (composed of professional staff to provide technical support to the Council and its committees).

22. Crowell, "NAFTA," p. 156.

23. See "Report on the GATT Symposium on Trade, Environment, and Sustainable Development," *Trade and the Environment.*

24. For details of the case, see Charnovitz, "GATT and the Environment."

25. Bhagwati, "The Case for Free Trade," pp. 18–23. See also the presentation of the case in Krutilla, "World Trade, the GATT, and the Environment."

26. From the preamble of the agreement establishing the WTO, available at www.wto.org.

27. For a consideration of the myriad cases that have been fought—and lost—on public interest grounds, see Wallach and Sforza, *Whose Trade Organization?*

28. For an examination of the early efforts of the Bank, see Le Prestre, "Environmental Learning at the World Bank"; and Piddington, "The Role of the World Bank."

29. See, for example, the well-known study on the Sardar Sarovar project: Morse and Berger, *Sardar Sarovar.*

30. The GEF is co-managed with the UN Development Programme and the UN Environment Programme, and many NGOs were disappointed at the Rio Conference in 1992 that the control of this fund was left in the hands of the World Bank. For an excellent discussion of the politics surrounding this decision, see Chatterjee and Finger, *The Earth Brokers,* chap. 10.

31. Daly, *Beyond Growth,* pp. 92–93. Daly also tells a very interesting story about the development of what he calls a "small environmental resistance movement" within the Bank: see pp. 8–10.

32. Wolfensohn, "You Can't Beat Us—So Join Us."

33. Wolfensohn made these comments in "The Debate on Globalisation," BBC News, Saturday, April 15, 2000. Transcript available at http://news.bbc.co.uk/hi/english/business/newsid_714000/714972.stm.

34. Ouattara, "Macroeconomics and Sustainable Development."

35. See Daly, *Beyond Growth,* pp. 158–159, for a discussion of the "language" of adjustment and the way in which the concept of structural adjustment demands a consideration of the two propositions suppressed (adjustment *of* what *to* what). When asked in this manner, it lays bare the project behind the IMF's strategy.

36. The OECD evolved out of the Organization for European Economic Cooperation (OEEC), an intergovernmental organization established in 1948 to assist with the economic growth of Western Europe, to administer North American aid under the Marshall Plan, and to oversee efforts to liberalize trade. The OEEC became the OECD in 1961 when Canada and the United States joined. The OECD involves itself in development aid, the provision of financial stability, and, of course, the encouragement of growth in international trade. It has continued to grow and now boasts thirty members: Australia, Austria, Belgium,

Canada, Czech Republic, Denmark, Finland, France, Germany, Greece, Hungary, Iceland, Ireland, Italy, Japan, Korea, Luxembourg, Mexico, Netherlands, New Zealand, Norway, Poland, Portugal, Slovak Republic, Spain, Sweden, Switzerland, Turkey, United Kingdom, and the United States.

37. OECD, *Economic Globalisation and the Environment*, p. 8.

38. Ibid., p. 25.

39. Ibid., p. 13.

40. For a comprehensive consideration of the OECD's efforts to get a Multilateral Agreement on Investment into operation, see Clarke and Barlow, *MAI: The Multilateral Agreement on Investment and the Threat to Canadian Sovereignty,* and also their book *MAI: New Global and Internal Threats to Canadian Sovereignty.* Most governments refused to acknowledge that the secret talks were taking place.

41. Shiva, a physicist, is one of the most articulate critics of biotechnology. Her writing concentrates on the corporate agenda and the impact it has on sustainable living and ways of seeing nature. She considers the current actions of the multinational agri-business firms as the latest in a line of colonizers of the developing world. See especially her books *Biopiracy* and *Stolen Harvest.* See also Sharma, *GATT to WTO,* chap. 5.

42. Shiva gives the example of Mayan peasants in Chiapas who are characterized as "unproductive" because they produce only two tons of corn per acre. The overall food output is, however, twenty tons per acre when the diversity of their crops is taken into consideration. Shiva calls the blindness to high productivity of diversity a "monoculture of the mind." See Shiva, "Poverty and Globalisation."

43. As quoted in ibid.

44. Ibid.

45. Greer and Bruno, *Greenwash,* pp. 29–30.

46. "EuropaBio—The Leaked PR Documents," available at www.home. intekom.com/tm_info/geleak1.htm. This document is well worth a read for insight into the way news programs get their coverage ("feed") about such issues directly from the corporations.

47. MacNeill, "Trade-Environment Links," pp. 7–8. The volume in which this article appears, although a publication of Canada's National Round Table on the Environment and the Economy, was sponsored by DuPont Canada. What better indication of the new relationship between business and government can there be, given the fact that DuPont is the largest chemical company in the world and has a woeful record on environmental affairs? For an excellent exposé, see Greer and Bruno, *Greenwash,* chap. 4. Among other things, MacNeill was a senior adviser to Maurice Strong at the UN Conference on Environment and Development in Rio, Secretary-General of the Brundtland Commission, and the primary author of *Our Common Future.*

48. MacNeill, "Trade-Environment Links," p. 8.

49. Strong, *Where on Earth Are We Going?* p. 199.

50. Schmidheiny, *Changing Course,* p. xi.

51. WBCSD, www.wbcsd.ch/whatis.htm.

52. Greer and Bruno, *Greenwash,* p. 29.

53. Ibid., pp. 33–35.

54. International Chamber of Commerce, *The Business Charter for Sustainable Development,* introd.

55. Toby M. Smith, *The Myth of Green Marketing,* p. 10.

56. Greer and Bruno, *Greenwash,* p. 25.

57. For Strong's description of his invitation to take over these roles, see his book *Where on Earth Are We Going?* chap. 14.

58. The cochairs of the commission were Swedish prime minister Ingvar Carlsson and former Commonwealth secretary-general Shridath Ramphal. The members were Ali Alatas, Abdlatif Al-Hamad, Oscar Arias, Anna Balletbo, Kurt Biedenkopf, Allan Boesak, Manuel Camacho Solis, Bernard Chidzero, Barber Conable, Jacques Delors, Jiri Dienstbier, Enrique Iglesias, Frank Judd, Hong-koo Lee, Wangari Maathai, Sadako Ogata, Olara Otunnu, I. G. Patel, Celina do Amaral Peixoto, Jan Pronk, Qian Jiadong, Marie-Angelique Savane, Adele Simmons, Maurice Strong, Brian Urquhart, and Yuli Vorontsov.

59. CGG, *Our Global Neighbourhood,* p. 169.

60. Ibid., pp. 214–215.

61. Ibid., p. 259.

62. Ibid., p. 261.

63. Ibid., p. 55.

64. For an in-depth critique of the CGG and the dangers inherent in their plan, see Broadhead, "Commissioning Consent."

65. Annan, "Address to the World Economic Forum in Davos, Switzerland," p. 4.

66. Annan, available at www.unglobalcompact.com.

67. Ruggie and Kell, "Global Markets and Social Legitimacy."

68. Greer and Bruno, *Greenwash,* pp. 23–24.

69. Scholte, "Beyond the Buzzword," p. 44.

70. "Statement of the International Peoples' Tribunal on Human Rights and the Environment," *Alternatives,* p. 113.

4

The Limits of
Regime Formation

AN ACCEPTANCE OF THE ESTABLISHED INTERNATIONAL ECO-
nomic order with its rhetoric of the benefits of globalization and trade
liberalization provides the backdrop for the concrete activities of the
green diplomats. The prevailing view of those seeking agreements in
the international diplomatic arena is one of orthodox multilateral bargaining to achieve shared goals with mutual benefits. The articulation of
the need for incremental steps toward such progress is embodied in the
writings of the scholars of regime formation.

In recent years, support for the wide range of environmental regimes
being negotiated and strengthened has grown, with an increased range
of actors assisting in their formation. The green diplomats (attending to
the needs and interests of the participating state parties) are joined by
scientists, nongovernmental organizations, and even representatives of
big business in an effort to develop the most effective agreement possible and to continue building on it to ensure that the arrangement lives
up to its promise. The progress made on a variety of issues and the apparent commitment to be inclusive of these nonstate actors are held up
as a significant improvement on bygone days of orthodox diplomacy
where the representatives of states would emerge from behind closed
doors and announce the creation of a new treaty or protocol designed
for mutual benefit but with a firm commitment to the preservation of
national interest.

The existence of problems of the magnitude of a deteriorating atmosphere has, it is true, led to a newer form of diplomacy. The complexity of the issues is outside the scope of expertise of even the most intelligent of state leaders and, as a result, the way is seen to be opening up

for participation of those with the relevant knowledge and expertise. For those celebrating the number of international agreements on environmental problems, the story is unfolding as it should: a greater degree of awareness of environmental problems, the allowance for an increased role of those with specialist expertise and interest, and an increased (albeit not perfect) awareness on the part of states that they must cooperate if they are to survive.

It is for many reasons difficult to critique the ongoing efforts of those engaged in negotiating environmental treaties. Who, for instance, would want to argue in all sincerity that the world is not a better place as a result of the fruits of their labor? The defenders of regime formation are doubtless correct to posit that if the current hot-button issues of international environmental deterioration (such as ozone depletion and global warming) were cast in terms of global economic trade relations or a deeply embedded way of thinking about science and nature, then representatives of states, international organizations, and nongovernmental groups would all have to throw up their hands in despair and give up on their efforts. It has been demonstrated on numerous occasions that the most likely way to secure support for an issue at a bargaining table around which are seated representatives of states with many different interests and problems is to frame the issue tightly, and to demonstrate that equitable rules are possible, desirable, manageable, and verifiable. Indeed, action taken in recent decades with a view to conservation measures and environmental protection has made a profound difference in the general awareness of issues and of the increased need to act.

The question remains, however, as to whether or not green diplomacy in this vein is enough. Can such incremental steps ever succeed in doing what is necessary to put an end to the human causes of environmental deterioration that are sanctioned (even encouraged) by the range of political, economic, and social actions and decisionmaking that are deemed acceptable within a completely separate compartment of international bargaining, namely, economic institution and regime building?

There are a number of serious limitations in this method for dealing with the vast array of environmental problems facing the world today. The acceptance of the existing institutions and ways of thinking are of course central and will be dealt with here. The deepening of the technical rationality so central to modern thought is evident with the celebration of scientific answers and the managerialist discourse that frames the issues for debate in international bargaining rooms. The optimism about supposed progress serves to mask the extent to which the environmental deterioration has deepened throughout the timeframe celebrated by both the practitioners of this incrementalist approach and the academic regime theorists. If we do not extend our field of vision we will be content with the smallest of incremental steps and will be so focused on the details of their negotiation that we will fail to gain insight into the irrational outcome of our supposedly rational calculations and bargaining techniques. With our eyes focusing on countless details and the wording of myriad clauses contained within the agreements reached, we will allow ourselves to be blinkered from the world around us, where the actual destruction continues.

In this chapter I will go to the heart of green diplomacy and will critically examine the case for regime formation that is the centerpiece of the practical efforts made by the incrementalists. I will argue that not only is the outcome of this international bargaining frequently much weaker in concrete practical terms than is often supposed, but also that the assumptions underlying the practice—objective knowledge, scientific reasoning, and the search for the technological fix—are the same as those that have produced the conditions for the deterioration of the natural world that is now the object of inquiry. I will examine the stages that are said to lead to the establishment of a successful environmental regime and explore in detail the attempts to construct regimes for atmospheric deterioration (both ozone depletion and climate change) in order to demonstrate that the practice itself is a clear example of a managerial discourse that serves to professionalize—indeed sanitize—the discussions of human impact on the natural environment. The relationship of knowledge to power is much more complex than the advocates of regime formation would have us believe, and it is time that the debate be taken out of the realm of technical fixing and placed in the broader consideration of the modes of thought at play in international society at large. That is to say, regime formation must be considered with the international push toward globalized trade practices based on the deregulated movement of transnationalized capital.

While the efforts of the green diplomat—dedicated to the articulation of solutions and the strengthening of resolve—are to be applauded, it must be acknowledged that the outcome is ultimately so flawed as to be virtually worthless. Indeed, to the degree to which it blinds us to truly radical, sustainable alternatives, such an approach is actually counterproductive. It is here that the incrementalist approach to the global environmental crisis receives its practical intent, and it is here that the failure of the structure of the solution proposed by the advocates of green diplomacy becomes crystal clear. This, then, is the story of the practical operations of green diplomacy at work.

REGIME FORMATION

The concept of regime formation as a practical solution for the building of cooperation among states (which are notoriously concerned with competition and the preservation of narrow national interests) became a central issue in the discipline of international relations by the 1970s. Although the concept of regime formation was not developed to examine interstate environmental cooperation exclusively, it has indeed become highly developed in this field of inquiry. The most widely used definition of *regime* will serve to establish what, precisely, is being referred to in this chapter:

> Regimes can be defined as sets of implicit or explicit principles, norms, rules and decision-making procedures around which actors' expectations converge in a given area of international relations. Principles are beliefs of fact, causation, and rectitude. Norms are standards of behaviour defined in terms of rights and obligations. Rules are specific prescriptions or proscriptions for action. Decision-making procedures are prevailing practices for making and implementing collective choices.[1]

States have, of course, long found ways to codify agreed-upon practices in order to bring a degree of predictability to their interactions. In the 1970s, however, the quest for knowledge and expertise on how best to guard the national interest while engaging in multilateral activity became much more prevalent in the academy. This interest was born of the need to understand the changes occurring in the international scene and the resultant transformation of relative power calculations. The apparent decline of the U.S. government's ability to control the operation of international arrangements as they had been defined in the aftermath of World War II was the impetus for U.S. academics to define better tools for understanding the shaping of international order. Focus was placed, as a result, on regime formation as a practice, as well as on the likely effect on the system.

Realists used the concept in an effort to cast light on the relationship between the decline of U.S. power (hegemony) and the erosion of existing regimes, especially those concerned with the international economic order as created by the postwar Bretton Woods regime. Liberal institutionalists challenged this so-called hegemonic stability theory by focusing on the way in which regimes could develop despite hegemonic decline. For the liberal institutionalist, the existence of myriad regimes could be used to call into question the realist view of states as nothing more than agents of power maximization. In turn, there ensued intense criticism of this institutionalist view of the development of the supposedly deeper form of international governance that, for them, regimes seemed to imply. Some argued, for instance, that regimes were inevitably structurally defined and could depend only on the distribution of power within the international system, an argument that cast profound doubt on whether or not regimes could be expected to develop as independent actors in the organization and operation of the international system.[2] Such arguments were designed to provide a necessary and salutary warning to "impressionable young hopefuls" who might be inclined to attempt to create the perfect world armed with tools of regime building.[3]

We need not concern ourselves here with the myriad academic debates between the various theoretical schools of thought.[4] It is enough to recognize that the focus on institution and regime building that was presented and developed by liberal institutionalists became the source of the optimism of green diplomacy and the basis of the strategy held out today as the most likely source of solutions to save us from global environmental collapse. In this framework, regimes must be seen as separate from both organizations (with a physical presence) and those international agreements that help to develop a regime but are a more limited and defined expression of legal commitment.[5]

The liberal institutionalist is concerned with the role of nonstate actors and strategies of negotiation, but of greatest concern is the development of an understanding of the conditions under which negotiations will succeed. Take, for example, Oran Young's attempt to move along the debate about institutional bargaining by offering a consideration of the likely determinants of success:

- when the issues lend themselves to contractarian interactions,
- when arrangements are available that all participants can accept as equitable (rather than efficient),
- when salient solutions (or focal points describable in simple terms) exist,
- when clear-cut and effective compliance mechanisms are available,

- when an exogenous shock or crisis spurs the negotiations on, and
- when effective leadership emerges.[6]

These conditions seem self-evident, and an examination of those instances of supposedly successful regime building doubtless demonstrates the veracity of the claim. It has, nonetheless, been important for the advocates of regime formation to attempt to push for agreements when these conditions quite clearly do not exist. Perhaps the "impressionable young hopefuls" have been infected by optimism and set forth to create a better world. In any case, it seems clear that for the most part, the ongoing activities toward the formation of environmental regimes take as a starting point (either implicitly or explicitly) the arguments put forward by the liberal institutionalists regarding the potential for institution building as a meaningful way of dealing with issues of shared concern. The task for the green diplomats then becomes one of attempting to determine the best way forward for realizing the promise of regime building even in the more difficult issue areas. As Thomas Bernauer has argued, "Institutions are choice variables. If the degree of success in international collaboration can be influenced by the institutions we establish and operate, we can be more successful if we know how to design institutions that produce the desired effect."[7]

The enthusiasm and positive thinking involved in the acceptance of this strategy are palpable, and one need not, as far as the green diplomat is concerned, go any further than the assumption that we will get better at designing the institutions as we learn more and more about which attributes they require to produce the desired effect. But such optimism is both limited and reinforced by the belief that the process, while inevitably slow and complex, is said to be the *only* solution open to us given the exigencies of world order. This is a circular logic that the green diplomat ultimately accepts: the world is as it is (i.e., anarchical and based on national sovereignty and interests), so we must find the best strategy for maximizing cooperation by building regimes to limit the worst excesses of the operations of the interstate system that have, in fact, been accepted as a given structure within which to work. But try they must: in this worldview incremental change is better than no change at all.

STEPS TO SUCCESSFUL REGIME FORMATION

Most strategies of incremental change contain a series of definable activities that are seen as the necessary and logical steps to success. The practice of regime formation is no different. There must be a definition of the issue before any action can be taken, and this quite logically leads to the necessity of gathering facts with which to make decisions. The resulting knowledge in turn demands serious efforts to bargain, and when the decisions have been made about the extent of the agreement, the negotiations are complete and the international community is left with a functioning regime that will have to be implemented and, because this is an ongoing process, will demand ongoing strengthening and revision. These steps of course overlap, but they are taken in this order nonetheless. Let us take each step in turn and examine the arguments of the adherents to regime formation.[8]

Framing the Issue

Quite logically, the first step toward securing international cooperation on a specific environmental issue is to identify the problem and to define it. In a sense, the struggle to get a specific environmental problem onto the agenda is the most crucial one and the manner in which it is framed is of equal import. The accepted way of doing this is to ensure that the issue is framed in such a manner that it is isolated from any broader consideration of the context within which the problem is occurring in an effort to make agreement on the specifics more likely. It is generally assumed by practitioners of regime formation and academics alike that the impetus for discussion will in all likelihood come from scientific information that, when it becomes available, highlights a problem that was previously unknown to exist. The nature of scientific inquiry also serves to limit the definition of a problem in highly specific terms due to the division of the various areas of inquiry into highly specialized categories of investigation. It should be emphasized, however, that the advocates of regime formation are not denying the political engagement of nongovernmental organizations or other interested actors in the placing of an issue on the international agenda, but there is nonetheless an emphasis on the weight of scientific evidence as the defining factor.

In a sense there are two things being considered here. First, the problem must become recognized as such, but second, it must be subsequently framed and defined in such a manner that it can be seen to require international efforts to rectify the consequences of the problematic situation. As Owen Greene argues, "[t]his is a major reason why science and 'knowledge production' processes are particularly important in environmental politics."[9] Clearly, no solution will be found if the problem is not identified, but what precisely does "knowledge production" entail?

Regime theorists—and indeed practitioners—have become increasingly aware of the extent to which scientific knowledge can be contested either by other scientists not yet convinced by the veracity of the evidence or, indeed, by those who have an interest in keeping an issue off the international agenda for more selfish reasons—major international corporations, for instance. The notion of knowledge production is a small step away from an acceptance of the view of the world that holds that there can be a straightforward articulation of facts that speak for themselves. Although there is an acceptance here of the need for good scientific information, the concept of epistemic community has been developed to illuminate the way in which information is translated into policy through the involvement of these so-called knowledge collectives.

Epistemic communities. Defined as a "network of professionals with recognized expertise and competence in a particular domain and an authoritative claim to policy-relevant knowledge within that domain or issue-area,"[10] the concept of *epistemic community* points to the increasing importance of the skilled expert in the formulation of international environmental policy. The obvious complexities of the range of environmental problems facing political leaders today lead many academics and practitioners of green diplomacy to the inevitable conclusion that there must surely be a stronger role for the scientific and technical experts in the formation of policy. Who, for instance, would suggest that any current head of state could show up at an international conference on global warming (or any other such important environmental issue) and speak with knowledge and confidence about the best way forward for the international community in tackling the problem? Here, as with society more generally, there is an intense reliance on "expert" advice and knowledge.

But the concept of epistemic community goes beyond merely the description of a technical or scientific expertise. Peter Haas points out that the epistemic community has

> (1) a shared set of normative and principled beliefs which provide a value-based rationale for the social action of community members; (2) shared causal beliefs, which are derived from their analysis of practices leading or contributing to a central set of problems in their own domain and which then serve as the basis for elucidating the multiple linkages between possible policy actions and desired outcomes; (3) shared notions of validity . . . and (4) a common policy enterprise—

that is, a set of common practices associated with a set of problems to
which their professional competence is directed.[11]

This list of the additional constitutive elements of the epistemic community is important, for it spells out quite clearly that this is not solely
a concern with value-free knowledge but clearly separates "truth" from
"consensual knowledge" and therefore opens the space within the
broader discussion of regime formation for an understanding of the values that practitioners (including scientists) have in the pursuit of knowledge for their own work. Haas and others have been concerned to consider the way in which these communities now operate transnationally
through a variety of networks (bureaucracies, businesses, scientific institutes, etc.) and have, as a result, increased influence in the coordination of both domestic and international policy. This work moves beyond
merely considering the pressure that can be exerted on decisionmakers
in that it seeks to examine the way in which individuals come to coa-
lesce around particular policies and work together to shape the way specific issues are seen in policy terms.

Those interested in understanding the complex process involved in
building international regimes and institutions are quick to demonstrate
that groups of like-minded individuals who seek knowledge about a
specific issue are important to policymakers for their ability to make
clear the range of options that are open to them and the likely consequences of choosing them. They are in no way seen as a threat to other
forms of political participation and/or expressions of democratic will
and should not, as Emanuel Adler and Peter Haas argue, "be mistaken
for a new hegemonic actor that is the source of political and moral direction in society. Epistemic communities are not in the business of
controlling societies; what they control is international problems. Their
approach is instrumental, and their life is limited to the time and space
defined by the problem and its solution."[12] Is this apparently benign
view substantially justified?

Fact-finding. In a sense, fact-finding can logically be considered as
part of the definition and framing of the issue, and it is essential that
these tasks not be seen as discrete but rather as overlapping. I use this
category to highlight the role of international organizations. For while
the role of epistemic communities continues to play an active—perhaps
even predominant—role in the deeper study of the issue at hand, the

involvement of a more broadly defined political intervener is seen as almost a necessity in order to ensure that the group of interested specialists continues to frame issues in a consistent and supportive manner. Organizations such as the UN Environmental Programme frequently play a key role in the articulation and dissemination of the best available evidence as it is collected and debated through a variety of channels (bureaucratic, academic, business, etc.), and when they are fully involved in the building of a case for international negotiation, their role can be of profound import.

While environmental interest groups or other political players are frequently involved in the quest to get an issue onto the international agenda and into the public consciousness, when it comes time to make the case for necessary international bargaining the decision is most often made on the basis of hard evidence as presented by credible members of the scientific community. As has been pointed out, the decision to move to the next step—that is, the actual negotiating of an agreement—can often be moved along quite effectively if there is an "exogenous shock or crisis" as mentioned in Oran Young's list of determinants of successful regime formation quoted above. State leaders will sometimes listen to demands made by environmental activists if they are backed up by "reasoned" scientific evidence, but the impact of a clear demonstration of the issue being framed—the presentation, for example, of an ozone hole—can move the regime building to its next stage quite quickly.

Negotiating the Agreement

Having been convinced of the need to seek an international agreement about a specific case—usually on the evidence presented by scientific experts—representatives of states will begin the long and often tortuous path to creating an effective international agreement. International negotiations are never easy: states seek to protect their interests as best they can in the face of calls for limits to their own maneuverability in policymaking areas. In any negotiations, the representatives of states will guard against taking any action that will have a negative impact on the popularity of the government at home or have what is perceived to be an unfair distribution of either costs or impacts. In terms of the diplomatic efforts, the most usual first step toward establishing a regime (with the principles, norms, and rules all in place) is usually the articulation of a very general commitment to the issue, often referred to as a framework agreement.[13] Getting states to at least agree that there is a problem can be difficult enough, so green diplomacy must make an effort to get this first piece of paper signed. An international agreement—even one with no real commitments or obligations—is the necessary prerequisite for the establishment of a regime with enforceable rules attached.

The period of bargaining and negotiation between the framework agreement and a legally binding set of rules is frequently as long as it is intense. The debates that rage over the minutiae of the details are inevitably embedded in much broader political debates that occur both at the domestic level as well as in international negotiating rooms. For instance, developing countries are frequently pointing out that international environmental negotiations can serve to limit their own quest for the levels of economic progress that have been reached in the North without, they are quick to note, much concern for the impact of that growth on the natural world. The international community is being forced to find ways to deal with such issues of distributive justice within the bargaining stage of regime formation.

The cases discussed below will demonstrate many of the problems of this stage of regime formation, but it is here that the green diplomat must work the hardest and maintain the commitment to the environmental issue under discussion. There are a range of actors who seek to influence the outcome of this process, with business lobbies and environmental activists being the two major groups seeking to shape the process.

Implementation and Strengthening

After the signing of an international agreement, the difficulties continue. States must ensure that their own domestic laws are brought into line with the international regulations. The implementation of the terms and conditions of any treaty is predicated on the full compliance of all the signatories, which, not surprisingly, is difficult to ensure or verify. Still, a regime can be said to be developing through the internationalization of the norms, principles, and rules by which states will, it is argued, feel under increased pressure to adhere to the regime. Compliance measures are developed and strengthened, as are the details of the agreement. Scientific information continues to develop, and as the epistemic communities, the international organizations, and the green diplomats all seek to respond to the latest information, suggestions for improvements are continually made through the meetings called to revisit and amend the treaties.

The open-ended nature of the regime development process is seen to guarantee that the incremental approach will ensure that the very latest information is given a hearing and that the international community will continue to make moves toward increasingly strong and all-encompassing agreements. Support for this form of environmental diplomacy is built through its method of dividing issues in such a way that incremental progress is possible. The hope exists, argues the incrementalist, that the successful attempts at regime formation will provide lessons to the practitioners so as to ensure an ever broadening network of international agreements designed to guarantee environmental protection.

THE CRITIQUE

Before describing the concrete attempts to formulate regimes to deal with ozone depletion and climate change, it is important to highlight some of the limitations with this practical expression of green diplomacy. There are two broad categories within which to describe the obstacles that stand between the promise of regime formation and its practical fulfillment. First, there are practical problems that limit the effectiveness of international bargaining on environmental issues. Many of these issues are raised by the supporters of the incrementalist approach themselves. These are, in fact, the problems that the green diplomat works diligently to overcome in an effort to ensure the best possible outcome of the negotiations. The second category of obstacles stems from the deeper limitations of the way of thinking that is exemplified by the advocates of regime formation. Here, I will discuss the way in which the practice of green diplomacy further deepens the very causes of the problem and thereby (unwittingly) is part of the crisis rather than a solution to it.

Practical Limitations

As mentioned earlier, neither the academics with an interest in nor the practitioners of regime formation have any illusions as to the difficult task they face. Many activists engaged in lobbying for the incremental steps feel frustrated at the exceedingly slow pace of the progress made. What keeps the process alive is the belief that there is really no alternative to the interstate bargaining epitomized by this practice and, further, that to give up hope on this exercise would inevitably lead to a worsening of the environmental situation.

Perhaps the most profound stumbling block is securing the necessary consensus that a problem even exists. Any degree of scientific uncertainty provides an easy excuse for elected leaders to avoid negotiations designed to change domestic practices. As seen above, the regime theorists point to the importance of an "exogenous shock" in turning complacent politicians into defenders of the environment, willing and able to undertake binding action to effect a change in the levels of environmental destruction.

The process of negotiating a strong and successful regime for any given environmental problem is dependent on a large number of states sharing a belief in the existence of scientific evidence about a particular environmental problem and, furthermore, being willing to negotiate. This may not sound like a huge stumbling block, especially when one considers an individual state's ability to argue at the table for an agreement that is in its own interests, but many states are wary of participating in such environmental discussions for a range of domestic political reasons. A state's own record on a particular environmental problem or the suspicion that other states are attempting to use environmental measures to gain an advantage in trade terms are perhaps the two most common responses. As mentioned, there is a legitimate fear on the part of developing countries that environmental protection of the global "commons" is being advocated at the expense of their own development. There are, as well, long-standing disagreements among states that make acting in concert extraordinarily difficult, especially on an issue that is often seen as having a place low on the agenda. In short, even getting the participants to the table is a difficult chore.

Once at the negotiating table, a range of stumbling blocks appear more evident.[14] The various pressures that a government comes under on the domestic scene must be borne in mind. Governments send their representatives to the negotiating table but inevitably seek to balance powerful interests at home. Indeed, the short-run calculations of most governments (an election timeframe) are in stark contrast to the type of long-range planning and vision that is demanded by the regime formation process. The state representative at the table will, in addition, be very aware of the various international coalitions and alliances that are being built in different issue areas, and institutional bargaining is inevitably caught up in this broader calculation of power sharing.

While aware of the difficulties of the negotiating process, the supporters of incremental change often point to the growing number of international environmental treaties that have been successfully negotiated and see within this trend a diminishment of the old-fashioned conception of the anarchical world order with states actively seeking to maintain control within the boundaries of the state. In fact, as Andrew Hurrell has argued, "[t]here is a marked preference for non-binding targets/guidelines which states are free to implement at whatever pace they see fit rather than the acceptance of firm and unambiguous obligations."[15] States have repeatedly refused to relinquish ultimate monitoring authority to an outside organization or agency. Such control over the issue calls into question the claims expressed by the regime advocates concerning a new form of cooperation and supranational authority in the area of environmental deterioration. Compare, for example, the weak international mechanism of these environmental agreements to those economic agreements discussed in the last chapter, with their legally binding dispute resolution mechanisms. Clearly, the reality here is one of a stronger role for the state, with its claim on technocratic power and the ability to oversee environmental management.[16]

In short, the participants at international environmental conferences celebrate if an agreement is reached and herald it as evidence of a new-found cooperative world order. However, environmental agreements inevitably contain provisions for self-monitoring and self-verification of domestic implementation of weak or vague treaties. It is little wonder that the natural environment has continued to degrade during a time of unprecedented international diplomatic activity.

Fundamental Problems

One of the beguiling characteristics of the liberal institutionalist variation of regime formation is its express intent of making the world a better place. The institutionalist challenge to the realist view of a world frozen in a competitive and anarchical international order has, on the face of it, a persuasively normative element that at least *appears* to accept the need for a fundamental rethink of the status quo organization of international society. The arguments for regime formation seem to be based on the separation of the *is* from the *ought to be*. The question then becomes: Given the degree to which both the regime theorist as well as the practitioner of green diplomacy accept the existing structures of the international system and celebrate the concept of sustainable development with all that it implies for a view of growth, economic expansion, and liberal trade markets, is the advocate of incremental change and institutionally defined limits representative of anything more than a weak and ultimately futile effort to stem the tide of the disaster? Is it, in fact, a continuation of an empirically grounded practice that is at its core highly suspicious of critical attempts to examine the assumptions that underlie the practice of regime formation?

A deeper critique of the incrementalist approach points to the tendency of green diplomacy to rely on a form of instrumental rationality to devise solutions for environmental problems. The prevailing view of the regime advocate is one that reduces complex and interrelated problems to individual problems suitable for the application of scientific knowledge as a solution. Issues that demand a consideration of values and choices become reduced to questions of a merely technical nature. Although the concept of epistemic community succeeds in raising awareness of the contested nature of scientific knowledge, it also tends to mask the extent to which the "administered society" of the modern bureaucratic state—with its dependence on technical solutions to individual problems—is becoming increasingly transnationalized.

With the discussion of epistemic communities, the regime analyst reinforces the prevailing worldview of scientific and technical rationality by privileging expert knowledge and assuming the discussion over possible solutions to be outside the realm of capability of the average citizen. Although it is true to say that the conceptualization of these so-called knowledge collectives, with their emphasis on interpreting information rather than simply uncovering truth, demonstrates a nuance of the more orthodox view of knowledge as *pure* rationality, it is nonetheless ultimately unsatisfying to anyone looking for a more holistic approach to the environmental problems. In fact, I would argue that the explicit awareness of knowledge construction as advanced by the scholars of epistemic communities fails to move us beyond technological determinism. The examination of the struggle for the power and authority to frame issues stops short of calling into question the basis of a specific type of knowledge with which to confront environmental problems.

In defending themselves against postmodern critics, the regime theorists are correct to point out that there is more to the world than merely word games, and that international relations is indeed more than a reflection of "discourses and habits."[17] Karen Litfin nonetheless makes the important point that these advocates of epistemic communities "tend to sidestep the *discursive* dimensions of knowledge."[18] That is to say, the concept of epistemic community may succeed in allowing us to seek a link between knowledge and power, but it concentrates on the actors themselves and fails to consider the social structure within which its participants are embedded. Indeed, the acceptance of the powerful concept of sustainable development serves to demonstrate the way in which the socially accepted bounds of thought can act to limit the scope of possible boundaries of action.

The attempt to depoliticize the phenomenon by arguing that the role of epistemic communities is not to be feared as a source of power because they are merely taking an instrumental approach to the problems facing them (as seen in the Adler and Haas statement quoted above) is extraordinarily telling. This argument goes beyond merely that of an appeal to trust the members of epistemic communities because they have specialized knowledge and an ability to translate that knowledge into practical policy solutions; instead it furthers the logic offered by the orthodox managerial language of the status quo.

The literature discussing the formation and operation of epistemic communities demonstrates a focus on institutional learning and in some cases even describes the impact in terms of evolutionary theory:

> The path-dependent evolutionary model implies that the effects of epistemic involvement are not easily reversed. To the extent to which multiple equilibrium points are possible in the international system, epistemic communities will help identify which one is selected. Subsequent outcomes reflect the initial vision of the epistemic community that helped frame and institutionalize the issue area.[19]

This quote points to something that should be of major concern to those seeking to make progressive claims for regime formation, namely that the framing of a way of seeing an issue is a powerful and powerfully limiting tool that, once embedded in a discourse, continues unseen and therefore (conveniently) unchallenged.

This instrumental rationality is of central import to the working of the *administered* state that the Frankfurt School members were so articulate in exposing. On the basis of this rationality, the issues faced are divided and subdivided until they are small enough pieces to manage, and *management,* after all, is the goal. The elevation of the expert and the goal of finding answers to delineated areas of inquiry have dramatically decreased our ability to challenge the solutions offered. At both the domestic and international levels, the environment has become an *object* of scientific investigation with the promised outcome being technological solutions to the various problems. Individuals are deemed the problem and the expert is the solution—almost a total reversal of the way in which the topic of ecology originally entered into the public consciousness and continues to be thought about by those involved in the ecology movement.[20] In the theory and practice of regime building, the expert frames the issue and provides the solutions to the politicians, who proceed to manage and oversee the system. The assumptions go unquestioned because questions outside the bounds of problems that can be technically managed have no place in the administered society. As Matthias Finger argues:

> [G]lobal environmental management is built on two implicit assumptions, both of which can be questioned: the first says that the pursuit of (industrial) development, even if sustainable, is desirable, necessary or inevitable. And in fact all the new global actors draw at least part of their legitimation from this implicit assumption. Another part of their legitimation is derived from the assumption that global management will be an adequate answer to global change. . . . [I]t is my conviction that global environmental management will fail. . . . [G]lobal environmental management is no alternative to the present crisis: global environmental management simply continues the "civilization of power."[21]

Now embedded in the logic of the rational-technical organization of life, the goals of green diplomacy appear to be a clear product of state power and exchange within, perhaps, an internationally administered society.

The concept of regime formation is a powerful one: It is articulated by scholars of international relations and acted upon by the practitioners of the incremental approach. It is a comfortable concept, for it encourages a belief (even a faith) in a managerial approach to environmental problems. For its academic celebrants, regime theory is presented as a progressive force because it is seeking to tackle the worthy cause of the degradation of the natural world while at the same time working within the realities of the system and therefore not succumbing to idealistic notions that cannot be met within the existing structures. It is, in short, applauded for walking a fine line between a realistic acceptance of the status quo and the utopian dreams of those who would change the world.

For the practitioner, the concept is useful for the focus it gives to myriad activities. What in many other cases would be known as a simple collection of international agreements or protocols becomes bounded, defined, controlled, and therefore of increased import when issues of governance are being discussed. While some scholars of international relations have expressed concern over the failure of the regime theorist to tackle tough issues,[22] an examination of the attempts to deal with the two major atmospheric problems, namely stratospheric ozone depletion and global warming, will amply demonstrate the true extent of the problems inherent in incrementalism.

THE CASE OF STRATOSPHERIC OZONE DEPLETION

The story of the creation of an international regime to protect the stratospheric ozone layer has been told repeatedly and is frequently used as a model case against which other efforts are to be measured and from which to draw lessons on the best way to deliver ourselves from a scenario of environmental ruin.[23]

It is true that this story can be told as a narrative of progress made in terms of international bargaining. Indeed, it has the makings of an epic tale: mighty corporate interests being forced to find alternatives to damaging chemical substances as a result of excellent and thorough scientific discovery while diplomatic bargaining and the concerted effort of an epistemic community convinced of its cause and willing to build transnational coalitions among fellow researchers prove that, far from the image of being under the influence of state interests, the scientific community can powerfully guide and shape a less knowledgeable governing elite. The story, which in its standard telling begins with the hypothesis put forward by two U.S. scientists about an apparently unnatural imbalance in the ozone layer, also maintains a place for the central figure of an energetic and determined leader—the executive director of the UNEP, Egyptian microbiologist Mostafa Tolba.

A retelling of the outlines of this epic tale is indeed required, but in this case it will be told from the point of view of a fundamental critique of the assumptions underlying the entire presentation of international environmental management. The myths that have developed around this particular example of regime formation (described by one specialist as "a striking instance of international cooperation")[24] will be measured against the ongoing deterioration of the atmosphere.

This story's beginnings must lie with the invention of the chemical compound that is the source of the destruction of the ozone layer. It is here that we see the first indication that the deeply embedded way of thinking about scientific progress is at the very root of the problem.

Chlorofluorocarbons (CFCs)—the class of chemical compounds at the center of this particular environmental crisis—were invented in the 1930s by General Motors. They were celebrated for the fact that they were nontoxic and stable, which is to say that they were nonreactive in the lower atmosphere. As such, they were seen to be a "perfect" chemical compound.[25] The characteristics for which they were praised were, alas, eventually discovered to be a serious problem for a different "segment" of the atmosphere, for while these chemicals are inert in the lower atmosphere, they rise through the atmosphere and break apart when exposed to strong ultraviolet radiation. This "perfect" chemical compound turns out to be, in fact, highly reactive in the stratosphere—that area between fifteen and thirty-five kilometers above us and about which most of us had heard nothing prior to the dire warnings that began to emerge in the 1970s.

Already we see the fallacy of the myth of scientific progress that has become the religion of modern societies. The technological ingenuity demonstrated by the creation of a chemical compound that would not be carcinogenic has led (inevitably?) to future problems. The technological fix, in other words, is not permanent and, as we will see later, invariably requires further "fixing."

The science of the phenomenon is relatively easy to understand: the chlorine atom contained in the CFC compound is "liberated" by ultraviolet radiation and subsequently destroys ozone molecules. A single chlorine atom destroys 100,000 molecules of ozone, if the current scientific understanding is correct.[26] It is important to note that a very long time passed between the development of the "wonder" chemical and the realization that destruction was occurring.

The initiation of concern began in the 1970s when James Lovelock developed an "electron capture device," which allowed for the measurement of trace gases in the atmosphere.[27] Lovelock found evidence of CFCs in the stratosphere, but he failed to link it to a chlorine reaction. The understanding of this linkage came a few years later when two researchers in the United States—Mario Molina and Sherwood Rowland—hypothesized that CFC emissions disrupted the natural ozone balance by reacting with, and breaking down, ozone molecules.[28] The findings contained in Molina and Rowland's 1974 paper set the research on the path that would direct and frame the development of the regime in the subsequent years.

Within three years, UNEP had established the Coordinating Committee on the Ozone Layer and was setting about ensuring that lines of communication among the community of scholars would be kept open. In March 1977, UNEP convened the International Conference on the Ozone Layer in Washington, D.C., and released their *World Plan of Action on the Ozone Layer,* a document that established the need for an international treaty. The building of a regime was beginning.

There was an immediate response to the Molina and Rowland paper in a number of countries, and the United States, by far the largest producer and consumer of the chemical compound, took an early lead in the issue and made moves to ban the use of CFCs in aerosol propellants.[29] As a result of early action, the total production of CFCs began to fall and continued to do so until the early 1980s, when the production of one of the CFC compounds (CFC-113) was increased as a solvent for computer chip manufacturing, a rapidly growing industry.[30] An increase in the ability of computer modeling to find solutions to the problems resulting from CFCs has been celebrated even as the increased activity in the computer industry has led to a greater increase in the production of CFCs. The irony of this situation is captured well by Richard Benedick's statement that CFCs "couldn't have occurred without modern science, without atmospheric chemistry, computer models, and projections."[31] While it is certainly the case that CFCs could not have been developed without modern science being directed by corporate interests, the claim that modern science is directing green diplomacy in a progressive manner is patently ridiculous.

A detailed and exhaustive examination of each stage of the negotiations is not necessary here. However, it is important to gain a sense of the pace of the international negotiations and some of the stumbling blocks that occurred along the way. After the initial burst of policy response among a number of states, the international discussions began slowly. By 1982, UNEP had established an ad hoc working group of legal and technical experts with the goal of drawing up a draft convention. By March 1985, the international community—at least some of its members—were prepared to sign a very weak framework convention in Vienna.

The conference in Vienna was a fractious one. The European participants were suspicious of the bans on production of some chemical compounds being proposed by the North American and Scandinavian countries and were proposing instead a production cap. In the end, the convention committed the signatories—of which there were only twenty plus the European Community—to protecting human health and the environment against any human activities affecting the ozone layer. No targets were set for the reduction of the chemical emissions, but the convention did establish the principle of research cooperation that led to the creation of joint programs and the establishment of mechanisms for the supply and sharing of information to international centers.

Despite its weakness, the Vienna Convention is celebrated for being the necessary first step on the long road to international efforts to deal with the shared problem of ozone depletion. In the standard telling of the development of the stratospheric ozone regime, it is crucial to establish the importance of the small but meaningful steps toward the successful resolution of the major differences. By beginning here with the depiction of original disputes among states that are then overcome through diplomatic bargaining, consensus among the players in the epistemic community, and effective leadership, the advocates of green diplomacy paint a picture of international cooperation. While the convention can indeed be seen as a step toward the formal compromises that were reached through later international negotiations, John Vogler is correct to point out that the "subsequent negotiations were essentially about finding a compromise that would accommodate the different industrial interests of the key producers."[32] While it is important to consider the way in which the scientific community came to understand and share goals and policy prescriptions, we should not lose sight of the fact that this initial attempt to reach agreement demonstrated the extent to which state participants were working to protect the commercial interests of leading chemical producers while examining the options for environmental protection; it was clearly the commercial interests that were at variance.[33]

Many commentators on the formation of this regime have celebrated DuPont's leadership role in helping to define the parameters of the problem and subsequently articulating a solution to the problem.[34] There is something quite unsettling about this presentation of DuPont's unilateral action in 1988 to cease production of CFCs as a heroic and selfless gesture. It is quite clear that DuPont had been working hard to find substitute chemicals and made its announcement in order that it could give weight to those arguing for a ban only when it was clear that it would be in a position to fill the market with its own substitute products. DuPont lobbied wisely to maximize its profit while at the same time sending a public relations message that the chemical industry was ahead of the game and acted in an environmentally sound manner *without* the need for any government regulation.[35] This magnificent "effort" has served DuPont extraordinarily well in subsequent campaigns to avoid public intervention in the chemical industry.

Despite the differences taking place within the chemical industry and among the North American, European, and Scandinavian countries leading the way toward an international agreement, the public became more involved shortly after the Vienna meeting when the world's media covered the discovery of the hole in the ozone layer above the Antarctic. This was the type of "exogenous shock" the regime theorists looked to to galvanize action, and it certainly acted as a spur to government activity in this case. The very public debates about the ozone hole necessarily led to calls for further research as well as to the more vocal activities of nongovernmental environmental organizations. Disputes within Europe emerged and the policy began to shift.[36]

Aside from the obvious repercussions of the increased discussion about the hole above the Antarctic, there is an interesting footnote to the discovery that should be considered in light of the deeper critique being offered here. The discovery was made by Joseph Farman (using a balloon carrying instruments to take measurements), who subsequently examined data that had been generated by NASA satellites and found that the ozone depletions had been detected but had been discarded by a computer program as being "aberrations."[37] The faith in science and technology to find answers to our many problems could perhaps be shaken by such an absurd situation: highly sophisticated technology ignoring an extraordinarily serious situation because "it" did not expect it.

Events moved more quickly—at least by diplomatic standards—after Farman's discovery. The science was framed successfully through a series of meetings and workshops held by the U.S. Environmental Protection Agency and by the UNEP, meetings that served to reduce the disagreements among atmospheric scientists and to develop "common scenarios" that "bounded the range of policies to be considered at subsequent government negotiations."[38] With the scientific community more or less in agreement, the attempt to give substance to the framework convention was undertaken before it had even been ratified by enough states to enter into force.

The participants at the 1987 conference in Montreal sought to develop measures to control consumption of the chemical compounds in question in addition to establishing targets for the reduction of their production. Trade with nonsignatories was restricted and in a novel approach to recognizing the responsibility of the overdeveloped world's major contribution to the problem, the developing countries were absolved of responsibility for meeting the targets for a full decade. Faith in science was once again reaffirmed with the determination that discussions would be ongoing and further scientific information about chemical compounds in the atmosphere would lead to future amendments to the Montreal Protocol. This promise has been followed up. A meeting held in London in 1990 led to the creation of a fund to subsidize the transition of developing countries to alternatives to ozone-destroying chemicals as well as to an agreement to tighten controls on the chemicals and add more compounds to the ever growing list of ozone-depleting substances.

Meetings of the state parties to the Montreal Protocol have continued to be held, and the list of chemical compounds covered and targeted for elimination grows ever longer. The participants have further accelerated the scheduled phaseout of some while constructing definitions of essential uses for others. Problems of use, recycling, exemptions, verification, and even the working of the multilateral fund continue to be discussed in these meetings designed to further strengthen the regime for protecting the ozone layer. Indeed, the entire process has a physical presence at the Ozone Secretariat based at UNEP. The office in Nairobi continues to oversee the process, receiving and analyzing data and information from the participating states on the production and consumption of the substances under consideration and monitoring the implementation of the agreements.[39]

For some, the existence of this ongoing process of shaping the agreements and moving with the advance of scientific awareness is reassuring: experts are looking after the environment—and us. But are the expert intervention and the willingness of states to bargain on the basis of it (assuming that they do) enough? It should be remembered that the original impetus for the creation of a regime was made possible by the development of a substitute for the chemical compounds that had been identified by the scientists. The group of substitute chemical compounds, hydrochlorofluorocarbons (HCFCs), also deplete the ozone layer—it just takes a little longer, as HCFCs have up to 10 percent of the destructive capability of CFCs.[40] Without these substitutes being developed, it is highly unlikely that the industry supporters of the agreement (notably DuPont) would have been so willing to go along with the whole plan.

There are other technological fixes being offered to help the troubled ozone layer:

- using a laser to "scrub" the CFCs from the atmosphere so they do not rise to the stratosphere,

- using infrared lasers to "blast apart" CFCs (also known as "atmospheric processing"),
- using planes to carry ozone into the stratosphere,
- firing "bullets" of frozen ozone into the stratosphere (which melt and replenish lost ozone),
- taking sulphur dioxide into the stratosphere (thirty-five metric tons per year) to reflect sunlight away from Earth, and
- covering most of the oceans with white Styrofoam chips to increase Earth's reflectivity and thereby reduce the temperature.[41]

Bearing in mind that CFCs were themselves designed as a technical fix, should we be so quick to applaud the efforts of giant chemical corporations that proclaim to have the answers, or to give valuable and scarce research dollars for these foolish attempts to counteract the destructive practices?

Another aspect of the Enlightenment scientific framework that has a bearing on this regime is the division of science into tiny, fragmented pieces for investigation. One of the leading researchers on CFCs in the atmosphere, Richard Stolarski, has talked about the reasoning behind choosing this particular area of study: "[It] looked like a nice, *quiet* piece of the stratosphere to cut off and maybe get a paper or two while we were learning and nobody would bother us."[42] Aside from what this says about the nature of academic research more generally, this quote vividly demonstrates the alarming ability to see the natural world as a series of individual problems. Bacon would recognize this vision and would celebrate its applicability. Alas, the impact of this is demonstrated by the fact that it took the state parties to the Montreal Protocol until 1998 before an effort was made to look at the ozone depletion issue in terms of global warming. The Ozone Secretariat proudly proclaimed:

> For the first time, the Parties are tackling the challenge of how to make policies to protect the ozone layer consistent with ongoing efforts to reduce emissions of the greenhouse gases that cause climate change. Several gases that are being used as ozone-safe replacements for CFCs—notably hydrofluorocarbons (HFCs) and perfluorocarbons (PFCs)—contribute to global warming and so are targeted for reduction under the 1997 Kyoto Protocol.[43]

As a result of our blinkered celebration of science finding the answer, the proposed solutions and technological fixes for one human-made catastrophe can further deepen the crisis in another area. It is unlikely that the proponents of regime formation will acknowledge that this is green diplomacy gone mad. An anniversary celebration of the Montreal Protocol reaffirmed the faith in the modern scientific method when it held a science colloquium to present the achievements in ozone depletion science and society's adaptation to the impact of the problem. The host of the celebrations, Canadian environment minister Christine Stewart, celebrated the "step-by-step approach" that was encouraging us all to "live within the limits of nature." Stewart's speech, furthermore, provides us with a superb restatement of the Enlightenment's scientific method and the total faith in it for achieving environmental goals:

> Science is the foundation and the driving force behind all decisions and all actions. After all, it was science that first alerted us to the problems of the thinning of our planet's natural sunscreen. It is science that has enabled us to track changes in the ozone layer. It is science that has identified the chemicals that are hurting the ozone layer. And, it is science that has provided and continues to provide guidance to policy-makers and industry on how to reduce and eliminate these harmful substances.[44]

Even in the narrow terms of its own defined task of arresting ozone depletion, however, celebrating the terms of the Montreal Protocol, with all its exceptions and allowances, is a perverse response. If every state adhered to the rules set out in it, the provisions would allow for another 10 million tons of CFCs to be released into the atmosphere, an amount that Litfin informs us would be equal to half of all production historically.[45] The U.S. Environmental Protection Agency calculated that if all states in the world participated, there would still be a threefold increase in stratospheric chlorine concentrations by 2075.[46] The ongoing discussions sometimes lead to exceptions, a notable example being the "specific-use" exemption for the U.S. space shuttle program allowed at the sixth meeting of parties in 1994.[47] A truly effective ozone depletion regime seems a long, long way off.

THE CASE OF CLIMATE CHANGE

While the international efforts to find a common strategy for dealing with stratospheric ozone depletion are widely celebrated as an excellent example of the potential for green diplomacy, the successful resolution of a regime for dealing with global warming has proven more elusive.

Despite the shadow that this particular effort at international bargaining casts over the status quo view of regime formation, the mainstream literature continues to focus on the bargaining undertaken by state actors, its outcome, and the efficacy of international institutions in the formulation of international treaties.[48]

The continual focus on the likely development of a regime to deal with this grave crisis and the standard presentation of the action necessary to get there in small but steady steps serve once again to exclude the very questions that should be central to any attempt to deal with the basic issue. It is essential to examine the ways in which the issue is being formulated and to point out the limitations inherent in this approach. It is furthermore crucial that we ask what, if any, pressure is being brought to bear in the calculation of state interests and what dangerous ways of thinking are being utilized to maintain support for the current logic of global economic relations. Most fundamentally, it is essential to consider in whose interests the participants at the bargaining table are acting.

While acknowledging that the achievement of an international regime to deal with global warming is a difficult proposition, the story of the issue is told by adherents of green diplomacy in a way that turns complex problems into technical issues that require little more than international bargaining in order to reach resolution. Of course political disputes among the participating countries are acknowledged, but once again the advocates of regime formation suggest—implicitly and explicitly—that although this may not be the fastest route to a successful plan for dealing with this shared environmental problem, it is the best we can achieve under the circumstances provided by the structures of the international order.

A recognition of the fact that human activities (such as the burning of fossil fuels) can have a significant impact on the chemical composition of the atmosphere is not particularly new. Many writers credit Baron Jean Baptiste Fourier with the early 1820s consideration of the greenhouse-like properties of the atmosphere. By the latter part of the nineteenth century, Svante Arrhenius was examining the anthropogenic sources of carbon in the atmosphere and was making the leap to a consideration of the ways in which human activities could possibly lead to a warming effect.[49] Despite this awareness, it was not until the 1970s that the issue was discussed at the level of international relations.[50] At Stockholm in 1972, climate issues were included in the discussions, and subsequent conferences—notably at the first World Climate Conference in 1979—served to place the issue on the agenda and in the collective consciousness of an increasingly environmentally aware public. But the real discussions surrounding the creation of the international consensus and the building of a regime did not gain any momentum until the 1980s. A conference held in Villach, Austria, in 1985 examined the impact of greenhouse gases in climate change. A conference was subsequently held in Toronto in 1988 that brought together government officials, scientists, industry representatives, and environmental NGOs from over forty countries. At this stage, the call for a move toward a convention to reduce carbon dioxide emissions was made and the quest for a legally binding regime was begun. Later that year the World Meteorological Organization (WMO) and the UNEP established the Intergovernmental Panel on Climate Change (IPCC) to assess the scientific and technical information related to human-induced climate change,[51] and in 1989 at a conference in the Netherlands there was a call for immediate international action to stabilize carbon dioxide emissions. A second World Climate Conference was held in November 1990 and witnessed dissent on the part of some participating states—notably the United States—to accept the arguments that targets and cooperative strategies would be needed to halt the environmental damage wrought by the emission of climate-changing gases. The UN General Assembly responded to the call from this conference with the establishment of the Intergovernmental Negotiating Committee (INC). The Assembly requested that the INC set to work negotiating a framework convention and complete the task in time for the Rio Conference in June 1992.

To fulfill its responsibility the INC held five sessions to prepare the Framework Convention on Climate Change (FCCC), which they indeed managed to draft by the Assembly's deadline. As an international agreement on an area of serious environmental concern, the FCCC does what most framework conventions do: it spells out in very vague terms the necessity of coming to a shared accommodation of a shared problem. It recognizes that there is a problem and sets an ultimate objective of stabilizing greenhouse gas concentrations in the atmosphere. Clearly, a detailed blueprint for action was not possible as a starting point, so the convention sets out a process for tackling the problem through regular meetings (known as a Conference of Parties [COP]), supported by a Secretariat. By establishing an institutional framework for discussions and an international political process for agreeing to specific actions, the FCCC put off the difficult issues for future negotiations to be based on scientific research and asked that, as a starting point, the parties to the convention provide an "inventory" of its "sources" of greenhouse gases and its "sinks" (the concept used as shorthand for the natural agents of greenhouse gas absorption). The FCCC also attempted to deal with some of the thorny issues surrounding the burden of responsibility by placing the major share on the rich countries of the overdeveloped North. Technology transfer, education, and a financial mechanism (entrusted to the Global Environment Facility at the World Bank in the first instance) were all issues included in the FCCC.

Within months of the Rio Conference, where the framework convention was opened for signature, Ted Hanisch (a member of the Norwegian delegation to the INC) posed the question: "Can we expect the Convention to produce adequate solutions or at least some significant steps toward protecting the atmosphere?" Hanisch's answer to his own question was a "qualified yes," and this response can be seen as representative of the response from the celebrants of green diplomacy.[52] Of course there was a recognition that the process would be slow and that some states would be resistant to change, but the overall assessment was that this was the necessary starting point, while the initial 155 signatures demonstrated a broad awareness of the importance of the issue and constituted a statement that future action would be forthcoming. Such is the nature of incremental change.

On its own terms, the development of the regime continued apace. The convention had been ratified by enough states to enter into force by March 1994, and the following year saw the first Conference of Parties in Berlin, where renewed focus was placed on the establishment of more concrete commitments. It was widely agreed that a protocol should be negotiated by the time of the third Conference of Parties in 1997, and negotiations took place in Berlin with that target in mind. The reports of the IPCC (its second assessment had been released in December 1995) provided a scientific backdrop to the ongoing negotiations, with the IPCC's offer of policy recommendations based on the best available scientific evidence. But much of the scientific evidence was being disputed by industry groups, and a number of countries (known as the JUSCANZ group—Japan, the United States, Canada, Australia, and New Zealand)[53] began to let it be known that they were not in favor of commitments that excluded the participation of developing countries and were moving away from the earlier agreement to recognize the so-called burden of responsibility.

What led to this shift? An examination of the behind-the-scenes lobbying in Berlin reveals the power of the giant industry lobby—the

Global Climate Coalition (GCC). Based in the United States and funded primarily by oil corporations, this organization was determined to stop the development of a protocol to the framework convention in its tracks. Indeed, along with the Climate Council (another industry lobby), the GCC accompanied the U.S. delegation to most meetings.[54] The corporations involved with the production of greenhouse gases have an enormous impact on policymaking in many countries, but nowhere more so than in the United States. The power of the fossil fuel industry acting in concert with the automobile industry demonstrates the degree to which the attempts to deal with the impact of climate change are held hostage to corporate profit margins.

In Berlin, the divergence among the participating countries was evident. States from the developing world were understandably concerned that they not be required to forgo their own economic development to compensate for the mess made by the overdeveloped world, and while the European Union (EU) and the Alliance of Small Island States (AOSIS) continued to demand a strengthening of the reduction targets of the industrialized countries, the stalling coalition led by the United States was resistant. Indeed, JUSCANZ refused to agree to the idea of targets and timetables for reduction, and the United States and Australia were against the mere mention of reductions in any agreed text.[55] And while the goal of the Berlin COP had been to strengthen the commitments of the framework convention, the best that could be achieved was the formal statement that the existing commitments were inadequate but the decision on the best way to strengthen them was deferred.

The JUSCANZ group was, as a result, seen by most other participating states (with the notable exception of the OPEC countries—for obvious reasons) as the major roadblock to defining the level of reduction of greenhouse gas emissions necessary to deal with climate change to any noticeable degree. On the demand of this group, the language of limiting greenhouse gas emissions began to be supplemented to allow for a business-plan type of strategy that might actually allow for a continuation of an increase in carbon emissions in overdeveloped countries. By focusing on the language of "sources and sinks," the Conference of Parties in Berlin began looking for ways of realizing the essential reduction of greenhouse gases without focusing solely on controlling emissions at the national level. Central to these efforts were debates over the issue of joint implementation, that is, a plan whereby developed countries could fund programs in developing countries (where they might be cheaper) in order that they meet their own targets for reduction somewhere else. It was agreed in Berlin that such action could be adopted on a voluntary basis but that no credits would be granted for emissions reductions—at least not at that time.[56] The support given to such solutions gave the blocking group encouragement for their future efforts.

An ad hoc working group was struck to take the Berlin Mandate and work out the details. The second Conference of Parties (in Geneva in 1996) failed to make much substantive progress, but a protocol was adopted at the third Conference of Parties in Kyoto in December 1997 and the establishment of the rules of the regime were set in motion. Under the terms of the Kyoto agreement, a commitment was made by industrialized countries to reduce emissions of six greenhouse gases, with a total reduction of 5.2 percent below 1990 levels by 2012.[57] Criticism was unleashed by environmental groups that this was far from adequate if any fundamental improvement was to be seen. The scientific evidence was fiercely contested inside and outside the negotiating rooms. The debate over the expert knowledge, however, is not the only point at issue. Those seeking fundamental shifts in environmentally destructive practices should be wary of allowing the debate to be shaped in such a limited manner.[58] While such targets can be strengthened within a system that establishes a program of incremental change based on evolving scientific "certainty," of longer-lasting and greater significance was the move toward what was described as "flexibility" in meeting targets through such mechanisms as joint implementation of targets, emissions trading, and the clean-development mechanism. These three mechanisms—described as innovative—were designed to assist the overdeveloped countries to reduce the costs of meeting their emissions reduction targets by purchasing reductions in other countries.

This move was widely celebrated by some green diplomats as a significant improvement on the earlier discussions of limits and reductions.[59] The language contained in these discussions is that of a free market approach and calculates everything in terms of "sources and sinks" and thereby reduces the complex discussions over human-induced climate change to discussion of a balance sheet that can be reckoned with ease: growth and increased exploitation of the natural environment seen as nothing more than an entry on a ledger. The picture being presented here is one of balance: if a country puts out an amount of carbon emissions, it must ensure that there are appropriate counterbalancing tendencies in the way of absorbing "sinks" (e.g., the ocean or trees) or an equitable reduction elsewhere through alternative technologies; if the polluting country does not have them, it must ensure that it pay others to provide the balance. The articulation of the catastrophe in terms of "sources and sinks" must surely be seen as an extraordinary manipulation of both image and language, a presentation of balance and harmony masking the very obvious imbalance that such destructive practices lead to. Moreover, it is interesting to contemplate the way in which this global double-entry bookkeeping style of dealing with the so-called sources and sinks further boosts—either deliberately or inadvertently—the presumed logic of globalization with its single marketplace calculation of human productivity, growth, and needs.

The only real hope of obtaining international agreement for the Kyoto Protocol was for the countries that were skeptical of the "flexible mechanisms" to give way to the group of countries willing to bring the entire process to a halt if this compromise was not made. The European countries, reluctant to take a path that could potentially allow a business-as-usual approach in those countries with the highest levels of carbon gas emissions, eventually agreed to the vague wording in the Kyoto agreement, but the tough decisions of putting flesh on the bones of the accord were put off until a future meeting in The Hague in November 2000.

The lead-up to the sixth Conference of Parties (COP-6) of the FCCC began in earnest when the fifth UN Global Climate Conference took place in Bonn in November 1999. One hundred sixty-six states came together to agree to a timetable for the promised cuts to greenhouse gas emissions. It was clear at this point that the idea of purchasing pollution credits and the other "flexibility" mechanisms were going to be a profound stumbling block.

The official purpose of the COP-6 meeting was to finalize the workings of the Kyoto Protocol so as to ensure that the convention could be ratified by enough states to enter into force.[60] The vagueness of the Kyoto Protocol has meant that regardless of the level of commitment, the lack of concrete detail on its operational mechanisms had prevented most states from taking the necessary steps to ratify it. The conference in The Hague was to change all this by making clear the details of the range of options open to participating states in reaching their targets. The avoidance of the difficult issues in Berlin, Geneva, and Kyoto had by necessity come to an end. The agreement on the details could be put off no longer.

Although only three countries had managed to reduce their own greenhouse gas emissions by the time of the meeting (Germany, Switzerland, and the United Kingdom), the majority of countries participating in the Hague meeting agreed with the EU's line that opening up the definitions of the flexible mechanisms to meet the demands of the United States and its deal-breaking allies would lead to a huge loophole that could be utilized by these countries to avoid taking substantial measures against greenhouse gas emissions at home.

Not much had changed with the U.S.-led coalition's demands for such a flexible approach. These countries sought to ensure that trading would be allowed in the emission quotas—allowing heavy fossil fuel users to buy shares from countries that had either managed to reduce fossil fuel use faster than expected or whose economies were in decline (the former Soviet Union clearly fits into this latter category). Canada and the United States led the way in demanding that credit be given to them for forests as "sinks." Canada argued that it should get a ton of pollution quotas for every ton of carbon dioxide absorbed by the country's forests.[61] This group of states was never going to agree that these mechanisms be merely supplemental to their domestic emission cuts; they were actively seeking ways to avoid the language of limiting growth.

When Jan Pronk, Dutch environment minister and host of the conference, offered a compromise paper that attempted to bridge the divide, he was scorned by those countries determined to agree to limits. His proposal was to allow forest projects to count under the clean-development mechanism, which would let industrialized countries meet their own targets by funding projects in developing countries. EU ministers argued that the proposed compromise would allow the United States to meet its Kyoto targets without reducing its emissions at all and that Pronk's proposal failed to respect the EU's "bottom line, which is to ensure that the environmental integrity and credibility of the Kyoto Protocol are safeguarded."[62] Several EU ministers believed that Pronk's plan would lead to an overall reduction of greenhouse gas emissions by a mere 2.2 percent by 2012 instead of the meager 5 percent promised by the Kyoto targets. Friends of the Earth reckoned that it would lead to a total increase in emissions and thereby completely undermine the entire Kyoto process.[63] Pronk's compromise was rejected by both the EU and the U.S.-led bloc of states.

While it is true that trees absorb and store carbon, there are numerous problems with this approach. It is, for instance, extraordinarily difficult to predict with any accuracy the stability of the process. When trees die, the stored carbon is released. How can we reliably monitor, quantify, and subsequently verify the "carbon sinks" in the manner suggested by the blocking coalition? There is additional uncertainty about the potential for "feedback"—that is, the effects of climate change that can amplify the negative consequences. Indeed, the difficulty of attaining accurate calculations is evident when we consider that the effects of global warming are already making the problems worse.[64]

A more substantial critique of the compromise offered by Pronk is of course necessary. The attempt to deal with forest "management" in this manner leads inevitably to a total commodification of such wilderness areas. It has been pointed out by some that this kind of calculation on the part of developed countries looking for trade-offs and developing countries desperate for cash credits would lead to both parties overlooking (or worse, deliberately ignoring) the people who either live in the forests or depend on them for their livelihoods. There has been some suggestion that natural forests would be cleared to make way for fast-growing eucalyptus plantations that would "soak up" carbon dioxide more quickly. This is the worst kind of bargaining with the natural world and a tack that will surely lead to the rapid and advanced destruction of the natural environment.

Nonetheless, the European participants continued to attempt to salvage something from the negotiations. After Pronk's failed attempt at compromise, the French participants led a delegation into talks designed to find an agreement that would allow the United States, Canada, and Japan to subtract the tons of carbon soaked up in domestic forests against emissions quotas.[65] Despite the French negotiator's ability in persuading the United States to dramatically reduce the amount of credit it sought, this last-ditch attempt failed when France's EU partners refused to back it, fearing it would represent a substantial retreat from their previous line.

By the end of the process, both Europe and the U.S.-led bloc were being criticized by the world's poorer nations for failing to find a joint solution. Quite clearly, however, the burden of responsibility for the failure lay with the blocking states, each of which refused any commitment to the establishment of a plan of action based on limiting their own greenhouse gas emissions. The desire for a market-based solution that would allow for pollution-as-usual for the world's largest consumers of fossil fuels was the real obstacle preventing the Conference of Parties from agreeing to the details of an administered plan of reduction.

Aside from the calamity that the blocking coalition of rogue states brought about at the Hague meeting, they also sought to undermine whatever residual belief existed in the necessity of seeking real limits to industrial growth as a way of dealing with atmospheric deterioration.[66] An increasingly bureaucratized, sterile, and commodified view of the natural world was evident at the Hague meeting, but within months, these international disputes became irrelevant. The newly elected U.S. president, George W. Bush, followed in his father's footsteps by placing the growth of the U.S. economy ahead of any environmental considerations. While Bush senior had been wary of the framework convention at the Rio Conference and had refused to sign it, his son extricated the United States from the Kyoto process, which his predecessor in the White House—Bill Clinton—had eased the country into. The green diplomats were thus faced with an enormous problem: the country that produces a full quarter of the greenhouse gas emissions was publicly denying the need for an international agreement to deal with the issue.

Despite the Clinton administration's failure to convince Congress of the need to sign on to the Kyoto Protocol, it had remained committed to international efforts to deal with the negative consequences of climate change. The presidency of George W. Bush has cast an even darker cloud over international efforts to find some level of international agreement to deal with the problem. It took Bush less than 100 days to announce his intention to drill for oil in the ecologically sensitive Arctic National Wildlife Reserve and to publicly declare the Kyoto process dead. This is clearly an administration determined to encourage unbridled economic growth based on increased use of fossil fuels. Indeed, for this administration, the environmentally suspect emissions-trading market discussed here is presented as an international conspiracy to force the United States to give money to poor countries or, worse still, to force Americans to give up their sport utility vehicles (SUVs). It has been estimated that by requiring a 15 percent improvement in the fuel efficiency of SUVs (less than three miles per gallon), the Bush administration could save more oil each year than the projected annual production coming from the Arctic National Wildlife Reserve.[67]

In July 2001 in Bonn, the parties to the Kyoto Protocol tried yet again to get a deal; in a manner of speaking they achieved their goal. Fearful of a complete collapse of the Kyoto process, the European countries gave in to the demands of the rogue group and the world was left with an agreement that could actually sanction an increase in greenhouse gas emissions. Celebration nonetheless ensued. Even green activists greeted the last-minute deal with relief and jubilation, convinced that a limited deal was better than no deal at all. Many of those present took delight in the ability of the conference to reach agreement in the face of U.S. intransigence and seemed to believe that the "successful" conclusion would be an embarrassment to the Bush administration. The

Bush administration was not, of course, embarrassed in the least; it is convinced that its position is the right one: the Kyoto protocol is "bad for American business."

While the academics concerned with regime formation and the practitioners of green diplomacy continue to focus on the necessary steps to realizing an international mechanism for limiting the anthropogenic causes of climate change, it is clear that they have a severely limited understanding of the obstacles to its achievement. The struggles over the framing of the science of climate change demonstrate the extent to which knowledge is contested. Far from the promise of the objective knowledge of the Enlightenment, guaranteeing a progressive move forward, the struggle to define the nature of the problem and its solution allows us insight into the behind-the-scenes struggle of private corporate interests to shape the discourse. Here we have an alliance of corporations dependent upon the continued increase in the use of fossil fuels literally buying its own scientific experts in order to shape the public debate and, further, pressure the green diplomats to act in a manner consistent with their own interests. And these interests demonstrate vividly the direct linkage of the growth ethic with environmental deterioration. However, even when that connection is made, the search for a technical fix to get us out of the problem is held up as the further promise of our Enlightened worldview. We can plant more trees to soak up the carbon, we can dump iron into the ocean, or we can just wait a little longer until a better solution comes along. We will fix it—we have done it in the past and we will do it again in the future. It is the human way, the incremental way, the Enlightened way. A solution is inevitable . . . or is it?

Is it not just possible that George W. Bush's withdrawal from the Kyoto process has demonstrated as clearly as anything could that greed and shallow thinking triumph over even the most limited and meager efforts of the incrementalist's plan to clean up the mess? With his myopic message to the American people that they could keep their energy-intensive way of life without facing any costs, the new president has ripped the Enlightenment fig leaf away from the modest plans of the green diplomats.

CONCLUSION

It is in the area of the atmosphere that the majority of international green diplomacy has been seen in the past two decades. It is with the two case studies examined here that we see the regime usually deemed the most impressive (ozone depletion) and the regime often seen as presenting the most intractable problems (climate change). But the process in other areas is similar, and attempts face the same challenges to find agreement.

Advocates of incremental approaches to environmental problems will continue to insist that there is no other option open to those struggling to find solutions to these shared problems in the "real world." *If* this is true, then it seems obvious that there is little hope for improvement, and academics and practitioners alike might just as well cease exhausting themselves with their efforts. For twenty years, the international agreements have done little more than act as a salve on our collective conscience and as a method for reaffirming our belief that continued growth is possible and that technological solutions will be found to save the day. The fact that HCFCs destroy the ozone more slowly than CFCs or that we can plant trees to suck carbon out of the atmosphere *should* be sounding very loud alarm bells about the adequacy of the technological fixes being offered by the experts. Indeed, the actions of the experts in one "segment" of the environment may well be having a deleterious effect on a different "segment." Such ongoing deterioration of the environment demonstrates quite clearly that the green diplomat really is fiddling while the atmosphere burns: the solutions offered do nothing to end the destruction, but the experts content themselves with the fact that they are stemming its tide.

This is clearly a case of the irrational being presented as rational, and the complexity of socially and economically embedded environmental problems being reduced to the relative simplicity of technical problems. Around the charts and the computer models, the "experts" plot the likely outcomes of different courses of action and cannot understand when "lay people tend to confuse global warming with other environmental problems, such as ozone depletion."[68] It is an important condition of their work that the modeling does not take into account any extraneous considerations or what is happening in other areas of inquiry. The statistics and measurements that have been gathered—or in more extreme cases assumed—serve to ensure our faith in the scientific model. What is wrong with this? Calculations surrounding our ability to survive in a dramatically altered natural world are presented rationally so as to deny the irrationality of the actions generating the crisis.[69] With the various constituent parts of the natural world carefully separated from one another, we witness scientists focusing on small measures to stem the tide of destruction. We are not allowed—for it would be un-scientific—to ask broader questions about the way in which the international society operates or what the root causes of the deterioration might be. Quantitative study and the answers it produces would be disturbed by such interventions that come from another dimension of thought—a dimension based on humility in the face of our responsibility for the destruction of the natural world.

Perhaps focusing on two ongoing attempts at regime formation is an unfair practice for a critic of the incrementalist program. Why not look at other regimes, dealing with other "issue areas"; after all, part of the beauty of the scientific rationalism that underpins these efforts is its reassurance that the natural world can be divided and subdivided in an effort to resolve specific crises and that such resolutions will have no adverse effects on other "pieces" of the natural world. Maritime pollution is considered separately from whaling and deep seabed mining. And there can be no suggestion that these issues be considered in conjunction with space debris or the military uses of outer space. And why, the regime defender would ask, would anyone possibly try to link efforts to agree to a convention on biosafety with anything else? The regime specialist will go one further:

> Although there is a natural and justifiable tendency to treat the mismatch between the scope of a regime and the dimensions of the underlying problem, perceived ecologically, as a source of ineffectiveness, the criticism can equally be regarded as impractical. There may be strong political reasons for avoiding the creation of all-encompassing regimes, however logically attractive they may appear. The epic attempt at codification involved in the Third Law of the Sea Conference is often now regarded as a precedent to be avoided.[70]

Here we can see not only a dismissal of the idea that the natural environment be considered more holistically in international efforts to deal with the anthropogenic causes of its deterioration, but also a rejection of the demand that all-encompassing treatments of an area (such as the ocean) be dealt with. No, the incrementalist will insist, the exigencies of the international system dictate that carefully delimited issues are the only rational and manageable way to obtain agreement among the actors in a fundamentally anarchical system.

In order to mount an effectively critical intellectual response to such assertions, we must, as a starting point, challenge the claim that objective knowledge will set us free. If there is any further need for calling this spurious claim into question, there are plenty of examples we can call to hand. Take, for example, the response of the Canadian government to early concerns about fish "stocks." Instead of reflecting on the changing nature and possible negative impact of new technology that was being designed to increase the catches of cod and the resulting boom in the profit margin of an expanding and professionalized industry, the bureaucrat responsible was adamant that progress was being made with absolutely no chance of repercussions from human activities: "I say it is impossible, not merely to exhaust them, but even noticeably to lessen their number by the means now used for their capture, especially if, protecting them during their spawning season, we are contented to fish them from their feeding grounds. . . . [T]here are no indications of exhaustion."[71] Setting aside for the moment the dramatically misguided approach to nature that is embedded in this notion of the natural world being nothing more than a storehouse for human enjoyment and consumption, the science presented by the "expert" was clearly and undeniably wrong.

To continue to claim that we have at our command the scientific tools to understand and ultimately control nature and that such knowledge is value-free and therefore outside the realm of political or economic interests, or indeed ethical or moral considerations, is demonstrably fallacious. The efforts of the incremental regime builders are, as a result, doomed to a future of defending their supposedly value-free science in the face of mounting evidence that their efforts are serving the very real commercial interests of those who wish to continue reaping benefits from a system based on exploitation and economic growth.

If the incrementalists respond with a plea that sometimes scientific knowledge needs more time to settle on the "truth" but that such agreement will inevitably be found, they unwittingly highlight the second facet of Enlightenment thought, which should now be challenged. The desire to solve any and every problem faced by society through recourse to technical knowledge is the logical by-product of the faith in the separation of fact and value. But if science is not "neutral" it can be turned and shaped to meet the needs of many or, more commonly, to facilitate the interests of certain groups.[72]

Other examples of the outcome of international environmental diplomacy can further serve to demonstrate the extent to which this practice reinforces the status quo organization of society—including the defense of capitalism that has become so deeply entrenched in the rhetoric surrounding sustainable development. Indeed, it has often been pointed out that many existing environmental regimes began as commercial

agreements. In many ways this should not come as a surprise. International negotiations to deal with a shared environmental problem have
often served as a means to finding mutually supportive ways to ensure
that no long-term harm will come to either economic growth or the
business interests dependent upon it. When the International Maritime
Organization (IMO) was given responsibility for implementing a treaty
on marine pollution, this ship-owners club was seen to be acting in its
own interests in establishing standards to prevent oil spills. But rather
than seeing this as a clear example of responsible economic enterprise,
we should be cognizant of the fact that the IMO has long been seen as
being selfishly anxious to limit responsibility or costs for prevention.[73]
Likewise, the involvement of giant multinational biotechnology corporations can be seen both directly and indirectly (through the influence
of national governments) in international discussions to agree to regulations for dealing with genetically modified organisms. This is not
pure science attempting to deal with potentially hazardous materials;
this is corporate control of biosafety with its prioritization of profits
over biodiversity.

The efforts toward greenwashing discussed in Chapter 3 are important to the ongoing process of gaining support for incrementalism.
When DuPont is presented as a champion of a regime to protect the
ozone layer while at the same time making the chemicals that destroy it,
we have come to the very edge of the age of irony. When the World
Business Council on Sustainable Development can present itself publicly as an agent for environmental assessment while lobbying behind
the scenes to ensure that the operation of the free market is seen as the
best strategy for realizing environmental standards, we can begin to expose the illogic of the supposed neutrality of instrumental rationality as
utilized and valorized by incrementalists.[74]

The economic calculations central to cost-benefit analysis—weighing
the relative short-term expense of dealing with environmental problems
against the potential expense for future generations—are merely one
more way that the incrementalists attempt to dazzle us with their sums
and projections. Discussions surrounding the so-called maximization
of society's welfare, which assume not only pure market operation but
the possibility of technological solutions down the road, lead to the
comfortable—but ultimately dangerous—belief that "there is no real
cause for alarm."[75]

The point is not just that these arguments are distressingly limited; the
illusory positive thinking upon which they rely serves to label alternative

views as utopian or idealistic, or counterproductive. The opposite of positive is most surely negative and, in the mainstream consideration of regime formation, incrementalism is seen as the only available step forward. Critiques of the status quo approach and its attached organizational structures and ways of thinking are indeed negative, but not in the sense implied by the defenders of regimes. The attempt to understand deeper causes and hidden dynamics is negative in the progressive, philosophical manner intended by dialectical argument. It is not negative in the sense that it merely breaks down or criticizes; it is negative in the sense that it recognizes the tension between the *is* and the *ought* and allows the space for a concerted effort to understand how particular ways of seeing have come to shape and possibly dominate society.

The implications for society (and for the natural environment) are profound if the sole task of the researcher is defined in such a way as to ensure that the organization of society goes unchallenged. The language of the incrementalist becomes a functional language and serves, as a result, to delegitimize critical and dialectical thought. The assumptions embedded in the mind-set, when sanctioned by both practitioners and intellectuals, become fixed and accepted in such a way as to deny the possibility of any other strategy for dealing with the situation at hand.

The conferences held to find solutions to shared international problems such as those described here are a good example of the rational technological society at work. The facts must be isolated from what Herbert Marcuse calls the "truly concrete context which makes the facts and determines their function" in order that they can be used to build uncritical technical solutions to the problems facing us.[76] The statistics and measurements are gathered and analyzed and subsequently presented to elite and exclusive gatherings of the dedicated representatives of the international community in order that collective action can be taken. The knowledge that this process is ongoing (separately and for each of the more serious problems) serves to reaffirm our faith in the ability of experts to find rational answers to specific problems and of policymakers to make enlightened choices among policy options in the common interest of humankind.

The problem with the acceptance of an unquestioned faith in the scientific fix has been argued in Chapter 1, and there is no need to reiterate the argument here. In terms of regime formation, however, we should keep these arguments in mind and develop a healthy skepticism about claims that the efforts to take well-defined (bite-sized) topics for control and management can lead to a successful solution for the myriad environmental problems. The environmental problems are larger than the cheerleaders of the incrementalist approach would have us believe. We cannot—indeed must not—regard the creation of international regimes for specific issue areas as a solution to the problems faced. We must instead articulate a challenge to the very idea of global environmental management and begin to make linkages against the wishes of the status quo diplomatic approach. As William Leiss argued three decades ago: "The goal of reversing the present self-destructive treatment of the environment cannot be separated from that of challenging the authoritarian decision-making powers vested in corporate and governmental institutions."[77] The patterns Leiss identified continue to exist and have been internationalized through the logic and practice of neoliberal economics. Resistance is necessary, but it must be built on a solid understanding of the embedded structures of thought and practice.

NOTES

1. Krasner, ed., *International Regimes,* p. 3.
2. See, for example, the classic presentation of this case: Strange, *"Cave! Hic dragones:* A Critique of Regime Analysis."
3. Ibid., p. 480.
4. For a variety of perspectives on regime formation, see Grieco, "Anarchy and the Limits of Co-operation"; Keohane, *After Hegemony;* Krasner, *International Regimes;* Keohane and Nye, "Two Cheers for Multilateralism"; Young, "Political Leadership and Regime Formation"; Young, "The Politics of International Regime Formation"; List and Rittberger, "Regime Theory and International Environmental Management"; Victor, Chayes, and Skolnikoff, "Pragmatic Approaches to Regime Building for Complex International Problems"; Vogler, *The Global Commons;* Osherenko and Young, "The Formation of International Regimes"; Little, "International Regimes"; and Bernauer, "The Effect of International Environmental Institutions." For a discussion of the possibility that a world environmental regime is being developed, see Meyer et al., "The Structuring of a World Environmental Regime, 1870–1990." For a critical examination of regimes that fits in with the broad themes of this book, see Paterson, "Radicalizing Regimes?"
5. For an interesting consideration of regimes in terms of international legal thinking, see Jurgielewicz, "International Regimes and Environmental Policy."
6. Young, "The Politics of International Regime Formation," pp. 366–374. See also Osherenko and Young, "The Formation of International Regimes," in which the authors set out a template of various hypotheses against which specific cases of regime formation can be tested.
7. Bernauer, "The Effect of International Environmental Institutions," p. 351.

8. For an explicit discussion of the steps toward successful regime formation, see Porter and Brown, *Global Environmental Politics,* chap. 3 (their steps are defined as issue definition, fact-finding, bargaining on regime creation, and regime strengthening). See also Greene, "Environmental Issues," pp. 325–327, for a slightly different set of steps: agenda formation, negotiating and decisionmaking, implementation, and further development.

9. Greene, "Environmental Issues," p. 325.

10. Haas, "Introduction: Epistemic Communities and International Policy Coordination," p. 3.

11. Ibid.

12. Adler and Haas, "Epistemic Communities, World Order, and the Creation of a Reflective Research Program," p. 371.

13. A framework agreement is usually seen as a very general statement of the shared goals of the participating parties to seek a solution to a common problem. It does not usually impose any binding obligations and is seen as being important for the reason that it signals the intention of the participating states to move forward to seek a treaty that would impose limits on activity. See Porter and Brown, *Global Environmental Politics,* p. 20.

14. For concise discussions of these practical problems, see Porter and Brown, *Global Environmental Politics;* and Hurrell, "International Political Theory and the Global Environment," p. 134.

15. Hurrell, "International Political Theory and the Global Environment," p. 138.

16. See ibid. See also Finger, "New Horizons for Peace Research."

17. Adler and Haas, "Epistemic Communities, World Order, and the Creation of a Reflective Research Program," p. 370.

18. Litfin, "Framing Science," p. 252 (emphasis in original). For an interesting discussion of the nature of social knowledge vis-à-vis regimes and their creation of norms, see Kratochwil, "Regimes, Interpretation, and the 'Science' of Politics."

19. Adler and Haas, "Epistemic Communities, World Order, and the Creation of a Reflective Research Program," pp. 372–373.

20. See, for instance, articles published in *Resurgence* or *The Ecologist.*

21. Finger, "New Horizons for Peace Research," p. 24.

22. Steve Smith, "Environment on the Periphery of International Relations." It should be noted, however, that Smith's argument in 1993 is curiously devoid of a critical theoretical awareness despite its claim to be focusing on the need to address the fundamental relationship between knowledge and power. For a critique of Smith's argument, see Hovden, "As If Nature Doesn't Matter." See also Saurin, "International Relations, Social Ecology, and the Globalisation of Environmental Change."

23. For the story of the ozone issue, see Benedick, *Ozone Diplomacy;* Haas, "Banning Chlorofluorocarbons"; Maxwell and Weiner, "Green Consciousness or Dollar Diplomacy?"; and Gribbin, *The Hole in the Sky.*

24. Haas, "Banning Chlorofluorocarbons," p. 187.

25. Ibid., p. 196.

26. For a simple explanation of the science, see Environment Canada, "Canada's Ozone Layer Protection Program," introd. See also the classic text, Gribbin, *The Hole in the Sky.*

27. For a fascinating account of this device and Lovelock's purpose in devising it, see Gribbin, *The Hole in the Sky,* pp. 40–43.

28. Molina and Rowland, "Stratospheric Sink for Chlorofluoromethanes."

29. For a detailed picture of the early U.S. regulatory action, see Maxwell and Weiner, "Green Consciousness or Dollar Diplomacy?"

30. Haas, "Banning Chlorofluorocarbons," p. 201.

31. Benedick, as quoted in ibid., p. 196.

32. Vogler, *The Global Commons,* p. 126. Despite his recognition of the role of corporations, Vogler still sees this as an "outstanding example of contemporary international environmental cooperation" (p. 127).

33. Maxwell and Weiner make this case admirably; see their article "Green Consciousness or Dollar Diplomacy?"

34. See, for example, Haas, "Banning Chlorofluorocarbons."

35. Doyle presents the facts surrounding DuPont's activities admirably; see his article "Hold the Applause."

36. For an interesting examination of the shifting of policy in Europe, see Brown, "Policymaking in International Organizations." While Brown acknowledges that initial British policies reflected the interests of the chemical industry—notably Imperial Chemical Industries (ICI)—the focus here is more on policy learning and policy brokers.

37. Haas, "Banning Chlorofluorocarbons," pp. 202–203. See also McKibben, *The End of Nature,* p. 38, for a discussion of this in terms of our assumption that nature changes slowly and the resulting inability to believe these anomalous readings.

38. Haas, "Banning Chlorofluorocarbons," p. 211. John Gribbin, it should be mentioned, believes that the scientific input into the policy process leading up to the Montreal meeting had virtually ceased; see Gribbin, *The Hole in the Sky,* p. 135.

39. For a comprehensive discussion of UNEP's role in the Montreal Protocol, see Downie, "UNEP and the Montreal Protocol."

40. Downie, "UNEP and the Montreal Protocol," p. 184.

41. McKibben, *The End of Nature,* p. 63.

42. Stolarski, as quoted in Haas, "Banning Chlorofluorocarbons," p. 192 (emphasis in original).

43. Ozone Secretariat, "Cairo Ministerial Meeting Links Climate Change and Ozone Solutions," p. 1.

44. Christine Stewart, "Speech Delivered on the Occasion of the Opening of the Ninth Annual Meeting of the Parties to the Montreal Protocol."

45. Litfin, "Ecoregimes," pp. 109–110.

46. Cited in Elliott, *The Global Politics of the Environment,* p. 57.

47. Ibid., p. 59.

48. See, for example, Feldman, "Iterative Functionalism and Climate Management Organizations"; Young, "Negotiating an International Climate Regime"; and Sebenius, "Designing Negotiations Toward a New Regime."

49. See, for example, Paterson, *Global Warming and Global Politics,* pp. 17–21; and McKibben, *The End of Nature,* pp. 7–8.

50. A description of the science of global warming is provided in virtually every paper and book written about the development of a climate change regime. For a superb description of the phenomenon with a focus on both naturally occurring and anthropogenic sources of greenhouse gases, see White, "Global Warming and the Greenhouse Effect," pp. 210–213. See also Paterson, "Global Warming"; and Retallack, "Kyoto." For an overview of the development of the FCCC and a broad view of the development of international activity in this area, see Vogler, *The Global Commons,* pp. 133–151; Elliott, *The Global Politics of the Environment,* pp. 60–73; Paterson, *Global Warming and Global Politics;* and Brenton, *The Greening of Machiavelli,* chap. 7.

51. The IPCC's work is divided into three separate Working Groups: the first deals with the scientific aspects of climate change; the second considers the vulnerability of the socioeconomic and natural systems to climate changes; and the third assesses options for limiting greenhouse gas emissions. There is also a Task Force on National Greenhouse Gas Inventories.

52. Hanisch, "The Rio Climate Convention," p. 63.

53. Elliott, *The Global Politics of the Environment,* p. 71; Paterson, *Global Warming and Global Politics,* pp. 69–70.

54. Paterson, *Global Warming and Global Politics,* p. 81.

55. Ibid., p. 69.

56. Elliott, *The Global Politics of the Environment,* p. 71. For an interesting discussion of the difficulty of realizing a successful international agreement based on individual national objectives and emission rights and bargaining, see Cooper, "Toward a Real Global Warming Treaty."

57. The six gases are carbon dioxide, methane, nitrous oxide, hydrofluorocarbons, perfluorocarbons, and sulphur hexafluoride. The emissions targets were set at varying levels. For example, the EU agreed to a collective reduction of 8 percent, the United States agreed to 7 percent, while Canada and Japan each agreed to 6 percent.

58. For an interesting examination of these issues, see Lutes, "Global Climatic Change." Lutes acknowledges the role of scientific knowledge in the discussions over solutions but argues for an explicit recognition of its socially constructed nature.

59. See Swart, "A Comprehensive Approach to Climate Policy," for a concise defense of the setting of quantitative objectives and implementation mechanisms.

60. To enter into force, the convention must be ratified by fifty-five parties to the convention, including annex 1 parties, accounting for 55 percent of carbon dioxide emissions from this group in 1990. The countries listed in annex 1 are the developed countries plus a number of countries—such as Croatia, Poland, and Latvia—that are undergoing the process of transition to a market economy.

61. Rolfe, "Canada's Game." For a consideration of the dubious scientific claims behind the idea of trees as "sinks," see Simpson, "Climate Change"; and Leggett, "Global Warming." For a further critique of Canada's stance on climate

change, see Broadhead, "Canada as a Rogue State"; and MacDonald and Smith, "Promises Made, Promises Broken."

62. EU Environment Commissioner Margot Wallstrom, "Climate Compromise Disappoints," BBC News Online, November 24, 2000, available at www. bbc.co.uk/hi/english/sci/tech/newsid_1038000/1038524.stm.

63. Friends of the Earth, "Six Reasons Why the Deal Is Junk," available at www.foecanada.org/campaign/cleanair/hague_001124c.htm.

64. Royal Society, "The Role of Land Carbon Sinks in Mitigating Global Climate Change." See also, McKibben, *The End of Nature,* pp. 27–29. For a discussion of the "plankton multiplier," see Leggett, "Global Warming," pp. 29–33.

65. Emma Ross, "Climate Meeting Ends Without a Deal," Associated Press, November 25, 2000.

66. The concept of "rogue" state has been used since the end of the Cold War, usually by Americans seeking to justify enormous military expenditure in the absence of an obvious threat to national security. But the fear of tanks rolling over the borders has, for many people, been replaced by new threats of pollution or environmentally irresponsible behavior. Any state that, for the purposes of gaining competitive advantage or of merely maintaining an unsustainable way of life, actively blocks, stalls, or otherwise subverts an international process designed to deal with shared problems becomes a threat to others by virtue of the destructive environmental consequences that result from such intransigence.

67. Roberts, "Bad Sports," p. 75.

68. Thompson and Rayner, "Risk and Governance Part I," p. 147. Thompson and Rayner are interested to consider the way people consider risk and develop their perceptions of environmental problems; they are not themselves representative of the uncomprehending experts. For consideration of the calculation of risk and debates within the field, see Douglas, "The Depoliticization of Risk"; Dunlap, "International Opinion at the Century's End"; Thompson, Rayner, and Ney, "Risk and Governance Part II"; and Bostrom et al., "What Do People Know About Global Climate Change? [Part 1 and Part 2]." These debates are exceedingly interesting for the way in which they cast the discussions about how people see the problems as well as their developing political sense of what should be done.

69. Marcuse made this point with regard to the strategies around nuclear deterrence; see his book *One Dimensional Man,* p. 190.

70. Vogler, *The Global Commons,* p. 179.

71. L. Z. Joncas of the Canadian Ministry of Agriculture, 1885, as quoted in Kurlansky, *Cod,* p. 123.

72. For a discussion of the contested nature of science and the struggle to frame environmental issues, see Hawkins, "Contested Ground"; Hannigan, *Environmental Sociology;* and Liberatore, "The Social Construction of Environmental Problems."

73. For a discussion of the IMO within the broader context of the creation of an "ocean regime," see Friedheim, *Negotiating the New Ocean Regime.* See also Greene, "Environmental Issues," for a brief discussion of the IMO's contribution

to environmental issues on the international agenda, along with other examples of action taken to facilitate economic interests.

74. For an interesting discussion of the role of transnational corporations in a range of international environmental regime efforts, see Finger and Kilcoyne, "Why Transnational Corporations Are Organizing to 'Save the Global Environment.'"

75. Beckerman, "Global Warming and International Action," p. 288. For a critical perspective on such thinking, see "Hot Air," *The Ecologist;* and Stirling, "Environmental Valuation."

76. Marcuse, *One Dimensional Man,* p. 190.

77. Leiss, *The Domination of Nature,* p. 21.

5

Reconsidering Utopia

IN ALL CORNERS OF THE GLOBE, THE PROMISE OF A NEW ERA OF environmental stability and increased prosperity are held out as the logical and inevitable by-products of both the practices of green diplomacy and the international economic arrangements being forged by proponents of deregulated international capitalism. Regional and global trade deals increasingly contain promises of environmental awareness and sustainability, and against the backdrop of these pledges the green diplomats continue to meet to agree on joint measures to deal with ecological degradation. This book has argued, however, that despite the lip service paid to environmental problems within the trade deals, the reality is that deregulated capitalism and the structures being established in its defense are bringing about a dramatic deterioration of the natural environment.

In fact, despite such routinely recycled protestations of ecological awareness from within free trade regimes, there remains a disturbing practical and popular disassociation between the green diplomacy of environmental agreements and the "greenback diplomacy" of trade deals. The public—especially but not exclusively in the industrialized countries—is presented with a picture of two separate forms of multilateral negotiations being undertaken in our best interests by "experts" in the distinct fields of economics and the environment. Yes, they are in some broad and vague sense aware and supportive of each other's aims and objectives—but no, an integrated approach is not considered to be necessary. The separation of the economic and environmental issues thereby continues comfortably in the public consciousness. The media reinforce the separation by carrying stories of green diplomacy and trade negotiations in different sections as though the outcome of one would have no impact on the other. Given the split in thinking that is, as I have argued, so deeply embedded in Western thought, this separation of issues is not surprising.

Despite the persistence, and pervasiveness, of this denial of fundamental connections between economic systems and environmental sanity, there is an increasingly loud chorus of voices insisting that there are indeed alternatives to the reality being presented. We live in an age of profound crisis, and it is leading to a massive renewal of the critical spirit in many societies around the world. Major, dynamically democratic alliances are being built to challenge the presentation of the inevitability of corporate globalization. The claim that it is through increasing trade and decreasing corporate regulation that we will most easily realize the promise of ecological sustainability is ridiculed by many—as is the claim that everyone, everywhere, desires the type of overdevelopment and commodified existence that we in the West champion and indulge in.

It is by no means clear that the voices on the margins of a wide variety of societies will succeed in their goal of presenting alternatives and gaining widespread acceptance of them. There are, as always, powerful forces of containment at work. As I argued in Chapter 2, the critique offered by the environmental movement of the 1960s and 1970s was absorbed all too easily, with the radical issues raised reformulated in such a way that the destructive practices and the structures underpinning them were left standing and, indeed, strengthened. Today's protesters have doubtless learned lessons from these previous attempts, but the situation they face is quite different; the battle lines are drawn internationally and the targets of protest are bigger and more remote from everyday life. In the 1960s, the local protest group could take aim at the resident corporate polluter; today, the decisions that impact on the environment are often made by representatives to trade arrangements hidden away from public view or by unelected trade tribunals not accountable to any democratic scrutiny. Likewise, the environmental problems themselves have become more complex. The ongoing destruction of local communities by resident polluters must be considered within the broader global context of ozone depletion, climate change, loss of biodiversity, and a series of other problems, the consequences of which may not be immediately apparent. The corporate greenwash campaigns send out powerful and reassuring messages, as does the language of responsible governmental action, embodied most succinctly in the concept of sustainable development.

Those intent on raising awareness of environmental issues in the overdeveloped countries face a public addicted to commodity consumption and fearful of the language of limits. In the underdeveloped countries the public is faced with government corruption, a lack of accountability, and the rigging of trade rules resulting in the elimination of truly sustainable practices: the undermining of small-scale traditional practices and local economies serving to guarantee transnational corporate access to resources and markets.

It is against the most reassuring of claims that the modern environmental protester must take aim: free trade will lead to prosperity and environmental well-being; sustainable development (in a form as articulated by the Bruntland Commission) will provide the guidance we need to ensure that the world's poorest people will gain access to a dignified life; incremental steps to global environmental action are the logical course of action; science and technology will provide the necessary answers for any seemingly intractable problems. The new protest movement must convince others that what is accepted as rational action is in fact irrational. It must furthermore stand up to the widespread belief that it is anti-progress, anti-technological, anti-individual, and anti-development. It is not sufficient to demonstrate a deep understanding of the current global structures or to merely offer a critique of the failed promise of green diplomacy. The protesters must convince millions of fellow citizens that the anti-globalization movement has workable alternatives that will be better for them and for the environment. This is a daunting challenge.

Throughout this book, I have sought to examine and critique the existing structures of society and the embedded ways of thinking that I believe have a bearing on the current state of environmental destruction. In doing so, I have attempted to highlight what Max Horkheimer calls the "breach between ideas and reality,"[1] that is to say, the breach between what an established system promises and what it in fact delivers. I have pointed to the illogic of the current promises of green diplomacy and argued that without rethinking the roots of the problem, this current method of dealing with global environmental problems can never be anything more than a method of slowing down the destructive practices responsible for the deterioration. I have illustrated the ideas, concepts, and indeed the societal structures that act to contain demands for a qualitatively different set of social relations, changes that would result in a healthier and more satisfying relationship with the natural world.

To offer alternatives is, of necessity, to undertake an exercise of the imagination. It is to break out from the constraints imposed by a worldview that seeks to reassure us that the existing reality is to be celebrated as the best possible model for the fulfillment of all human beings regardless of where they might be, or with what alternative model of community they might currently be living. It is perhaps ironic that the use of the concept of sustainable development may well have an unintended consequence. Faced with the well-publicized reality of a rapidly worsening environmental situation, the more the concept is used to claim that the current goals of unending growth and resource extraction are the key to finding an environmental Shangri-La, the more the inherent illogic of its program becomes evident. It also, as I argued in Chapter 2, provides insight into what should be the goal—namely, truly sustainable development. Because nonrenewable resources cannot, by their very nature, be sustainably used, a focus then becomes placed on alternatives. Because the current environmental problems have been caused by unchecked growth, further growth can no longer be presented as the answer. And because the deregulation of capital leads to the search for the locale with the lowest environmental standards in order that profit can be maximized, such deregulation can no longer be presented as the way forward for raising environmental standards. The tension within the concept of sustainable development thereby becomes extraordinarily useful in moving forward with structural and theoretical alternatives.

Clearly my critique of green diplomacy goes much further than merely a concern with the speed or effectiveness with which the international community develops its action plans for dealing with global environmental problems. Such a critique would conclude with nothing more than suggestions for how to improve the current attempts to use multilateral activity within the given set of structures of the international economy. Such analyses continue the separation and compartmentalization of issues, seeing no conflict between the standard growth model and a protected environment. Instead, I have argued that the backdrop of an international trading system—one based on economic growth, capital mobility, and guaranteed corporate rights—against which green diplomacy takes place, comes from, and further deepens, destructive practices based on an unsustainable view of nature. It is a system that asks us to believe that the Enlightenment worldview—with its confidence in a dualistic scientific method and faith in technological fixes—alongside economic structures that celebrate competitiveness, resource extraction, and unlimited growth, will provide the vision necessary to take the entire world into a bright new future of environmental growth and increased wealth. It is incumbent upon any critic of this status quo system, then, to offer an image of a viable alternative based on a reformulated scientific view, alternative economic ideas, and a suggestion of where the movement might come from to inspire the debate necessary to shift the political agenda toward a more environmentally sound and egalitarian project that will shatter the way of seeing interests in terms of domination—human and natural.

As I will argue in this chapter, it is high time to examine "the historical alternatives which haunt the established society as subversive tendencies and forces,"[2] and to highlight the possibilities for a realistic worldview that would move beyond the limits of green diplomacy. I will begin by offering insight into an image of science illuminating the critique I offered in Chapter 1, pointing to the possibility of a new direction for scientific inquiry. Such a revitalization is eloquently advocated by a number of innovative, progressive scientists disturbed by the inherent destructiveness of Enlightenment methods and mind-set. I will then link these radical ways of thinking to Herbert Marcuse's insistence on the need for a new science—a concept for which he has been criticized, but which I believe should be revived and renewed in relationship to the challenges facing us today.

A consideration of the economic alternatives being put forward in many parts of the world is also essential, given the obvious relevance they have for true sustainability. There are some surprisingly detailed and profound suggestions being offered for changes to economic structures both within countries and between them. In addition to domestic attempts to build true sustainability, protest networks that have grown up around the violence of the existing international system provide inspiration and goals for an alternative internationalism capable of delivering freedom, progress, and environmental sustainability.

Because the struggle to expose the blocked progressive tendencies of any society is a difficult task, it is essential to continue to point to the powerful forces deployed to ensure their containment. Although I will focus on the alternatives that are both reasonable and possible, it is important to temper this optimism with a healthy dose of intellectual skepticism. In short, I will point to the hurdles that lie in the path of the very many people around the world sharing in the struggle to achieve a truly sustainable society in which to live, and I will consider the chances of this international protest movement in achieving its goals.

NEW SCIENCE AND ENVIRONMENTALISM

Environmentalists are frequently accused of being anti-technology and anti-science. Those who seek a fundamentally different engagement with the natural world and insist on an understanding of the social context within which scientific inquiry is conducted are accused of being naïve waifs desirous of a return to a simpler past or a rural idyll. And although there has long existed a romantically charged opposition to Enlightenment science (powerfully articulated by the Romantic poets themselves), there is far more to the current critiques of the social uses of science than this stereotype would have us believe. Critical Theory once again allows us to move beyond the simplistic "either-or" scenario of "progress" versus a "return to the past."

As was argued in Chapter 1, the early Frankfurt School writers put forward a critique of Enlightenment science and its methods that was neither romantic nor unrealistic. Examining the outcome of a form of reason that separates subject from object and holds that human knowledge can be complete, Theodor Adorno and Max Horkheimer point to the way in which the "multiplicity of forms is reduced to position and arrangement, history to fact, things to matter."[3] The implications of this are clear for them: "Thinking objectifies itself to become an automatic, self-activating process; an impersonation of the machine that it produces itself so that ultimately the machine can replace it. Enlightenment has put aside the classic requirement of thinking about thought."[4] Such a mind-set allowed science to be perceived as being beyond politics or social struggle—merely a technique for investigation and nothing more.

Marcuse then offered a view of technology as possessing great positive potential if undistorted by social structures based on commodification, profit, and manufactured needs. In his view, science and technology are never outside the social context and are inevitably used to increase and solidify existing power relations. The use of science and technology in the service of modern society then functions at the expense of the more progressive uses to which they could just as easily be directed, given a radical change in social context.[5] The logical conclusion of Marcuse's argument is that science and technology cannot and will not change their form until they are released (or wrested) from the demands of a repressive society. To take a simple but currently relevant example, we need look no further than the uses to which the scientific community are put in the George W. Bush administration.

Bush claims that the development of alternative energy technologies is too expensive to contemplate, so the administration seeks to develop plans for oil drilling in the pristine Arctic National Wildlife Reserve in an effort to meet the ever growing energy needs of the United States. At the same time, the administration offers billions of dollars of contracts to military technology companies to develop the necessary equipment to in turn develop a national missile defense program designed to shoot down incoming intercontinental ballistic missiles emanating from threatening "rogue" states. The fact that the countries most frequently cited (Iraq, Iran, North Korea) do not have the capability (or likely the desire) to fire the missiles for which the shield is being designed is not mentioned.

Taking this example, we can only imagine the framing of the debate if environmentalists controlled the White House. The citizens of the United States would be asked whether they wanted $100 billion to go to a missile defense system that probably would not work and would in all likelihood lead to a destabilization of international relations and a possible arms race in space, or alternatively, whether they wanted $100 billion put toward the study and application of energy resources that would halt (or dramatically limit) the need to go looking for more fossil fuel resources and would assist with the global efforts to decrease greenhouse gas emissions, providing communities with more control over their energy needs and so leading to true sustainability.

The protest against the expenditures on anti-ecological and militaristic technologies is at least in part due to the fears of the population that if the current energy plan is not carried out, the cost of keeping gas-guzzling vehicles on the road will be prohibitive. Their material interests are part of the social fabric, which then encourages a debate along the lines desired by powerful interests. Likewise with the missile shield: a manufactured fear of being exposed to acute international danger results in a largely uncritical response to massive expenditures in the interests of weapons manufacturers. The manipulation would have to be recognized at a popular level before society would demand en masse that science be directed toward peaceful needs and ecologically sustainable projects.

This was the bind that Marcuse chronicled in *One Dimensional Man.* Being locked into the language, logic, and rhetoric of a society makes it difficult to see the irrationality of it. And Marcuse may well have been correct to argue that the development of a new science will follow a change in social relations. Nonetheless, it is doubtless the case that scientific change and debate can also act as a destabilizing force, opening broader debates and so assisting with the charting of a course toward a fundamentally altered set of social, economic, and political power relations.

There has been, in recent years, an increase in the number of voices within various fields of science seeking to call into question the reductionist scientific method so cherished since the Enlightenment. This destabilization of scientific orthodoxy accomplishes a number of things. First, the challenge opens up a space from within which to question the priorities to which science is directed within society. Second, it demonstrates that scientific inquiry is not—can never be—an objective exercise outside the power structures of any given society. Third, it provides insight into the reality that scientific language has come to reflect and reinforce a worldview that is inherently aggressive and that seeks to control and dominate nature (human nature included) at enormous environmental and social costs.

The space clearly does not exist here for a comprehensive examination of the many scientists who have challenged Enlightenment orthodoxy with a view toward redirecting science and technology toward more ecologically sustainable and less manipulative ends. A brief introduction to some of those whose arguments are particularly suited to the environmental theme will serve to make the point.

Fritjof Capra's *The Tao of Physics* pointed to a holistic view of science by drawing on Hindu and Buddhist thought. His engagement with the ecology movement has been invaluable and he continues to write passionately about both science and society. In a recent article, Capra very effectively challenged the manipulated concept of sustainability by making clear its inherently progressive quality. "What is sustained in a sustainable community," he argues, "is not economic growth or development, but the entire web of life on which our long-term survival depends. A sustainable community is designed in such a way that its ways of life, businesses, economy, physical structures, and technologies do not interfere with nature's inherent ability to sustain life."[6]

At a more expressly political and ideological level, biologist Richard Lewontin has been at pains to point out that science is a "supremely social institution, reflecting and reinforcing the dominant values and views of society at each historical epoch."[7] Lewontin echoes the Frankfurt School when he makes explicit the essential relationship between modern science and the development of industrial capitalism and argues that "science has replaced religion as the chief legitimating force in modern society."[8] In Lewontin's view, science can quite clearly be seen to be molded by the economic and social forces of society. As a result, commercial interests are masked as pure scientific inquiry. By exposing this social reality, Lewontin provides us with the insight needed to call into question the presented picture of a rational objective science.

Quite possibly the most comprehensive reconsideration of scientific method is that offered by the late physicist David Bohm, who set out to challenge the fundamentals of the fragmented view of reality that dominates both scientific thinking and society at large and is responsible for so much destruction. Bohm started with this reasonable premise:

> We have seen that fragmentary thinking is giving rise to a reality that is constantly breaking up into disorderly, disharmonious, and destructive partial activities. Therefore seriously exploring a mode of thinking that starts from the most encompassing possible whole and goes down to the parts (subwholes) in a way appropriate to the actual nature of things seems reasonable.[9]

Throughout his writings, Bohm's concentration on "wholeness" presents the necessity of what amounts to a revolution of thought. A lengthy quote is essential to demonstrate the complexity and interconnections of his argument:

> Of course, the prevailing tendency in science to think and perceive in terms of a fragmentary self-world view is part of a larger movement that has been developing over the ages and that pervades almost the whole of our society today: but, in turn, such a way of thinking and looking in scientific research tends very strongly to re-enforce the general fragmentary approach because it gives men a picture of the whole world as constituted of nothing but an aggregate of separately existing "atomic building blocks," and provides experimental evidence from which is drawn the conclusion that this view is necessary and inevitable. In this way, people are led to feel that fragmentation is nothing but an expression of "the way everything really is" and that anything else is impossible. So there is very little disposition to look for evidence to the contrary. . . .
>
> [W]hen men try to separate some aspect of nature in their practical technical work, a similar state of contradiction and disunity will develop. The same sort of thing will happen to the individual when he tries to separate himself from society. True unity in the individual and between man and nature, as well as between man and man, can rise only in a form of action that does not attempt to fragment the whole of reality. . . .
>
> What is the use of attempts at social, political, economic or other action if the mind is caught up in a confused movement in which it is generally differentiating what is not different and identifying what is not identical? Such action will be at the best ineffective and at worst really destructive.
>
> Nor will it be useful to try to impose some fixed kind of integrating or unifying "holistic" principle on our self-world view, for, as indicated earlier, any form of fixed self-world view implies that we are no longer treating our theories as insights or ways of looking but, rather, as "absolutely true knowledge of things as they really are."[10]

The implications for society are clear: until we begin thinking very differently—and Bohm is advocating something much more than a radical paradigm shift—the destructive tendencies of Western society will continue. He describes and critiques a worldview that allows fragmentation of knowledge in destructive ways (the separation of ozone science from climate change science, for example) and warns of the dangers of merely trying to identify a new mind-set that would provide a new totalizing logic with which to undertake research.

Bohm furthermore makes explicit the implications for language itself, the grammar rules of which bring about a fragmentation of thought. The subject-object-verb structure of language reinforces the worldview that in turn imposes its logic on scientific (and social) inquiry. Bohm considers, for example, the deceptively simple, uncontroversial sentence "It is raining" and asks us to consider where the "it" is that is "doing the raining."[11] By pointing out the way in which language shapes our worldview, he establishes the necessary conditions through which a language more appropriate to *wholeness* could be conceived of. He offers us the concept of *rheomode* (essentially a flowing language) and demonstrates by example the impact language has on our view of the world.[12]

Bohm's presentation of the need for a radical break in the current scientific mind-set, then, asks us to consider the impact the current system of thought has on language, on education (playing a role in maintaining the status quo),[13] and on human creativity.[14] Bohm's works constitute in themselves a holistic, nuanced, and comprehensive challenge to the established scientific method, which is so easily absorbed by established society for its own use.

Compare the above examples of new thinking to the popular writings of E. O. Wilson. Wilson's recent bestseller *Consilience* is held up as a "tract for our times."[15] Wilson's attempt to offer a unifying vision of science is dependent, however, upon a view of the world that directly maps onto that of Francis Bacon. By "consilience," Wilson means the linking of knowledge across disciplinary boundaries in an effort to gain "total" knowledge. Declaring his belief in the ability of human reason to "attain the grail" of objective truth, Wilson is looking for the ways to overcome the stumbling blocks to realizing the promise of Enlightenment science held out by Bacon and others. He likens the Western scientific method to human nature and reduces all of culture and art to little more than the transmission of information. Absent from Wilson is any awareness of the power of the dominant way of viewing the world;

there is nothing poetic or aesthetic here, just a view that holds that science is on a progressive path to total knowledge. The reductionist method is mistaken for a holistic approach because it seeks to draw the component parts of the disciplinary scientific discoveries together. Wilson does argue for a "unity of knowledge," but his unity is to be the result of reductionist thought from many areas being reassembled through synthesis:

> The greatest challenge today, not just in cell biology and ecology but in all of science, is the accurate and complete description of complex systems. Scientists have broken down many kinds of systems. They think they know most of the elements and forces. The next task is to reassemble them, at least in mathematical models that capture the key properties of the entire ensembles. Success in this enterprise will be measured by the power researchers acquire to predict emergent phenomena when passing from general to more specific levels of organization. That in simplest terms is the great challenge of scientific holism.[16]

No part of life is exempt from Wilson's view that objective knowledge is possible and offers a way for the bridging of the sciences and the humanities as part of his overall goal. Human nature, political life, the economy, and even ethnic conflict are reducible to cause-effect scientific understandings. Wilson's contempt for social scientists stems from his belief that they "have never been able to embed their narratives in the physical realities of human biology and psychology, even though it is surely there and not some astral plane from which culture has arisen."[17] It is a testament to the limitations of the mainstream view that Wilson's ideas can be presented as a breakthrough to a science more responsive to the needs of society. *Consilience* well serves the needs of those who seek to contain radical thought.

Marcuse was doubtless correct to argue that the purposes to which science and technology are directed cannot change before a radical alteration of economic relations. Critical thinking from within scientific disciplines, however, has the potential to destabilize the prevailing mind-set and thus contribute to movements for broader social change.

ECONOMICS AND SUSTAINABILITY

The belief in the inevitability of the current international economic system is a difficult one to challenge effectively. It is true, however, that vast protests of recent years have begun to destabilize the status quo presentation of the so-called phenomenon of globalization. Although the adherents of the neoliberal revolution of the 1980s and 1990s have only to point to the history of capital market integration to argue that it forms a seamless web of economic logic, there now seems to be an increasing awareness that a number of rather more progressive (or merely *different*) projects had to be shut down in order that the "inevitable" could occur. Upon examination, the "inevitable" is shown to be the result of myriad decisions taken in the belief that efficiency and prosperity are best realized through free market trading and a reduction or elimination of constraints on business operations. The realization of the emptiness of the rhetoric of inevitability is spreading, and the challenge to its flawed logic is based on arguments of the unsustainable nature of the project and a profound opposition to the conflation of standard-of-living indicators and quality of life.

There is no need to revisit the arguments made in Chapter 3 about the human and ecological costs of the neoliberal project. However, a few central tenets of my argument regarding the destructiveness of the prevalent economic growth model are worth restating. Crucially, this model—which we have seen to underlie current green diplomatic efforts—seeks to promote a global trading system based on the unconstrained mobility of capital. Such a system guarantees a move away from belief in the necessity of local production for local needs and instead inspires policies and economic activities fulfilling the needs of transnational corporations. This transformation has been encouraged by the dictates of international financial organizations (the IMF and the World Bank in particular, but also regional economic development banks and other international institutions), which have insisted on the transition to export-based economies as a precondition for economic assistance. Poorer countries have been forced into such positions through the Structural Adjustment Policies with catastrophic results in environmental, social, and economic terms.

Despite its glittering promises, this economic growth model has not worked to alleviate poverty but has instead served to amplify existing inequalities and further widen the disparity between rich and poor within most societies and, as well, between developing and overdeveloped countries. The figures on this growing disparity make it impossible for the proponents of the neoliberal model to argue with any credibility that the project is accomplishing what it claims.

PROTEST: NORTH AND SOUTH

Protests against the neoliberal worldview are increasingly prevalent in both the overdeveloped and the underdeveloped worlds. In the over-developed world, the impetus for change arises from the realization that an affluent society does not provide many people (perhaps even most) with the contentment they crave. Feelings of emptiness and frustration are experienced by many who are seen by all standard indicators as "successful." For those in the industrialized countries who have been "restructured" (made redundant or find themselves in unfulfilling work), the struggle for survival at minimum wage becomes an uphill battle. The increased corporate control of all aspects of life, the increasing gap between rich and poor, the decrease in the availability of meaningful employment, and the disintegration of the environment have led to widespread disenchantment with the oft-repeated proclamation that society is moving in the right direction.

Protest is developing, then, in myriad places and taking a number of forms. For some people, it is sufficient to attempt a massive shift in lifestyle in an effort to regain a greater sense of meaning for their life. The "simple living" (or "living lightly") movement is a clear example of this attempt to reclaim deep contact with the values and rhythms of community, family, and self-sufficiency. Significant increases in psychological disturbances are leading many to find solutions to the current situation through a range of therapies. For others, protest takes the form of attempting to get others to realize the emptiness of the overconsumption of society and the concomitant commodification of self.[18]

It is, however, the effort to expose the illogic of the existing system, and the attempt to present and inspire alternatives to it, that pose the most profound threat to the status quo and its support for destructive practices. Attempts to wrench open the debate by presenting workable alternatives are the real substance of a vibrant revolt against the environmentally destructive system, one capable of linking negative protest with a positive map for the future. The building of linkages across various divides (class, race, nationality, etc.) is essential if the movement is to succeed in its destabilization of the status quo. The extent to which this constitutes the emergence of a transnational movement (an international counter-hegemonic struggle) is not yet clear. What is clear, however, is that all over the world groups are beginning to challenge neoliberal orthodoxy and see in it the roots of serious environmental, social, and economic problems.

In the overdeveloped world, protesters against the corporate agenda are presented as selfish protectionists—comfortable middle-class folk attempting to preserve their own way of life in the face of a challenge from the poorer people of the world, who are, the orthodox story goes, at last making a breakthrough to "modernity." While a portion of those protesting certainly can be said to fit this description, far more are expressing concern about the fate of their fellow human beings in other parts of the world who are falling victim to the neoliberal agenda and who are themselves rising up to take action against the increased corporate control of their lives.

The huge number of protest movements attempting to save ways of life not fitting into the Western model of development cannot all be chronicled here.[19] For the purposes of my argument, however, it is helpful to select a few very different struggles and reflect on the lessons they offer as we search for a new internationalism.

India: Narmada Dam

India presents a wealth of inspiration to those looking for arguments to level against the dominant model of development as woven into the model of deregulation. From the Chipko movement to the 1999 Intercontinental Caravan—a group of 500 farmers protesting against the global financial system and the impact of biotechnology (specifically, genetically modified seeds and their devastation of traditional agriculture) who took their rally to Europe to protest against the G-8—citizens' groups from India are putting their Gandhian tradition to work.[20] Any of these protests could be introduced here to display the impact of the Western model of development and the resulting resistance in defense of a threatened way of life. But there is one struggle of particular relevance to our theme. The protests over the massive dam project for the Narmada River bring together in microcosm the arguments about scientific and technological "advancement," the calculation of economic growth, the role of international financial organizations, the needs of small communities, and the resulting protests to refuse a definition of progress that obliterates a way of life that has been truly sustainable throughout history.

People often speak of the struggle against the Narmada Dam as though it constitutes a single problematic development project. It is, alas, far bigger than this, with over 3,000 dams involved. The misrepresentation is partly due to the understandable preoccupation of the

Narmada Bachao Andolan (NBA; Save the Narmada Movement) with the Sardar Sarovar Project (SSP)—one of the megadams in the project, the building of which will displace over 300,000 people and will deprive hundreds of thousands more of their livelihoods. This, alongside the other megadam, the Narmada Sagar, has been the focus of the movement for a number of years.[21]

The arguments over the dams are familiar to anyone who has studied the postcolonial history of India. The debates at Independence were between those of a Gandhian persuasion who believed that the future lay in small, self-sufficient communities (Gandhi feared the oppressiveness he believed inherent in technology), and those who countered with arguments of a rather more orthodox Western way of measuring progress. This latter mind-set was best represented by India's first prime minister, Jawaharlal Nehru, who early on proclaimed the Bhakra Nangal, India's largest dam, "the temple of Modern India," and sought a massive project of dam-building to demonstrate India's modernity.[22]

Standing firmly behind Nehru's vision, the current government argues that the dams are necessary for the development of India. They promise that benefits will be seen in the region, that the displaced villagers will be offered land compensation and resettlement, and that the lost forests will be restored through reforestation. From the point of view of those people living along the shores of the Narmada, there is little comfort in these claims. The resettlement projects have been a dismal failure in the places where they have been tried, leaving the "oustees" without their sustainable livelihoods and forced into artificial and substandard communities. It is no surprise that, as the negative impact of the dam projects became ever more apparent, protesters would return to Gandhi's critical spirit and awareness in order to force into the open the cost of modern development—and identify who, in reality, is being asked to pay.

What is crucial in this debate is the refusal of the protesters to accept standard indicators of growth, progress, and an acceptable quality of life—or, indeed, to accept the credibility of those who present such information:

> What movements like the ones in the Narmada valley are further questioning is the tyranny of the official "expert"—the economist, the engineer, the consultant—who assumes that his/her model is the only truth. They are demonstrating how this arrogance has reduced complex natural and social systems into commodities, into fragments that need to be given a monetary value and subsumed in a cold equation.

This attitude has also erased all sensitivity to his historically evolved systems of land and water management—that those who are marginal to the dominant model are capable of identifying more sustainable alternatives and that even if this knowledge has been eroded, a dialogue between traditions (the modern with the traditional, for example)—should be the accepted principle.[23]

Management, "expertocracy," a denial of democratic dialogue, and a celebration of a destructive way of thinking are the features of the Indian government's commitment to this dam project. They are faced with protesters who eloquently question the logic of the decisions being taken and the way in which they are put into action. After hearing that a dam was to be built in their region without consultation with the villages most affected, a group of people from eight villages had this to say:

> Our habitat is not a wasteland . . . as claimed by the Polavaram project authorities. We are not poor and primitive. We are being condemned to backwardness. We are peasants and we grow Jonna (sorghum), Mackkajonna (maize), rice, mirch, tobacco, dals, etc., of several varieties. We grow a variety of crops with bio-fertilisers and rain water. The crops we grow are not only free from poisonous chemicals, but also give good yields. We do not wish to allow the loss of livelihood and fertile lands.
>
> We are the people of the forest and nature. Forests are the abode of sacred spirits. They are the source and part of our economy—our daily food, agriculture, livestock, housing, implements; our belief system and worship; our song and dance; and our life world. Our practices, lifestyles and beliefs protect nature and are shaped by it.
>
> We have festivals for the produce of all plants. . . . We consume vegetables, cereals, pulses, mohua and several other things only after conserving the same for the next season.
>
> We do not like to lose our life dependent on nature for one based on and dictated by money.
>
> We do not approve of the project also because it has violated our right to decide how we like to live. Projects that affect life and the future of our children and the tribe as a whole cannot be decided by anybody other than us. That same government attempts to do so is a violation of our fundamental right and we reject such acts.[24]

This brief excerpt from a powerfully written appeal to a distant and unresponsive government links many issues of import for India, and for the developing world more generally. The international trade deals and finance packages that encourage export-driven "industries" are undermining the country's ability to produce enough food for its own market.

This artificially created deficiency leads to hope being placed in the promise of unnaturally produced, genetically modified foods to make up for the loss of sustainable farmland—a loss leading to mass suicides of farmers in some regions because of the failure of the crops and the destruction of traditional farming practices.[25]

Who, then, has the answers? The experts, or the people whose sustainable way of life is being threatened by the decisions of distant and unrepresentative governments and the corporate community to whom they look for investment and ideas? Arundhati Roy poses it this way:

> Indians are too poor to buy the food their country produces. Indians are being forced to grow the kinds of food they can't afford to eat themselves. . . . Certainly India has progressed, but most of its people haven't. Our leaders say that we must have nuclear missiles to protect us from the threat of China and Pakistan. But who will protect us from ourselves? What kind of country is this? Who owns it? Who runs it? What's going on?[26]

Food production, agribusiness, militarism, control, and democratic accountability: all subjects that should be the backdrop to green diplomacy but that rarely, in fact, enter the minds of those focused on the details of incremental steps to a more sustainable environment. To echo Roy, *what's going on?*

The protest movements in India have had some success with their campaign. The World Bank—which has been a major source of financing for the Indian government's dam projects over the years—was so embarrassed by the growing public mobilization that it responded by appointing an independent commission to study the Narmada projects. Eventually, the Bank's funding was withdrawn. The project continues, however, and all means of protesting are rebuffed by an indifferent government. At the time of writing, the NBA continues its struggle in the face of recent government announcements that the height of the dam will be increased from 90 to 100 meters by June 2002, submerging still greater areas of land and displacing thousands more. The NBA and thousands of its supporters have vowed to continue the pacifist struggle against this inhumane and environmentally destructive decision.[27]

Nigeria: Ogoniland

The resistance movement offered by the Ogoni people in the southern region of Nigeria presents a tighter focus on the actions of corporations and governments complicit in the oppression they bring. The issue was brought to the attention of the world's media in late 1995 when the articulate president of the Movement for the Survival of the Ogoni People (MOSOP), Ken Saro-Wiwa, was hanged along with eight fellow leaders.

MOSOP's Bill of Rights, presented to the government and the people of Nigeria in October 1990, goes to the heart of the movement's demands. By seeking political control of their own affairs, the Ogoni argue that it should be in their power to protect their environment and ecology from degradation. In referring to "incompetent indigenous colonialism," they call for a new political order in Nigeria that would allow devolved responsibility while, at the same time, the Bill of Rights would reaffirm ideas of coexistence, cooperation, and national progress; this cannot be seen as a statement to incite ethnic division but is rather a celebration of a "democratic Nigeria, a progressive multi-ethnic national, a realistic society of equals, a just nation."[28]

MOSOP's peaceful protests against the devastating environmental consequences brought to their subsistence farming communities by Shell Oil were massive: 300,000 people (out of a total population of 500,000) raised their voices in January 1993. This was a powerful and passive movement that sought to highlight the conflict between an industry bent on resource extraction for the profit of distant shareholders and the impact that such "environmental terrorism" was having on their valuable farmland. In this case, little effort was made to hide the relationship between the corporation and the government, with the latter using its monopoly on "legitimate" violence in an attempt to suppress the uprising.

What is of import for our broader discussion is the way in which a local protest highlighting the dangers of corporate control of government reached a huge international public. The case of Ogoniland's suffering became a central part of a much larger effort to target Shell Oil in particular and oil corporations in general for their appallingly anti-environmental and inhumane policies.[29] The Ogoni's pacifist stance and their articulate demands led to a better understanding of the actions of transnational oil companies and the impact they have on the sustainable existence of millions of people around the world. Because of the nature of the problem, the focus of the protest was—simultaneously and inextricably—local and global.

Canada: Nunuvut

This is a different case from those explored above in the sense that the creation of Nunuvut (meaning "Our Land" in Inuktitut)—a territory in the Canadian Arctic—can be seen as a long-overdue legitimation of traditional hunter-gatherer rights within a modern nation-state. This is not a protest movement akin to the others discussed here, but it nonetheless provides an instructive example of an attempt to restore balance to a damaged lifestyle in the face of overwhelming pressures.

The history of the treatment of the Inuit peoples of this region by the colonial settlers of the country can only be described as horrific. Decades of official attempts to force the Inuit into a style of life unsuited to their cultural traditions left a devastating legacy, particularly with regard to forced resettlement and a "residential school" system that forbade the speaking of native languages and took children from their homes and communities to be educated—often abusively—in "Western" ways: a policy, in essence, of cultural extermination and erasure from history.

Although the creation of Nunuvut is one among a number of recent examples of land-claims agreements in Canada, it represents "the most ambitious attempt in the history of the encounter between colonists and hunter-gatherers to secure coexistence at the frontier."[30] Over 350,000 square kilometers of land in the eastern Arctic has been turned over to the self-governance of its native population—people with a fundamentally different way of seeing the human relationship to nature. Their story thus provides us with a powerful boost to our imagination—a liberating understanding that the bureaucratic, planned, unequal, and ecologically unsustainable society measured by numerical growth indicators is *not* the only way to see the world. After a long-drawn-out and often terrible struggle against "the inevitable," the Inuit have attained a version of self-government that clearly bears the imprint of their contact with the colonizer, but that also recognizes their own form of modern society. Nunuvut has a legislature, but one without a party structure. Decisions are reached through the time-honored manner of consensus. A Department of Sustainable Development—which includes a recognition that public participation in decisionmaking is essential—continues to consider the problems facing the Inuit people while they attempt to identify strategies for the conservation of land, water, and resources—many of which are eagerly sought by mining companies with a very different interest and ethos.[31]

Mexico: Chiapas

The Zapatista movement has generally been presented in the mainstream media as an old-fashioned guerrilla rebellion. The images most often presented are of masked gunmen occupying towns and seeking to overthrow a democratically elected government. The failure of the press and politicians to grasp the significance of the Zapatista's search for justice in the face of the Mexican government's efforts to institutionalize neoliberalism (through NAFTA) is not, however, preventing the movement from garnering a great deal of attention around the world, or stopping its beliefs and approaches from being rapidly and actively translated into the language of myriad struggles.

The best place to begin to understand this new form of protest is to peel back the layers of the orthodox presentation of the Zapatista as a group of "armed insurgents." Let us start with their masks, which, although assumed by many to be worn simply to protect "criminals" from identification by the authorities, are in fact worn to illustrate the "defacing" political reality that the indigenous peoples of Chiapas are "invisible" and unseen by the policymakers. Having struggled for centuries over issues of land reform and economic justice, the people of this region said, "Enough is enough!" (Ya Basta!) and took control over their own lives when it became obvious that NAFTA would commercialize every aspect of their existence and dismantle their system of communally owned and shared land.

Although the Zapatista rebel forces did indeed seize several towns in Chiapas the day that NAFTA went into effect, the similarity of this movement with a typical armed rebel movement ends there. Inspired by the conviction that "it is not necessary to conquer the world; it is sufficient to make it new," their purpose is not "to usurp power but to exercise it."[32] This reclaiming of a political space in which people can define their own power has been a powerful motivating force, and its echoes have been heard in other resistance movements around the world. Based as it is on the demand for respect, dialogue, and participation in the direction of society, the movement also amounts to a profound rejection of the destructive logic and principles of neoliberal economic policy: rampant profiteering, attacks on labor and environmental standards, and extended rights and freedoms for big corporations.

Practicing their own principles of dialogue and mutual respect, the Zapatista have not only taken their message to the Mexican people but have invited others to teach them; they have at no point taken a superior, all-knowing attitude, and they ask only that others listen as well as speak. When the previous Mexican government reneged on a number of key promises, the Zapatista fell silent, refusing the indignity of one-sided discussion. Their ongoing commitment to true democratic principles has been inspirational for many Mexicans, and fire for the imagination of many radicals.

The Zapatista's broad appeal stems in part from the articulate and profoundly moving statements and declarations made by Subcomandante Marcos, through whose voice the Zapatista's message is often heard. These statements—often in the form of poetry or parable—are subsequently translated for dissemination through the Internet. Through his use of beautifully crafted poetry and prose, Marcos has proclaimed that "our word is our weapon,"[33] as indeed it is a powerful part of any resistance movement.[34] An important element of "knowing" that is denied by the technocratic rationality of modern society is the knowledge that stems from art in its many forms. As Fred Knelman argues, "Poetry, art and music are surely other legitimate ways of achieving understanding, totally different in form and substance from the purely scientific. And the creative can reveal what science cannot."[35]

The Zapatista's courageous stand against NAFTA, and the Mexican government's willingness to sacrifice principle for profit, led to massive international support from people who felt that they were fighting the same cause. The Zapatista invited those who dare to contemplate alternatives to an "Intercontinental Meeting for Humanity and Against Neoliberalism." Consider the following excerpt from Marcos's welcoming message at the inaugural ceremony, where he first sets out a communal project and then offers direction for the meeting:

> *We,* who nourish the heart with the bitter bread of hope.
> *We,* who see in the past a lesson to be learned and not an obstacle, who turn toward yesterday to learn, not to repent.
> *We,* who look at the future as something that is built on the present, who hope for a tomorrow for everyone.
> *We,* who balance fear with shame, prudence with courage, indifference with memory.
> *We,* human beings, who exist (who defy power), who want to transform La Realidad and change it into something better, something new, something good.
> *This is the fight for La Realidad:* Some want to build it, others want to destroy it.
> *They want to destroy it* with the absurdity of denying it through oblivion, destruction and death.
> *We want to build it,* with the absurdity of rebuilding it through history, creativity, and life.
>
> This is the dilemma that we have come to think about and begin to speak about, the dilemma of La Realidad. This is a fundamental and

definitive theme, for humanity and against neoliberalism. In order to solve this dilemma, we have to face a very powerful enemy, cloaked in neoliberalism. Its crimes recognize no national borders; they represent the globalization of despair. Neoliberalism offers us a new world doctrine: surrender and indifference as the only means of inclusion; death and oblivion as the only future for those excluded; ignorance and arrogance as the only government; crime and impunity as the highest law; robbery and corruption as the main industry; assassination as the source of legitimacy; lying as the supreme god; prisons and graves for those who are not willing to follow.

War always. That is neoliberalism. But its power is also based on our weakness. To our lack of alternative proposals, they offer the continuation of the nightmare. We must go beyond lamentations and propose new possibilities. We did not invite you here to accumulate complaints. We did not call on you to embody our misfortunes or to bring a continental dimension to our nightmare. We invited you to multiply our hopes. We called upon you to lessen our hardships, to give hope a continental dimension. Don't let our enemy's grotesque and terrible image dull the mirror where we seek our own road. Let's not hide arbitrariness and laziness within ourselves, covering them up under the daily crime of a world order that turns history, nations, and individuals into dust. Let's not offer a new nightmare under a different guise. Let not the complicated political geometry, which multiplies centers and extremes ad infinitum, signify impunity for the errors committed. We did not come today to change the world. We are here today with the most modest of purposes: to make a new world.[36]

This is a movement with a difference, engaged in a struggle for difference. It seeks to shatter conventional images of power and insists on democracy at every level. The invitation for people to recognize that they too are Zapatista if they are engaged in struggle—wherever they may be—has been powerfully received. And while the media tend to report the anti-globalization meetings (be they in Seattle, Prague, Washington, D.C., Davos, or Quebec City) as undisciplined groups of protesters who do not even know what they stand for, this coverage demonstrates a willful lack of awareness of the movement's message and approach. Many of the people on the street are intuitively or consciously following this new theory of *Zapatismo;* they are demanding a dialogue of respect and are saying Enough! to discussions behind closed doors about decisions that fundamentally alter the world in which we live. And they are a political force and influence—locally and globally—to be reckoned with.

DIFFERENT STRUGGLES, SIMILAR DANGERS

These diverse movements share a commitment to preserving a home-land and the corresponding way of life upon which its survival is built. The way of life in each case is based on a view of sustainability that puts it at odds with a "worldview" that uses economic measurement techniques revealing nothing of importance about quality of life, cul-ture, or sustainable existence and based instead on accelerating rates of resource extraction and environmental destruction.

These cases also demonstrate, more clearly than any number of charts and graphs, that green diplomacy fails in its goal precisely because it sets an agenda so limited as to be meaningless. The best set of incremental policies in the world to slow global warming, for instance, will not—in-deed cannot—deliver a plan for sustainable development to the world. These examples of protest also share a reinvigoration of the notion of "commons" in a way that seriously challenges that offered by green diplomacy. In the sterile language of resource management, the "com-mons" is nothing more than an area over which no state has the "right" of development.[37] But in these cases—and in many, many others around the world—there is a reclamation of the commons as a local area for the per-petuation of shared knowledge and the nurturing of natural habitat.[38]

Finally, these cases utilize a discourse that places the notion of sus-tainable development firmly within the concept of ecological justice. Questions of power, distribution, and economic and social justice are central to each, generating a corresponding need to expose power rela-tionships serving to marginalize, repress, and dominate alternative ways of being.

Notwithstanding the undeniable potential of such movements to ef-fectively highlight and oppose oppression, it would be foolhardy to see within these cases a salvation for the current state of the world's envi-ronmental affairs, and those who are looking for food for the imagin-ing of alternatives must be wary of making such examples into some-thing they are not. The struggle in the Narmada has been profound and has had some success. The brutal truth remains, however, that the process of dam-building is ongoing and the displacement of people con-tinues apace. There is no victory in sight for the many communities in India who are struggling against the politics of "big" development. Leaving aside the linkages this case offers us to a militarized, bureau-cratized, sanitized, and corporatized government, the simple struggle to live a traditional sustainable life is severely challenged by those who would ask that small communities sacrifice for the greater common good.

As for the Ogoni battle, we must recognize the limits of a boycott against such a powerful global corporation as Shell Oil. The greenwash of corporate practice is all too often successful, and many people are unwilling or unable to look to the reality behind the slick advertising campaigns. Shell Oil has been successfully reinventing its image as a corporation sincere about human rights and willing to put principles above profit.[39] Laughable, yes—but also successful. Shell won the World Environment Center's "Gold Medal for International Corporate Environmental Achievement" in 2001. The award was given to celebrate Shell's "Sustainable Development Management Framework"—a set of guidelines designed to integrate sustainable development into the way they do business.[40] The award prompted MOSOP to launch a petition against the company.[41]

The importance of oil and gas development projects within the international financial institutions continues to have a profound impact on the lived experience of many Africans. If we look at the World Bank funding, for example, we can see that there exists a continued policy of supporting those projects of interest and profit to transnational oil corporations—with Shell certainly among them. For while the Bank has plenty of literature proclaiming that it has moved in the direction of assisting with projects for nonrenewable energy resources, the statistics tell quite another story. The ratio of World Bank financing for fossil fuels projects to renewables in the period 1992–2000 was sixteen to one.[42] Meanwhile, groups such as Oilwatch continue to make explicit the many ways petroleum companies consistently and systematically violate human and environmental rights in their quest for profit.[43]

Nunuvut is, likewise, not an idyll, and to portray it as such can be more than misleading: it can lead to false hope and great disappointment. The Inuit, in bargaining with the Canadian government, were forced into a position of giving up mineral rights over part of the territory. One senses there will be battles in the future that continue the long discussions about the role of resource "development" within traditional hunter-gatherer societies. Perhaps of greater import, however, is the rather obvious point that regardless of how sustainable the Inuit are in their own communities, they are living in a world in which the actions of others can severely limit their own potential for a long and happy traditional lifestyle. For if the rest of the world continues with its consumption of carbon fuels, global warming will kill off the traditional Inuit life-style. The Canadian Arctic is already reporting vast changes in its cli-mate patterns, and the orthodox development ethos, if unchanged, will lead to an erosion of the traditional Inuit lifestyle as severe as any colo-nial invasion or act of genocide.

Serious dilemmas and temptations are faced by any alternative movement basing its strategy on a vision that runs contrary to the dom-inant project around it. There is always the possibility of co-option into the orthodoxy. Although there is no indication that the Nunuvut gov-ernment will sell the mineral wealth of their land to the highest bidder, it is important to recognize the inducements that will be placed before them in order to raise money to cover the costs of providing for the many pressing social needs of the population.

Instructively disturbing in this regard is the fate of the protest move-ment led by aboriginal leaders in Canada's Northwest Territories through-out the 1970s against proposals to build pipelines to carry gas and oil through the environmentally pristine Mackenzie Valley to markets to the south. This was an emotional issue for Canadians, suddenly confronted with the usually hidden social costs of a project, like so many others, de-signed to allow the continuation of a wasteful consuming lifestyle. The government of Pierre Trudeau established a commission to examine the impact such a pipeline would have on the environment and on the people of the North. Thomas Berger headed the commission and consulted widely across Canada, and the report sold well, an unusual phenomenon for a public inquiry document.[44] But this was no ordinary government report; it was a passionately written report—complete with hundreds of photo-graphs—that managed to convey the complexity of development issues and that sought to give voice to the concerns of the people who feared for their communities, their lifestyle, and their environment. The report juxta-posed the conflicting ideas of the Arctic as a homeland for people and as a frontier for industry, thereby encapsulating the ongoing conflict between ways of seeing a natural environment. By considering the "white man's mission not only to tame the land and bring it under cultivation, but also to tame the native people and bring them within the pale of civilization,"[45] Berger successfully placed the discussions about the future of Arctic oil and gas exploration into their proper intellectual, cultural, and historical contexts. His report was clearly intended to inspire a fundamental rethink about the inevitability of pushing into new frontiers, the ability of tech-nology to solve problems, the use of wilderness for profit, and the cultural impact and political disenfranchisement that result when a way of life is eroded, suppressed, or conquered. In the end, Berger rejected the "white" view of the North he sums up so admirably:

> In all the years of contact between the two societies, the white man still sees the North from his own point of view, and he still wishes to conquer the frozen and waste spaces that he sees, with roads, mines, drilling rigs, gas wells and pipelines. He dreams of the technological conquest of the northern frontier.[46]

Two decades later, some of those formerly opposed to the pipeline project are in powerful positions within the government of the Northwest Territories, including the premier, Stephen Kakfwi. Kakfwi, however, is now actively involved in a campaign to convince the Alaskan government to use the route through the Mackenzie Valley instead of an alternative route through Alaska and the Yukon in order to get their gas to the markets in the lower forty-eight states.[47] Couched now in terms of creating a level playing field and taking advantage of the renewed interest in oil and gas exploration in the Arctic, the discourse has shifted dramatically. What went wrong? Certainly, the environmental risks cited by Berger continue to exist. His commitment to alternative definitions of development, and his commitment to *listening* to those who live in the region, were tempered, however, by the fact that he did not rule out the possibility of a pipeline in the future or its attendant energy development plans. This aspect of his report, however, can hardly be blamed: the report as a whole provided tremendous ammunition to those fighting to save the environmental and sustainable lifestyles. It is certainly sobering to recognize that some of those individuals to whom Berger did indeed listen have now adopted the language and goals of the frontier and renounced (or at least placed in secondary place) the language and goals of maintaining a homeland.[48]

"We have never had to determine what is the most intelligent use to make of our resources. We have never had to consider restraint," Berger argued at the conclusion of the Commission's report. "Will we continue, driven by technology and egregious patterns of consumption, to deplete our energy resources wherever and whenever we find them? Upon this question depends the future of northern native people and their environment."[49] The question is now being answered by the government of the Northwest Territories in the affirmative.

The Zapatista movement commands our attention and respect because of the complex view of power it offers as a way forward. But those who would live a sustainable life in Mexico continue to live with poverty, oppression, and destruction. Grinding poverty and ill health are widespread, and although the government of Vincente Fox may well be able to come to an accommodation with the Zapatista, it is difficult to see how the movement can be declared a winner if the free trade deal that has brought the neoliberal model to Mexico is extended to all of the Western Hemisphere—a NAFTA desire that is, as I shall consider below, gaining support throughout the region. While there may be a great deal of "imagining" taking place at the grassroots level, there is a distinct lack of it at the bureaucratic and governmental levels.

In qualifying our enthusiasm for inspirational attempts to resist the orthodoxy, we should also bear in mind the danger of seeing success stories when there are many more cases of resisters being silenced. As an added precaution, anyone seeking sustenance for their imagination must be careful to avoid romanticizing the way of life being presented, enshrining it as an alternative that must never grow or change—a paradoxically colonial exercise in museum-piece analysis that we can indulge in when feeling wistful or destabilized by *our own* situation.

To give an example of the first pitfall, we need look no further than the nomadic peoples of the Peruvian rainforests, who have not engaged in a highly publicized case against transnational oil companies but whose case may well end up as tragically as that of the Ogoni.[50] And even if the Ogoni somehow achieved all their goals tomorrow, a celebration of their success would have to be matched by the realization that it is often the high-profile cases that find resolution or some form of justice. Another aspect of this romanticization is the tendency for activists outside the situation to examine a struggle without considering the possibility that they too are complicit in the destructive practices being resisted. To take the Ogoni case again is fair, for an examination of the use of fossil fuels is obviously central to their struggle: the root of the problem, in short, is the profit margin of a company seeking to bring oil to customers at a cost that will allow them to continue in a lifestyle that is ultimately responsible for environmental deterioration. The issue of personal consumption should not—indeed must not—be avoided by anyone seeking solutions for the current rate of environmental destruction.

Romanticizing tendencies can also be strong within a protest group, stunting its capacity to grow and develop. I think my point can best be made by giving voice to the words of Rachel Attituq Qitsualik, an Inuit journalist:

I think people are making a mistake when they try to box Inuit culture into the "caretakers of the Arctic" role that has become sexy and politically correct over the years.

Are we to assume that Inuit somehow sprang, utterly complete, from the snow and ice, from the tundra and hills? Are Inuit less capable than other human beings of appreciating their entire planet—the vibrant green of rainforests; the undulant gold of desert dunes; the resinous scent of pines; or the yeasty perfume of fruit orchards?

In this sense, I think we could learn from our aboriginal neighbours to the south, the First Nations peoples. Theirs, almost universally, is a philosophy of Earth as parent, a living whole from which no living or unliving thing is unconnected. In the past, some Inuit peoples too had developed a similar outlook toward existence.

All Inuit were at least aware of the Land, but they originally conceived of the Land as the entire world—not merely an Arctic chopped up into political and cultural zones. Even more inclusive were the Angakkuit, who encapsulated all of existence within the concept of "Sila," the wind-breath-air-force that pervades and animates all things. . . .

Every year, there are more and more mosquitoes in the south. One of the reasons for their increase is the lack of frogs, who normally eat them. But the frogs are disappearing. No one knows exactly why. Some think the ultraviolet light leaking through a depleted ozone layer is killing them. Others think that chemicals are stunting the growth of tadpoles, who never reach adulthood. But no one knows. . . .

My point is that Inuit now live in a larger world than they used to, and they need not fear stepping out into that world. If Inuit are to care about the land, they must come to realize that the land they think of now includes the rest of the globe. As humans, which is what "Inuit" means, their heritage is not only an Arctic one, but a great global heritage.

Steadily the world is becoming a vast community, a community that is only enriched by the contributions of any single culture within it. Inuit have a lot to offer—a heritage of adaptation, practicality, common sense, and sheer toughness.

If we can only invoke the old way we used to view the world, as a limitless expanse, and ourselves as belonging only to that vastness, then perhaps we can assist these younger cultures of the world in reversing some of the damages that has been done to it. . . .

Some principles of Inuit environmental philosophy are much needed in the world today. The basics take the simplest form: Give back what you take. Don't take more than you need. Leave some for those coming after you.

But we have to sort ourselves out first. An idea, like a tool, is only as good as those who wield it.[51]

The most important thing is to recognize and listen to the struggles of people in different locations who are falling victim to the results of a vicious and inhumane economic system, a system that results in destruction of cultures and environment. To continue to recognize this, and to struggle on behalf of others, is *not* romanticism, as Hugh Brody so eloquently argues:

> To celebrate the qualities of a system, and to identify the many ways in which that system secures a successful relationship between people and their lands, as well as among the people themselves—this is to identify the real, not to perpetuate the romantic. Nor is it romanticism to express concern about a system's decline, to convey people's dismay about being dispossessed, to affirm their rights to keep their lands, languages and customs.[52]

THE ANTI-GLOBALIZATION MOVEMENT: HAUNTING THE STATUS QUO

Any discussion of the increasing range of protests against the destructive practices of neoliberalism would not, of course, be complete without a consideration of the anti-globalization movement. Without having a specific locale or even a coherent set of arguments to ground its protest on, this movement challenges corporate power and increasingly weak (or unwilling) governmental responses to it. In many ways it can be seen as an umbrella for the myriad sites of resistance that take aim at the increased corporate control over all aspects of society with such deleterious effects on the environment, and on social and political spaces in all corners of the world.

Recent discussions of the growth of the anti-globalization movement tend to begin the chronicle with the mass demonstrations outside the WTO meetings in Seattle in late 1999. This is misleading. Although many of us may have been unaware of the action in the streets, the direct protests against the policies of large international organizations and closed economic clubs have been taking place for a long while. Mass protests against the appalling consequences of the World Bank/IMF's Structural Adjustment Policies began in earnest in the late 1980s. In Venezuela (1989), in Morocco (1990), in India (1992), and in Bolivia and Chiapas (1994), people found their voices—and when they did, they protested loudly.[53]

Seattle was, it is true, different. Having presented its agenda as inevitable and of immense benefit to the poor and downtrodden of the world, the WTO was leaving itself exposed to such dramatic demonstrations of rejection. Of course it is true that splits were apparent among the participants too, but it was the battle on the street that made headlines and brought the debates over the direction of the international economy into the homes of millions of people who had not protested, who had assumed their governments were looking after their interests.

Much has been written about the potential for this new direct-action political force to destabilize existing power structures—both national and international.[54] Here, it is important to consider the possibility that this new movement could act as a substantial force for change, one that will inspire a radical rethink of the very premises of the neoliberal orthodoxy and thereby inspire the building of a more just and environmentally sound international economic order.

The picture presented in the mainstream media is one of a ragtag band of leaderless and basically idea-less resisters, a form of anarchistic tourism with protesters out to have fun and disrupt democratically elected officials whenever and wherever they meet. As Charles Krauthammer raged about the Seattle protests, "you had your one-world paranoids. . . . And you had your apolitical Luddites, who refuse to accept that growth, prosperity and upward living standards always entail some dislocation."[55] The reality, of course, is quite different.

To demonstrate the concrete options that the protesters are presenting, it is worth examining an important example that has produced both very public protest and the very hard work that building an alternative to a powerfully dominant set of ideas entails.

Free Trade Area of the Americas

The current efforts under way to expand the North American Free Trade Agreement to other countries of the Western Hemisphere (except Cuba) provide us with an encapsulation of the efforts both of those who favor deregulated international commerce and of those who recognize the environmental and social costs involved in the project. While the representatives of the governments of the participating countries struggle with the likely outcome of the trade deal, an amazing group of activists from around the hemisphere has been undertaking a study of its own. The suggestions made by the Hemispheric Social Alliance are, as I hope to show, practical and truly sustainable. But most important, its articulation blows the cover off the status quo presentation about the inevitability of the globalization project.

The process to find a strategy to extend trade throughout the hemisphere got under way in late 1994 at the Summit of the Americas in

Florida. The declared goal was to create the largest free trade zone in the world—a linkage of economies incorporating 800 million people. In Chile in 1998, the Free Trade Area of the Americas (FTAA) was formally launched with the establishment of nine working groups to consider the major areas of negotiation. It should come as no surprise that the undertaking is one encouraged by the United States and bears all the hallmarks of the destructive economic and environmental practices that have been pointed to in this book. Despite the fact that some governments in the hemisphere are concerned about the provisions of the negotiating text presented in Quebec City in 2001, it is fair to say that the structural power and authority of the United States, combined with uncritical governmental subscription to advancing economic growth through international cooperation, have led to a widespread belief that this is the only possible way forward.

While the U.S.-led project of corporate freedom is presented at an uncritical level as being inevitable, the Hemispheric Social Alliance offers an alternative that truly "haunts" the established society precisely because of its concrete suggestions of how governments could put together an agreement to foster truly sustainable development and serve the interests of the majority rather than a minority of interests.[56] Perhaps of greater import, this network provides every indication that groups in the overdeveloped and underdeveloped regions in the hemisphere recognize a joint cause to fight for. This is not a case of workers in industrialized societies attempting to protect their jobs at the expense of their poorer counterparts in the developing world. Instead, there is a clear recognition both that internationalism can serve the interests of peoples across the hemisphere, and that these interests are at risk if the project of deregulating international capital is the project pursued. So, what then do they offer?

The vision presented in the discussion paper, titled *Alternatives for the Americas* and drafted for the Summit of the Americas in Quebec City, is a thoughtful and comprehensive document (close to 100 pages), rigorously challenging the "logic" of globalization, exposing the interests behind the deregulation mania, and detailing the effects of the neoliberal orthodoxy and the likely consequences of its program.

One of the most striking aspects of this alternative project is the way in which it gives voice to the important issues silenced by the official FTAA process. The negotiating areas established through working groups included investment, finance, intellectual property rights, agriculture, market access, services, and dispute resolution. The Hemispheric

Social Alliance points out that a number of rather important topics are missing: human rights, environment, labor, immigration, the role of the state, and gender. Giving voice to the important interconnections among these issues breaches the imposed logic of the "inevitable" process of globalization as claimed by the champions of the FTAA process itself.

It is clearly not possible to describe the full range of suggestions contained in the alliance's document, but the "general principle" sums up nicely the essential perspective:

> Trade and investment should not be ends in themselves, but rather the instruments for achieving just and sustainable development. Citizens must have the right to participate in the formulation, implementation and evaluation of hemispheric social and economic policies. Central goals of these policies should be to promote economic sovereignty, social welfare, and reduced inequality at all levels.[57]

Why does "free trade" fail to uphold this "general principle"? The document answers the question succinctly:

> This dominant free trade approach . . . argues that the global market on its own will allocate and develop the best possibilities for each country. Thus, free trade does not simply involve opening ourselves to global trade; it also entails renouncing our role as active subjects in determining our future, and instead allowing the market to decide the future for us. According to this view, it is unnecessary for us to envision the kind of nation we want to be or could be. We only need to eliminate all obstacles to global trade, and the market itself will take on the task of offering us the best of all possible worlds.[58]

This is the imagining of alternative projects that is so dangerous to the prevailing worldview. As soon as voice is given to alternatives, it makes the presentation of the "inevitability" of current projects doubtful. By insisting that it is not against progress, development, or trade, the alliance successfully posits itself as an equivalent project, but one that takes a different set of principles as its starting point and adopts an accordingly distinct set of criteria against which success is to be judged.

The alliance insists on greater democratization, and its explication of what this means goes far beyond the limited understanding presented by the governments of the region. Democratization of debates and decisionmaking is a necessary precondition, but far more important, citizens must participate in the formulation, implementation, and evaluation of economic and social policies. A central part of the effort to reinvigorate democratic ideals stems from the insistence that corporate rights have gone too far and have become a threat to the very substance of the democratic process. Mechanisms must be added to ensure that public control over economic and other decisionmaking is maintained and that local efforts to achieve economic sustainability are protected from corporate attempts to externalize costs. Here we see clear expression given to demands for the raising of standards, not competing on the basis of lowering them. We see sustainability become real in terms of concrete policies to produce incentives to move in directions that value the natural environment and, importantly, the social world too. There are other general headings under which the alliance insists on true progress—decreasing military expenditure, recognizing human rights within the broader context of existing international instruments as well as within trade agreements (i.e., encompassing a "democracy clause"), and reducing inequalities both within and between states.

But how? Let us consider the formal proposals for dealing with the environmental crisis facing the hemisphere as a fair representative of the types of concrete proposals on offer. The alliance insists that environmental costs be internalized—that is to say, the cost of producing goods should include the costs to the environment. Environmental sustainability is not only to be considered in terms of economic accords but addressed as an "overarching dimension and perspective" throughout such agreements.[59] The concept of sustainable development thereby loses its buzzword tendencies and opens up the possibility of a holistic perspective including an articulation of the limits to growth within the consideration of social equity. In addition, the alliance argues that

- environmental costs should be dealt with equitably by acknowledging the different responsibilities based on historical contributions to the current problems,
- goals and timelines for ending the trade of products that harm the environment should be established,
- the precautionary principle (rather than risk assessment) should be supported,
- trade should encourage production close to the site of consumption,
- social and ecological dumping should be rejected,
- foreign investment should be channeled toward sectors in which sustainable development can be strengthened,
- companies and investors should be regulated to ensure compliance with a country's objectives,

- foreign investors should be held to the highest environmental standards, and be obliged to share technologies, and
- sovereign rights that allow the restriction of investment that aggravates social or environmental problems should be protected.[60]

To specify such guiding principles as a way of evaluating governmental and intergovernmental action is an obvious starting point for a reclamation of green politics. First, it refuses to accept the claim that there is only one way to organize international trade—that is, releasing corporations from responsibilities in order to foster investment. Second, it establishes at both local and global levels the recognition that economics and ecology are to be linked in a very different way than the proponents of the neoliberal model would have us believe. Here we see an implicit belief that green diplomacy is ultimately a futile project if the action is taken without regard to the realm of international activity and multilateral bargaining that undertakes agreements allowing the wholesale destruction of communities and ecosystems. Policy prescriptions for trade relations, as a result, have a direct impact on the global environment.

The alliance offers a number of specific recommendations that would serve the environment much more effectively than do current efforts at regime formation. It recognizes, for example, that forests are *homes* to indigenous peoples and traditional communities—not merely resources for trade. In this clear statement of principle, the alliance presents a radical challenge to the consideration of natural resources as nothing more than commodities, while at the same time exposing the harm done by the neoliberal export model to both people and the natural environment. The policy implications are clear:

- any movement toward an FTAA must "consider forests as varied and complex ecosystems,"
- trade and investment agreements should be subordinated to international environmental agreements as well as to national policies on conservation of biodiversity (this includes, of necessity, the participation of the local populations in the decisionmaking on such policies),
- environmental and agricultural subsidies that favor the indiscriminate use of forests should be eliminated—especially subsidies for large-scale monoculture, and
- a system of certification of sustainable forest products should be promoted.[61]

So, instead of a group of diplomats negotiating a toothless forest management regime, this discussion demonstrates the necessity of going to the root of the problem. The solution to the destruction of forests—with all it implies for atmospheric health and biodiversity—challenges both the way of thinking about the issue as well as the economic system that encourages the exploitation of this "resource" at a huge environmental and human cost.

The alliance's discussion of biodiversity and intellectual property is similarly radical. For while the green diplomats expend effort to construct a regime to deal with serious threats to biodiversity, they fail to recognize the major cause of the destruction: trade arrangements designed to allow the corporate ownership and exploitation of all genetic resources. Again, the critique of the neoliberal threat to biodiversity provides practical suggestions:

- reject the process of privatization of natural resources,
- reject intellectual property rights on lifeforms,
- protect collective rights of local communities in conservation, breeding, and cultivation of biodiversity within a broad framework of defending indigenous rights,
- ensure that the ILO convention, which protects inalienable rights of people to full autonomy in decisions over traditional habits, is given preeminence,
- provide local communities with the right to veto projects that exploit resources in such a way as to threaten their economic, social, and cultural lifestyles, and
- guarantee the free circulation of knowledge and access to genetic resources, reject bioprospecting projects, and compensate communities that create and conserve biodiversity.[62]

All of these goals can be written into trade deals that take as their starting point the interests of citizens rather than corporations.

In its consideration of energy, the alliance advocates the elimination of subsidies (indirect and direct) for fossil fuel energy and a redirection of investment toward clean-energy projects. There are proposals to ensure that mining projects do not have a negative impact on communities or the environment, that the intensive use of chemicals for monoculture agricultural production for export is ended through a reorientation of investment toward agroecological technologies, and that the self-regulation of industry in controlling trade in dangerous substances is ended. In all of these areas and in many others (labor, foreign investment, agriculture, etc.), citizen participation in the decisionmaking process and respect for communities are seen as being of paramount importance. It is nothing short of a redefinition of internationalism and, as such, its realization would provide an appropriate backdrop for a green diplomacy of substance to take place.

I have focused extensively on this particular effort at presenting alternatives not least because it encapsulates the integration of the different facets of "real life"—lived experience—into a consideration of policy and thereby refuses to accept the sanitized, unreal language of the corporate project. It insists on a view of governments as servants of people rather than of business elites and thereby attempts to reinvigorate the critical spirit of real democracy. Furthermore, it provides concrete suggestions for the measurement of progress in real human terms without advocating a simple blueprint to be used in all societies. It has, rather, set out a full account of the possibilities inherent in the existing society, drawing on the benefits of existing structures where appropriate and calling for the rebuilding of others where necessary. Perhaps of greatest import is the clear demonstration this effort has offered for the ability of groups to link up across the international divides when the goals are shared, but to do so in the interests of preserving the strengths of the local communities. Finally, it does not present itself as having the answer to all the issues being discussed, but rather as part of an ongoing democratic discussion among people within and between states. These are ideas for discussion—not dictates from above.[63]

This presentation of the Hemispheric Social Alliance is not intended to imply that it is the only such group.[64] It is, however an impressive and important coalition, the actions of which successfully display a powerful image of the possibility of articulating a detailed set of alternatives to the neoliberal policies routinely presented as inevitable. The increasing number of such networks provides exciting evidence of the internationalization of protest and resistance to the dominant economic "juggernaut."

The People-Centered Development Forum (PCDF), founded by David Korten, is another excellent example. Taking as its central organizing principle a notion of *justice* and insisting on very different indicators of development and progress than those offered by GNP and GDP, the forum stresses the necessity of equitable development, inclusiveness in decisionmaking, true sustainability, and a sense of progress as "social, intellectual and spiritual advancement that reflect[s] the quality of life."

This movement, as in the case of the Hemispheric Social Alliance, is building transnational networks.[65] What is essential here is the reclamation of both the ability and the right to protest *and propose;* to demand "a world," as Marcos would say, "in which there is room for all."

And the movement would appear to be growing in both strength and influence. The annual World Economic Forum is now shadowed by a most amazing gathering called the World Social Forum (WSF). The distance between the goals of these two forums could not be wider. While the World Economic Forum is a meeting place for the celebrants of the corporate-led, free market version of globalization, the WSF offers a venue for those who seek a cooperative and inclusive form of internationalism aware of the ecological needs of the planet. For the past two years (2001 and 2002), the WSF has met in the Brazilian industrial port town of Porto Alegre, a town that is itself run through a participatory process based on neighborhood assemblies.[66] Organizers of this year's event believe that 60,000 people attended—tripling last year's figure. This is surely a movement on the rise.[67]

In the face of the ongoing media presentation of the protesters as ill-informed advocates of "utopia," it is essential to recall that "what is denounced as 'utopian' . . . is that which is blocked from coming about by the power of the established societies."[68] The detailed proposals emanating from such groups as the Hemispheric Social Alliance demonstrate exactly what is being blocked. It is the conviction that a radically more equitable and just future is both desirable and obtainable that drives the various protest movements.

NOTES

1. Horkheimer, *Eclipse of Reason,* p. 182.
2. Marcuse, *One Dimensional Man,* pp. xi–xii.
3. Adorno and Horkheimer, *Dialectic of Enlightenment,* p. 7.
4. Ibid., p. 25.
5. For a further consideration of the responsibility of scientists for the use society makes of their work, see Marcuse, "The Responsibility of Science."
6. Capra, "The Challenge of Our Time," p. 18. See also *The Tao of Physics.* For Capra's understanding of the relationship between mental processes and science, see "Systems Theory and the New Paradigm." In this work, Capra succinctly points to the life-destroying tendencies of modern science.
7. Lewontin, *Biology as Ideology,* p. 9.
8. Ibid., p. 8.
9. Bohm, "Postmodern Science in a Postmodern World," p. 350.

10. Bohm, *Wholeness and the Implicate Order*, pp. 15–17.

11. Ibid., p. 29.

12. There are similarities between Bohm's work on language and that of Marcuse. Marcuse was insistent that the increasingly sterile language of the administered state (the acronyms, the technical language, etc.) led to a worldview that blocked critical thought. Consider, for example, Marcuse's argument that "[l]anguage not only reflects these controls but becomes itself an instrument of control even where it does not transmit orders but information; where it demands, not obedience but choice, not submission but freedom. This language controls by reducing the linguistic forms and symbols of reflection, abstraction, development, contradiction; by substituting images for concepts. It denies or absorbs the transcendent vocabulary; it does not search for but establishes and imposes truth and falsehood." See *One Dimensional Man*, p. 103.

13. Bohm, "Human Nature as the Product of Our Mental Models."

14. Bohm and Peat, *Science, Order, and Creativity*. In this work, Bohm and Peat are concerned to discuss what would be involved in a general release of human creative energies. Again, the linkages to Marcuse are important, although Marcuse was more concerned with the ways in which art can transcend the established society and create a new sensibility and critical awareness. See Marcuse, *The Aesthetic Dimension; An Essay on Liberation; Counterrevolution and Revolt;* and of course, *One Dimensional Man*.

15. Tickell, "A Tract for Our Times," p. 56.

16. E. O. Wilson, *Consilience*, p. 93.

17. Ibid., p. 202.

18. For a consideration of the attempts to link ecological well-being to psychology, see Roszak, *The Voice of the Earth*. See also Samuels, *The Political Psyche*, for a discussion of the linkages between political beliefs and depth psychology. On the efforts to raise awareness about our consumption patterns and the advertising that presses us on, see any issue of *Adbusters*.

19. For an interesting discussion of both the issues and the many sites of resistance, see Brecher and Costello, *Global Village*.

20. Guha and Martinez-Alier, *Varieties of Environmentalism;* and Raj and Choudhury, *Contemporary Social Movements in India*. The members of the G-8 are Canada, France, Germany, Greece, Italy, Japan, Russia, and the United States.

21. For the most wonderfully passionate description of the project and the resistance to it, see Roy, *The Cost of Living*. See also Drèze, Samson, and Singh, eds., *The Dam and the Nation*.

22. Nehru, quoted in Esteva and Prakash, "Re-Routing and Re-Rooting Grassroots Initiatives," p. 118. Nehru's belief did not hinder him from having an important view of tribal rights that was designed to prevent values being imposed from outside. For a discussion of this, see Dhagamwar, "The NGO Movement in the Narmada Valley." I would argue that Nehru failed to see the contradiction in the policies he was pursuing and that the logic of the modernization plans was virtually guaranteed to have a negative impact on the small tribal communities whom he sought to protect. For an interesting presentation of the different approaches of Nehru and Gandhi, see Guha and Martinez-Alier,

Varieties of Environmentalism, chap. 8. Guha and Martinez-Alier argue that the environmental movement has tended to present the differences between Nehru and Gandhi too simplistically and comes from a "cowboys and Indians" vision of history.

23. Kothari, "Dams on the River Narmada," p. 5.

24. This excerpt is from an appeal drafted and approved in March 1995 at a regional meeting in Malkangiri district. It was translated by Bharath Bhushan and reproduced in *Lokayan Bulletin*, "To Withdraw Polavaram Dam," pp. 84–85.

25. For a discussion of the impact of genetically modified organisms on traditional farming in terms of "corporate colonialism," see John Vidal, "The Seeds of Wrath." See also the discussion in Chapter 3.

26. Roy, *The Cost of Living*, p. 22.

27. NBA press release, "Sardar Sarovar Dam Height Cannot Be Raised! NBA to Fight Tooth and Nail," January 28, 2002, available at www.narmada. org/nba-press-releases/january-2002/ssp.height.html.

28. The Ogoni Bill of Rights can be found at www.mosopcanada.org/info/mosop0370.html.

29. For an excellent consideration of the trials and tribulations of the Shell boycott, see Yearley and Forrester, "Shell, a Sure Target for Global Environmental Campaigning?" On the human rights aspect of the Shell-Nigeria link, see Sachs, *Eco-Justice;* and Connors, "Environmental Racism."

30. Brody, *The Other Side of Eden*, p. 313.

31. It should also be noted that one of the compromises made by the Inuit in getting the deal with the Canadian government was to relinquish mineral control of a portion of the land.

32. Marcos, *Our Word Is Our Weapon*, p. xxv.

33. See ibid.

34. For a thoughtful presentation of Marcos's poetry in the context of political struggle, see Higgins, "The Zapatista Uprising and the Poetics of Cultural Resistance."

35. Knelman, *Every Life Is a Story*, p. 47. The space does not exist here for a consideration of Marcuse's concept of an aesthetic dimension and its importance in transcending existing social reality and envisioning alternative realities. See, for example, Marcuse, *One Dimensional Man*, and also Marcuse, "Art as a Form of Reality."

36. Marcos, *Our Word Is Our Weapon*, pp. 99–100.

37. The debate has long raged over the idea of the "commons." Garrett Hardin kicked off the debate in 1968 with his controversial argument that herdsmen sharing a commons will act to maximize their own share and thereby the "freedom in a commons brings ruin to all." See Hardin, "Tragedy of the Commons," p. 104. For its application at the level of international relations, see Soroos, "Conflict in the Use and Management of International Commons"; Imber, *Environment, Security, and UN Reform*, chap. 3; and Wijkman, "Managing the Global Commons." A critique is easily leveled against Hardin's argument that he is assuming selfish, atomized action, which does not, in fact, exist in all communities. For a brilliant critique of Hardin's view, see Shiva,

"The Violence of Reductionist Science." It is nonetheless interesting to contemplate the way in which the international system operates—through its neoliberal policies of competition and profit—to encourage states to act in the selfish way depicted by Hardin's parable.

38. For an interesting consideration of the traditional meaning of the term *commons* compared to the misappropriation of it by Brundtland, see Chatterjee and Finger, *The Earth Brokers,* pp. 25–27.

39. For a fascinating look at the ad campaign that speaks of "profits and principles" and argues that "[a]t Shell, we are committed to support fundamental human rights. . . .We invest in the communities around us to create new opportunities and growth," see Wiwa and Rowell, "Some Things Never Change."

40. World Environment Center (WEC), "2001 Jury Citation: WEC Gold Medal for International Corporate Achievement." Shell is one of the funders of the WEC.

41. See the MOSOP (UK) website for the letter sent to the World Environment Center on January 29, 2001, protesting the award, available at www.nigerdeltacongress.com/iarticles/movement_for_the_survival_of_the.htm.

42. I am indebted to Daphne Wysham (Institute for Policy Studies) for this statistic. The exact amount was $15.7 billion to $1 billion.

43. See the Oilwatch Declaration on Human Rights, which was made public in 1998. Oilwatch is a network of ecological, human rights, religious, and local organizations established in 1995. See their website at www.oilwatch.org.ec/main.html.

44. It is interesting to note that Berger was also one of the four people on the World Bank's independent review of the Narmada Dam project.

45. Berger, *Northern Frontier, Northern Homeland,* p. 85.

46. Ibid., pp. 112–113.

47. McKenna, "NWT Woos Alaska on Pipeline." There are, of course, a range of views expressed by the elders of the various northern communities. There are disputes about the degree of ownership and control over the project as well as over environmental safeguards. For an examination of some of these debates, see Girard, "Pipe Dream." For a consideration of the minimal scope allowed for public participation, see Gleeson, "Pipeline Process Under Fire."

48. For a hard-hitting look a the consideration of arctic oil within the Western development ethos, see Livingston, *Arctic Oil.*

49. Berger, *Northern Frontier, Northern Homeland,* p. 200.

50. Yearley and Forrester, "Shell, a Sure Target for Global Environmental Campaigning?" p. 137.

51. Qitsualik, "My Mother Earth Article."

52. Brody, *The Other Side of Eden,* p. 146.

53. For an interesting discussion of these various protests, see Brecher and Costello, *Global Village,* chap. 5.

54. For further information about the movement and the politics behind it, see Barlow and Clarke, *Global Showdown;* "Lori's War," *Foreign Policy;* Retallack, "After Seattle"; and Bray, "Web Wars." For an invaluable depiction of the growth of the movement and all that it is set against, see Klein, *No Logo.*

55. Krauthammer, "Return of the Luddites," p. 25.

56. The Hemispheric Social Alliance was formed at the Summit of the Peoples of the Americas in 1998 and includes the Inter-American Regional Organization of Workers (which includes the AFL-CIO, the Canadian Labour Congress, the Brazilian Central Unico dos Trabalhadores, etc.), the Latin American Coordinator of the Rural Organizations (CLOC), the Interamerican Platform on Human Rights and Democracy, the Gender and Trade Network, national multisectoral citizens networks (including the Alliance for Responsible Trade, the Mexican Action Network on Free Trade, Common Frontiers, the Chilean Alliance for Just and Sustainable Development, the Brazilian Network for a Peoples' Integration, the Peru Chapter of the Hemispheric Social Alliance, and the regional Civil-Society Initiative on Central American Integration), and representatives of the sectoral forums held at the summit. For this list and further details, see the website of the Hemispheric Social Alliance at www.art-us.org/hsa.html. This alliance is formalized to the extent that there is a governing council (consisting of some forty organizations) that meets at least yearly and acts to set policies and strategies. There is also an operating committee that implements decisions. This is an impressive movement that works diligently to educate the public.

57. Hemispheric Social Alliance, *Alternatives for the Americas*, p. 4.

58. Ibid., p. 6.

59. Ibid., p. 15.

60. Ibid., pp. 15–16.

61. Ibid., pp. 17–18.

62. Ibid., pp. 18–19. The document actually gives many more such suggestions; this is merely a representative list.

63. The Hemispheric Social Alliance was not content to leave Quebec having made its own case. The follow-up critique of the document released by the official delegates is equally detailed and thoughtful. See Hemispheric Social Alliance, "The Free Trade Area of the Americas Exposed."

64. There are a wide range of ideas being articulated. Some seek merely reform of the WTO, others are more radical. But most suggestions articulate the need for a massive shift in our mind-set. See, for example, Cavanagh, Wysham, and Arruda, *Beyond Bretton Woods;* Hines, *Localization;* Newell, "Environmental NGOs and Globalization"; Daly, *Beyond Growth;* and Korten, "The Mindful Market Economy," for some very obvious steps to make economics more human.

65. In this case, the official linkages are with Positive Futures (United States), the New Economics Foundation (United Kingdom), the Development Resources Centre (South Africa), the Center for Alternative Development Initiatives (Philippines), and the Network of the People-Centered Development Forum. See the PCDF website at www.iisd.org/pcdf.

66. Juniper and Wainwright, "Alternative Visions That Are Worlds Apart," p. 26.

67. "Alternative Forum in Brazil Winds Up."

68. Marcuse, *An Essay on Liberation*, pp. 3–4. This is the quote that closed Chapter 1.

6

Conclusion

THE CURRENT STATE OF THE ENVIRONMENT AND THE EXISTING mechanisms for dealing with the crisis facing the international community have led to the appearance of a number of books offering insight into the most promising solutions for the seemingly insurmountable problems. The advocates of regime formation share with green diplomacy an unwillingness to go beyond the current structures of the system in a quest for solutions to the environmental crises facing us. Through a celebration of incremental changes in international behavior, we are asked to set aside our unreasonable demands for radical change in the interest of dealing with "reality." We are advised to steer clear of dead-end paths to utopia, and concentrate instead on the possible solutions within the practical limits of the current system.

It has been my contention throughout this book that such a request is ultimately misguided. The desultory results of this incrementalist approach demonstrate that the promises of green diplomacy have not been realized and, more important, cannot be achieved because of the inherent flaws in the construction of the issues under investigation. The limits accepted by green diplomacy are not predefined and immutable; they are the results of conscious decisions taken by governments. The refusal to think beyond these limits is a failure of both will and imagination. It is nothing short of an acceptance of the status quo and, as such, plays the role of justifying the destructive practices that produce the environmental problems being examined.

The international treaties that have been negotiated through the efforts of green diplomacy have failed demonstrably. The regime created to deal with ozone depletion leaves us with nothing but a slowing of the destruction and the request that we have faith in yet another technological fix. The biological diversity of the planet continues to diminish, the forests continue to be clear-cut, the climate continues to change. And the actions taken to deal with the resulting crises continue to be undertaken in isolation from each other—as though the natural world can be carved up into discreet areas for investigation and, indeed, for healing. Presenting the actions of these dedicated diplomats as the best that the international community can possibly achieve is a denial of the interrelatedness of these issues and a refusal to examine the broader goals of Western industrial society and the corporate interests that drive the economic growth model.

The advocates of incrementalism would have us believe that economic growth will serve to eliminate the problems caused by economic growth. We are told that sustainable development, defined by and furthered through liberal economic principles, is the answer to our dilemma. The system that proclaims it and puts the necessary legislation and trade deals together to ensure it, however, leads irrevocably to the destruction of any sustainable, small-scale community that dares to challenge its monolithic vision. In short, we are asked to believe that the system of thought, economic practice, and scientific rationality is "just the ticket" to lead the world—the entire world—into a bright new future of environmental sustainability and an increase of prosperity and justice for all. The entire project is presented as being, of necessity, one of top-down politics with little or no room offered for citizen participation beyond that of the ballot box. Furthermore, those who seek to maintain the present course of action have enormous power and influence to shape the debate in an extraordinarily limited fashion.

Some green diplomats doubtless see serious problems with the dominant economic growth model, but there is little room for the advocacy of alternative structures within the established system to bring environmental treaties into effect. In addition, it must be acknowledged that the problem is deeper than economics. Indeed, our customary way of seeing the world and organizing our knowledge stems from and serves to reinforce the damaging economic practices that have been examined here.

Green diplomacy as it is currently constituted simply cannot successfully fulfill the demands of its stated task. The goal of institutionalizing international agreements with the aim of qualitatively improving the world's natural environment will not happen as long as the solutions are sought within the reductionist method of inquiry that allows issues to be artificially separated from one another.

The result of the approach is one in which the "fixing" in one area can create problems in another area. There is little awareness of the fact that much attention is given to seeking solutions for problems that are themselves the product of technological fixes of an earlier age. The faith in our ability to come up with answers that *this time* will work would be an example of admirable determination were it not so dangerous. The comfortable language of *management* and *control* soothe us and keep us from demanding an approach that would go to the root of the problem. Indeed, it must be acknowledged that such expertise is rare given the current educational structures—at least in the overdeveloped world—which are also based on the same division of the sciences and the natural world into microsubjects.

The existing theory and practice of regime theory and green diplomacy play an important role in the overall attempt to depict a managerial discourse designed to promote confidence in the system, in prevalent ways of thought, and in the human ability to control the natural environment. Despite the determined and honest efforts of those involved in the practice, then, green diplomacy serves as an important part of the picture presented to reassure and soothe us that we are on the right track. We are not.

The ascendancy of a new scientific model would help us put the currently dominant one into its proper perspective and would lay bare its limitations. The promise has long been held out that we are "progressing" toward a sustainable future while the evidence points in the opposite direction. But such a shift is difficult to contemplate. Although there are scientists challenging the mental models that limit our field of vision, the deeply embedded nature of science and technology benefits the technocratic, managerial society. Scientists who attempt to make explicit the power of reductionist techniques and methods are often shunned, ignored, or marginalized. It is important that the critical voices on the margins be listened to and actively promoted wherever and whenever possible.

The new protest movements do not accept the givenness of this state of affairs and are in turn seeking to rejuvenate a political discourse that takes as its starting point the irrationality of the currently dominant neoliberal discourse. At various sites around the world an attempt is being made to point to the fallacy of the promises made and, further, to imagine workable alternatives that place the environment and local communities above corporate profit. By calling into question the absurdity of a discourse that would have us believe that deregulated international capitalism, with its attendant overconsumption of resources and minimal environmental and labor standards, is a magic recipe for ecological sustainability, the protesters force us to consider our own complicity in destructive practices.

It is clear that the odds are stacked in favor of the forces behind the neoliberal project. Armed with consoling concepts such as sustainable development and the supposed promise of green diplomacy, those behind this process present the case to the various publics in terms of the need to construct rules for fair play and the ability of the free market—extended globally and operating without hindrance from governments or local communities—to usher in a new era of promise, justice, technological progress, and equity. The extension of mass culture and corporate branding seek to ensure that this message of hope is extended far and wide. Furthermore, the project is presented as an inevitability with no possible gain to be made by resisting it.

Through a demonstration of what sustainable development really means, the protesters against the building of the Narmada Dam in India share much common ground with the Zapatista movement in Mexico: both offer a glimpse of a more balanced approach to sustainable living. At a different site, the Inuit communities who bear the consequences of the destructive practices that lead to global warming (but no responsibility for them) articulate an alternative that encourages us to reconsider our place in nature. Meanwhile, the Ogoni people in Nigeria struggle against a state infrastructure that acts in the interests of multinational oil corporations rather than in the interests of people and their natural environment, with dire environmental and human consequences. In these places and many, many others, demands are being made against the claims of justice, equality, freedom, and sustainability, which are placed at the center of the free market ethos and which are not—indeed cannot be—realized due to the contradictions inherent in the project. In a sense, what each protest group participates in constitutes an act that seeks to liberate the intent of the concept of sustainable development and, in doing so, turns it against the forces that have utilized it as a technique of stabilization.

The gap between the theory and practice of the neoliberal project is clearly evident for anyone wishing to look, but an awareness of failed promise is not sufficient grounds for a transformation of the system. The undermining of the irrational logic is of necessity the first step, and the presentation of alternative possibilities that capture the imagination of a vast majority of the public is also required. A protest that shakes the very foundations of the given society, however, is both necessary and difficult. It is one thing, for instance, to expose the (il)logic of a system that creates sweatshops full of people engaged in making branded goods for people on the other side of the world; it is entirely another to raise the awareness of the reality to such an extent that large numbers of people refuse to go along with the branding and say "enough" to manufactured needs.

Consciousness raising is, arguably, having some success at the current time. The anti-globalization movement has made it through the barriers erected by a corporate media intent on managing the message. Through the use of street theater, humor, and corporate awareness campaigns, and the presence of the sheer numbers of protesters willing to face off against Darth Vadar–like lines of police clad in riot gear, the images make it onto televisions across the world.

Likewise, some success has been had in the articulation of alternatives, although these have not been as widely disseminated as their proponents doubtless hoped. Increasingly, the protesters are presented as a ragtag group of people who want to go to a big party, or who have no real understanding of the intricacies of global politics, or who are simply selfish in the face of a changing international marketplace that lets the formerly oppressed peoples of the so-called third world into a system of fair trade rules.

The arguments of the mainstream—corporate, governmental, and even diplomatic—can be exposed as being irrational, but a protest that seeks to destabilize the dominant logic (both scientific and economic) will have to be profound and dedicated. The shaking of foundations is never easy, even in the face of mounting evidence that backs the cause. The most likely result of the current protests will be a minimal adjustment on the part of the governments and international institutions. Enough will be offered that the system appears to respond to demands; such adjustment is typical and will placate the majority of the population, whose concerns are being raised but who either fear the language of limits and alternatives or know little about the details of the issues and are content with a little "fixing." The protesters themselves must keep their eyes on the ultimate prize, the creation of a just, democratic, and fulfilling society that allows diversity and debate and that directs science and technology to the fulfillment of human needs rather than to the tools of war and the satisfaction of shallow demands.

The language of commodification is all around us and it is easy to see the logic of exchange value creeping into every aspect of life. The pressure is on in the corridors of environmental regime formation to bring the interstate bargaining into the marketplace with the discussions of "flexible mechanisms" and market values of carbon gas emissions. At the current time, most governments of the world are resisting this particular commodification, but the pressure is clearly on them to give way to the dominant polluters. A refusal to allow the total absorption of all that lives and breathes into commodified logic is an essential component of the myriad struggles against corporate control and must be placed front and center in the debate.

The destructive tendencies of the current international system—the system that underpins green diplomacy—are made apparent with the tools offered by Critical Theory. The absorptive tendencies of the status quo are being challenged by a growing protest movement that is actively pointing to the possibilities for a radical transformation of the existing social, political, and economic structures that are binding the neoliberal system together:

> The growing opposition to the global domination of corporate capitalism is confronted by the sustained power of this domination: its economic and military hold in the four continents, its neocolonial empire, and, more important, its unshaken capacity to subject the majority of the underlying population to its overwhelming productivity and force. . . .
>
> Now, however, this threatening has been loosening up, and an alternative is beginning to break into the repressive continuum. This alternative is not so much a different road to socialism as an emergence of different goals and values, different aspirations in the men and women who resist and deny the massive exploitative power of corporate capitalism even in its most comfortable liberal realizations. The Great Refusal takes a variety of forms.[1]

Anyone assuming this quote is an extract from something written recently can be forgiven for the mistake. Full of optimism that at last a force was growing that was threatening to destabilize the structures of an exploitative, corporate society, Marcuse penned these thoughts in the late 1960s. Alas, it is offered here to temper the optimism that is building in some areas. This is not to deny the possibility that fundamental change can result from the actions of the various movements active today, for that, I believe, is the only way the system will change. Furthermore, in a number of significant ways, today's anti-globalization movement—in its various manifestations—is substantively different from the movement spoken about in the above quote. Greater awareness exists about the potential costs of the dream of scientific advancement.

Massive transnational corporations such as Monsanto and Novartis attempt to sell their message that genetically modified and bioengineered foods are a miracle with which to feed the world. But these messages, or rather advertisements, fall jarringly on a skeptical public wary of corporate control of food and the increasing evidence of the dangers implicit in tinkering with the fundamentals of life. Farmers, once enamored with the possibility of huge profits and the promise of a better environment resulting from less pesticide use, find that they are struggling with so-called superweeds as a direct result of their own actions. Cynicism sets in and leads to a more receptive public for the protesters' claims, which no longer seem outlandish.

Equally, the pompous claims of elected officials around the world that trade negotiations will not lead to lower labor, environment, or human rights standards are left looking ridiculous when corporations are successful in forcing changes in domestic legislation that does just this. Widespread distrust of politicians and their promises is the result, and fewer and fewer people bother to vote, trying but failing to see much substantial difference between the leading political parties.

A younger generation begins to look more closely at the promises made by the "brands" they purchase, and begins to take issue with the exploitation—of both workers and consumers—lying behind them. Naomi Klein may be overstating things when she argues that "as more people discover the brand-name secrets of the global logo web, their outrage will fuel the next big political movement, a vast wave of opposition squarely targeting transnational corporations,"[2] but then again, she may not be overstating the power of *that* particular idea to galvanize young people into action, to *refuse* to participate in the system that enslaves others and fails to bring them the happiness promised by the ad campaigns.

And from those struggling most directly with the costs of transnational corporate practice, the cry is being heard louder and more clearly with each passing day: *Enough!* Strategies now exist for getting out the word that in bygone eras (including the 1960s) would not have been heard. The tactics used by the Zapatista in resisting the neoliberal model as they seek to rewrite the Mexican constitution are replayed in dozens of other struggles, in the poetry of Subcomandante Marcos inspiring different movements in different locales, and over the Internet ensuring that the heavy hand of the "law" cannot erase the message. The Internet may not be the answer to global struggles, but it is a mighty useful tool.

My point is simply this: unlike previous attempts to shake the established order, this movement has built-in diversity and promotes the essential component of democracy—the right to be heard. This is an integrated movement in the sense that most people, in most parts of the world, can be appealed to on the grounds that they are in some way or other a victim of the corporate greed, government complacency, or environmental destruction that are by-products of the neoliberal system. There are no generational, gender, or location differences here. There are different struggles with different objectives, but all together they form a chorus demanding a voice, and that voice will be difficult to suppress.

The real, ongoing struggle for both social and environmental justice is a world away from the expert-filled corridors of green diplomacy. As I have argued throughout this book, the impoverished, managerial ethos and practices of the major environmental regimes are part of the crisis green diplomacy seeks to address. However painful and distressing the realization may be, for the sake of an effective struggle for social transformation and ecological recovery we are obliged to pass a damning verdict: green diplomacy is part of the problem, not the solution.

NOTES

1. Marcuse, *An Essay on Liberation*, p. vii.
2. Klein, *No Logo*, p. xviii.

Bibliography

Adler, Emanuel, and Peter M. Haas. "Epistemic Communities, World Order, and the Creation of a Reflective Research Program." *International Organization* 46 (1) (Winter 1992): 367–390.

Adorno, Theodor W., and Max Horkheimer. *Dialectic of Enlightenment*. London: Verso, 1997. [Originally published in 1944.]

Agger, Ben. "On Science as Domination." In *Domination,* ed. by Alkis Kontos. Toronto: University of Toronto Press, 1975.

Alford, C. Fred. *Science and the Revenge of Nature: Marcuse and Habermas.* Tampa: University of South Florida Press, 1985.

"Alternative Forum in Brazil Winds Up." BBC News, February 5, 2002. Available at http://news.bbc.co.uk/hi/english/world/americas/newsid_1802000/1802305.stm.

Annan, Kofi. "Address to the World Economic Forum in Davos, Switzerland." January 31, 1999. Press Release, SG/SM/6881, February 1, 1999.

Atkinson, Adrian. *Principles of Political Ecology.* London: Belhaven Press, 1991.

Bacon, Francis. *The New Organon and Related Writings.* Ed. by Fulton H. Anderson. Indianapolis: Bobbs-Merrill, 1960. [Originally published in 1620.]

Baldwin, Robert A., ed. *Neorealism and Neoliberalism: The Contemporary Debate.* New York: Columbia University Press, 1993.

Barlow, Maude, and Tony Clarke. *Global Showdown: How the New Activists Are Fighting Global Corporate Rule.* Toronto: Stoddart, 2001.

Barnett, Jon. "Destabilizing the Environment-Conflict Thesis." *Review of International Studies* 26 (2) (2000): 271–288.

Bate, Jonathan. *The Song of the Earth.* London: Picador, 2000.

Bauman, Zygmunt. *Modernity and the Holocaust.* Ithaca: Cornell University Press, 1989.

Baylis, John, and Steve Smith, eds. *The Globalization of World Politics: An Introduction to International Relations.* Oxford: Oxford University Press, 1997.

Beckerman, Wilfred. "Global Warming and International Action: An Economic Perspective." In *The International Politics of the Environment: Actors, Interests, and Institutions,* ed. by Andrew Hurrell and Benedict Kingsbury. Oxford: Clarendon Press, 1992.

Benedick, Richard Elliot. *Ozone Diplomacy: New Directions in Safeguarding the Planet.* Cambridge: Harvard University Press, 1991.

Benthall, Jonathan. *The Limits of Human Nature.* New York: E. P. Dutton, 1974.

Benton, Ted. "Marxism and Natural Limits: An Ecological Critique and Reconstruction." In *The Greening of Marxism,* ed. by Ted Benton. New York: Guildford Press, 1996.

Berger, Thomas R. *Northern Frontier, Northern Homeland: The Report of the Mackenzie Valley Pipeline Inquiry.* Vol. 1. Toronto: Lorimer, 1977.

Bernauer, Thomas. "The Effect of International Environmental Institutions: How We Might Learn More." *International Organization* 49 (2) (Spring 1995): 351–377.

Bhagwati, Jagdish. "The Case for Free Trade." *Scientific American* 5 (269) (November 1993): 18–23.

Bhushan, Bharath, trans. "To Withdraw Polavaram Dam." *Lokayan Bulletin* 11 (5) (March–April 1995): 83–86.

Bohm, David. "Human Nature as the Product of Our Mental Models." In *The Limits of Human Nature,* ed. by Jonathan Benthall. New York: E. P. Dutton, 1974.

———. "Postmodern Science in a Postmodern World." In *Key Concepts in Critical Theory,* ed. by C. Merchant. Atlantic Highlands, N.J.: Humanities Press, 1994.

———. *Wholeness and the Implicate Order.* London: Ark, 1980.

Bohm, David, and F. David Peat. *Science, Order, and Creativity.* London: Routledge, 1987.

Bostrom, Ann, M. Granger Morgan, Baruch Fischhoff, and Daniel Read. "What Do People Know About Global Climate Change? 1. Mental Modes." *Risk Analysis* 14 (6) (1994): 959–970.

Bray, John. "Web Wars: NGOs, Companies, and Governments in an Internet-Connected World." *Greener Management International* (24) (Winter 1998): 115–129.

Brecher, Jeremy, and Tim Costello. *Global Village: Economic Reconstruction from the Bottom Up.* Boston: South End Press, 1994.

Brenton, Tony. *The Greening of Machiavelli: The Evolution of International Environmental Politics.* London: Earthscan and Royal Institute of International Affairs, 1994.

Broadhead, Lee-Anne. "Canada as a Rogue State." *International Journal* 56 (3) (Summer 2001): 461–480.

———. "Commissioning Consent: Globalization and Global Governance." *International Journal* 51 (4) (Autumn 1996): 651–668.

Brody, Hugh. *The Other Side of Eden: Hunter-Gatherers, Farmers, and the Shaping of the World.* London: Faber and Faber, 2001.

Bronner, Stephen Eric, and Douglas Kellner. *Critical Theory and Society: A Reader.* New York: Routledge, 1989.

Brown, Leann. "Policymaking in International Organizations: The European Union and Ozone Protection." In *International Organizations and Environmental Policy,* ed. by Robert V. Bartlett, Priya A. Kurian, and Madhu Malik. Westport, Conn.: Greenwood Press, 1995.

Capra, Fritjof. "The Challenge of Our Time." *Resurgence* (203) (November–December 2000): 18–20.

———. "Systems Theory and the New Paradigm." In *Key Concepts in Critical Theory,* ed. by C. Merchant. Atlantic Highlands, N.J.: Humanities Press, 1994.

———. *The Tao of Physics.* London: Wildwood House, 1975.

Carson, Rachel. *Silent Spring.* New York: Fawcett Crest, 1962.

Cavanagh, John, Daphne Wysham, and Marcos Arruda. *Beyond Bretton Woods: Alternatives to the Global Economic Order.* London: Pluto Press, 1994.

Charnovitz, Steve. "GATT and the Environment: Examining the Issues." *International Environmental Affairs* 4 (3) (Summer 1992): 203–233.

Chatterjee, Pratap, and Matthias Finger. *The Earth Brokers: Power, Politics, and World Development.* London: Routledge, 1994.

Churchill, Derek, and Richard Worthington. "The North American Free Trade Agreement and the Environment: Economic Growth Versus Democratic Politics." In *Greening Environmental Policy: The Politics of a Sustainable Future,* ed. by Frank Fischer and Michael Black. London: Paul Chapman, 1995.

Clark, Ann Marie, Elisabeth J. Friedman, and Kathryn Hochstetler. "The Sovereign Limits of Global Civil Society: A Comparison of NGO Participation in UN World Conferences on the Environment, Human Rights, and Women." *World Politics* 51 (1) (October 1998): 1–35.

Clarke, Tony, and Maude Barlow. *MAI: The Multilateral Agreement on Investment and the Threat to Canadian Sovereignty.* Toronto: Stoddart, 1997.

———. *MAI Round Two: New Global and Internal Threats to Canadian Sovereignty.* Toronto: Stoddart, 1998.

Clinton, Bill. "Remarks by the President to the Fifty-second Session of the United Nations General Assembly." September 22, 1997.

Clow, Michael. "Sustainable Development: Our Next Path of Development, or Wishful Thinking?" *British Journal of Canadian Studies* 11 (1) (1996): 1–10.

Cobb, Clifford, Ted Halstead, and Jonathan Rowe. "If the GDP Is Up, Why Is America Down?" *The Atlantic Monthly* 276 (4) (October 1995): 59–78.

Colás, Alejandro. "The Promises of International Civil Society." *Global Society* 11 (3) (September 1997): 261–277.

Commission on Global Governance. *Our Global Neighbourhood: The Report of the Commission on Global Governance.* Oxford: Oxford University Press, 1995.

Commoner, Barry. *The Closing Circle: Nature, Man, and Technology.* New York: Knopf, 1971.

———. "Motherhood in Stockholm." *Harper's Magazine* (June 1972): 49–54.

Connors, Libby. "Environmental Racism: Australia, Shell, and Nigeria." *Social Alternatives* 16 (2) (April 1997): 50–52.

Cook, Chris, ed. *Pears Cyclopaedia, 1997–1998.* London: Penguin, 1997.

Cooper, Richard N. "Toward a Real Global Warming Treaty." *Foreign Affairs* 77 (2) (March–April 1998): 66–79.

Cox, Robert W. "Social Forces, States, and World Orders: Beyond International Relations Theory." In *Neorealism and Its Critics,* ed. by R. O. Keohane. New York: Columbia University Press, 1986.

Crowell, George H. "NAFTA: Potential Environmental Impact." In *The Environment and Canadian Society,* ed. by Thomas Fleming. Toronto: ITP Nelson, 1997.

Daly, Herman E., ed. *Beyond Growth.* Boston: Beacon Press, 1996.

———. *Economics, Ecology, Ethics: Essays Toward a Steady-State Economy.* San Francisco: W. H. Freeman, 1980.

———. "The Perils of Free Trade." *Scientific American* 269 (5) (1993): 24–29.

———. *Toward a Steady-State Economy.* San Francisco: W. H. Freeman, 1973.

Davidson, Eric A. *You Can't Eat GNP: Economics As If Ecology Mattered.* Cambridge, Mass.: Perseus, 2000.

de Bell, Garrett, ed. *The Environmental Handbook.* New York: Ballantine/ Friends of the Earth, 1970.

"The Debate on Globalisation." BBC News, April 15, 2000. Available at http://news.bbc.co.uk/hi/english/business/newsid_714000/714972.stm.

Dhagamwar, Vasudha. "The NGO Movement in the Narmada Valley: Some Reflections." In *The Dam and the Nation: Displacement and Resettlement in the Narmada Valley,* ed. by Jean Drèze, Meera Samson, and Satyajit Singh. Delhi: Oxford University Press, 1997.

Doran, Peter. "Earth, Power, Knowledge: Towards a Critical Global Environmental Politics." In *Boundaries in Question: New Directions in International Relations,* ed. by John MacMillan and Andrew Linklater. London: Pinter, 1995.

Douglas, Mary. "The Depoliticization of Risk." In *Culture Matters: Essays in Honor of Aaron Wildavsky,* ed. by R. J. Ellis and M. Thompson. Boulder: Westview Press, 1997.

Downie, David Leonard. "UNEP and the Montreal Protocol." In *International Organizations and Environmental Policy,* ed. by Robert V. Bartlett, Priya A. Kurian, and Madhu Malik. Westport, Conn.: Greenwood Press, 1995.

Doyle, Jack. "Hold the Applause: A Case Study of Corporate Environmentalism." *The Ecologist* 22 (3) (May–June 1992): 84–90.

Drèze, Jean, Meera Samson, and Satyajit Singh, eds. *The Dam and the Nation: Displacement and Resettlement in the Narmada Valley.* Delhi: Oxford University Press, 1997.

Dubos, René. *Reason Awake.* Columbia: Columbia University Press, 1970.

Dunlap, Riley E. "International Opinion at the Century's End: Public Attitudes Toward Environmental Issues." In *Environmental Policy: Transnational Issues and National Trends,* ed. by Lynton Caldwell and Robert V. Bartlett. Westport, Conn.: Quorum Books, 1997.

Eckersley, Robyn. *Environmentalism and Political Theory: Toward an Ecocentric Approach.* London: UCL Press, 1992.

Ehrlich, Paul. *The Population Bomb.* New York: Ballantine, 1968.

Ekins, Paul. *A New World Order: Grassroots Movements for Global Change.* London: Routledge, 1992.

Elliott, Lorraine. *The Global Politics of the Environment.* London: Macmillan, 1998.

Ellul, Jacques. *The Technological Society.* New York: Knopf, 1964.

Ellwood, Wayne. "Building a Green Economy." *New Internationalist* (278) (April 1996): 7–13.

Environment Canada. "Canada's Ozone Layer Protection Program." Available at www.ec.gc.ca/ozone/protect/index_e.html.

Esteva, Gustavo, and Madhu Suri Prakash. "Re-Routing and Re-Rooting Grass-roots Initiatives: Escaping the Impasse of Sustainable Development for the Narmada." *Lokayan Bulletin* 9 (3–4) (May–August 1991): 113–125.

Evernden, Neil. *The Natural Alien: Humankind and Environment.* 2nd ed. Toronto: University of Toronto Press, 1993.

Feldman, David Lewis. "Iterative Functionalism and Climate Management Organizations: From Intergovernmental Panel on Climate Change to Intergovernmental Negotiating Committee." In *International Organizations and Environmental Policy*, ed. by Robert V. Bartlett, Priya A. Kurian, and Madhu Malik. Westport, Conn: Greenwood Press, 1995.

Finger, Matthias. "Environmental NGOs in the UNCED Process." In *Environmental NGOs in World Politics: Linking the Local and the Global*, ed. by Thomas Princen and Matthias Finger. London: Routledge, 1994.

———. "New Horizons for Peace Research: The Global Environment." In *Perspectives on Environmental Conflict and International Relations*, ed. by Jyrki Käkönen. London: Pinter, 1992.

———. "NGOs and Transformation: Beyond Social Movement Theory." In *Environmental NGOs in World Politics: Linking the Local and the Global*, ed. by Thomas Princen and Matthias Finger. London: Routledge, 1994.

Finger, Matthias, and James Kilcoyne. "Why Transnational Corporations Are Organizing to 'Save the Global Environment.'" *The Ecologist* 27 (4) (July–August 1997): 138–142.

Foster, John Bellamy. "Marx and the Environment." *Monthly Review* 47 (3) (July–August 1995): 108–123.

Friedheim, Robert L. *Negotiating the New Ocean Regime.* Columbia: University of South Carolina Press, 1993.

George, Jim. *Discourses of Global Politics: A Critical (Re)Introduction to International Relations.* Boulder: Lynne Rienner, 1994.

Gill, Stephen, and David Law. *The Global Political Economy: Perspectives, Problems, and Policies.* Toronto: Harvester-Wheatsheaf, 1988.

Girard, Daniel. "Pipe Dream." *Toronto Star,* July 21, 2001.

Gleeson, Richard. "Pipeline Process Under Fire: Producers Welcome, Public Not." *Northern News Services,* July 13, 2001. Available at www.nnsl.com.

Greene, Owen. "Environmental Issues." In *The Globalization of World Politics*, ed. by John Baylis and Steve Smith. Oxford: Oxford University Press, 1994.

Greer, Jed, and Kenny Bruno. *Greenwash: The Reality Behind Corporate Environmentalism.* New York: Apex Press, 1996.

Gribbin, John. *The Hole in the Sky: Man's Threat to the Ozone.* London: Corgi Books, 1988.

Grieco, J. "Anarchy and the Limits of Co-operation: A Realist Critique of the Newest Liberal Institutionalism." *International Organization* 42 (3) (Summer 1988): 485–507.

Grundman, Reiner. "The Ecological Challenge to Marxism." *New Left Review* (187) (May–June 1991): 103–120.

Guha, Ramachandra, and J. Martinez-Alier. *Varieties of Environmentalism: Essays North and South.* Delhi: Oxford University Press, 1998.

Haas, Peter M. "Banning Chlorofluorocarbons: Epistemic Community Efforts to Protect Stratospheric Ozone." *International Organization* 41 (1) (Winter 1992): 187–224.

———. "Introduction: Epistemic Communities and International Policy Coordination." *International Organization* 46 (1) (Winter 1992): 1–35.

Habermas, Jürgen. *Toward a Rational Society: Student Protest, Science, and Politics.* London: Heinemann, 1971.

Hanisch, Ted. "The Rio Climate Convention: Real Solutions or Political Rhetoric?" *Security Dialogue* 23 (4) (1992): 63–73.

Hannigan, John A. *Environmental Sociology: A Social Constructionist Perspective.* London: Routledge, 1995.

Hardin, Garrett. "The Tragedy of the Commons." In *Economics, Ecology, Ethics: Essays Toward a Steady-State Economy,* ed. by Herman E. Daly. San Francisco: W. H. Freeman, 1973. [Originally published in *Science* 162 (3859) (1968): 1243–1248.]

Harding, Stephan. "Exploring Gaia." *Resurgence* (204) (January–February 2001): 16–19.

Hawkins, Ann. "Contested Ground: International Environmentalism and Global Climate Change." In *The State and Social Power in Global Environmental Politics,* ed. by Ronnie D. Lipschutz and Ken Conca. New York: Columbia University Press, 1993.

Held, David. *Introduction to Critical Theory: Horkheimer to Habermas.* London: Hutchinson, 1980.

Hemispheric Social Alliance. *Alternatives for the Americas.* Discussion Draft no. 3. Available at www.asc-hsa.org.

———. "The Free Trade Area of the Americas Exposed: Civil Society Critique of the Official Draft Text Preliminary Analysis of the FTAA," Discussion Draft no. 1, January 2002. Available at www.asc-has.org/pdf/ftaa_analysis_eng.pdf.

Henderson, Hazel. *Creating Alternative Futures: The End of Economics.* New York: Perigee Books, 1980. [c.1978.]

Higgins, Nicholas. "The Zapatista Uprising and the Poetics of Cultural Resistance." *Alternatives* 25 (3) (July–September 2000): 359–374.

Hines, Colin. *Localization: A Global Manifesto.* London: Earthscan, 2000.

Hodson, H. V. *The Diseconomics of Growth.* London: Pan/Ballantine, 1972.

Horkheimer, Max. *Critical Theory: Selected Essays.* New York: Seabury Press, 1972. [English translation.]

———. *Eclipse of Reason.* New York: Seabury Press, 1974. [Originally published in 1947.]

"Hot Air: Global Warming and the Political Economy of Threats." *The Ecologist* 27 (1) (January–February 1997): 2–4.

Hovden, Eivind. "As If Nature Doesn't Matter: Ecology, Regime Theory, and International Relations." *Environmental Politics* 8 (2) (Summer 1999): 50–74.

Hurrell, Andrew. "International Political Theory and the Global Environment." In *International Relations Theory*, ed. by Ken Booth and Steve Smith. Cambridge, England: Polity Press, 1995.

Imber, Mark F. *Environment, Security, and UN Reform*. London: Macmillan, 1994.

International Chamber of Commerce. *The Business Charter for Sustainable Development*. Available at www.iccwbo.org/home/environment/charter.asp.

International NGO Forum. "People's Earth Declaration: A Proactive Agenda for the Future." Available at www.iisd.ca/sd/principle.

Juniper, Tony, and Hilary Wainwright. "Alternative Visions That Are Worlds Apart." *Guardian Weekly*, February 8–14, 2001.

Jurgielewicz, Lynne M. "International Regimes and Environmental Policy: An Evaluation of the Role of International Law." In *International Organizations and Environmental Policy*, ed. by Robert V. Bartlett, Priya A. Kurian, and Madhu Malik. Westport, Conn.: Greenwood Press, 1995.

Kellner, Douglas. *Critical Theory, Marxism, and Modernity*. Baltimore: Johns Hopkins University Press, 1989.

———. *Herbert Marcuse and the Crisis of Marxism*. Berkeley: University of California Press, 1984.

Keohane, Robert. *After Hegemony: Cooperation and Discord in the World Political Economy*. Princeton: Princeton University Press, 1985.

Keohane, Robert, and Joseph Nye. *Power and Interdependence: World Politics in Transition*. Boston: Little, Brown, 1977.

———. "Two Cheers for Multilateralism." *Foreign Policy* (60) (1985–1986): 148–167.

Klein, Naomi. *No Logo: Taking Aim at the Brand Bullies*. Toronto: Knopf, 2000.

Knelman, Fred. *Every Life Is a Story: The Social Relations of Science, Ecology, and Peace*. Montreal: Black Rose Books, 1999.

———. "What Happened at Stockholm?" *International Journal* 28 (1) (1972–1973): 28–49.

Korten, David. "The Mindful Market Economy." *Resurgence* (200) (May–June 2000): 16–19.

Kothari, Smitu. "Dams on the River Narmada: A Call to Conscience." *Lokayan Bulletin* 9 (3–4) (May–August 1991): 1–10.

Krasner, S. D., ed. *International Regimes*. Ithaca: Cornell University Press, 1983.

Kratochwil, Friedrich. "Regimes, Interpretation, and the 'Science' of Politics: A Reappraisal." *Millennium: Journal of International Studies* 17 (2) (1988): 263–284.

Krauthammer, Charles. "Return of the Luddites." *Time* 154 (24) (December 13, 1999): 25.

Krutilla, Kerry. "World Trade, the GATT, and the Environment." In *Environmental Policy: Transnational Issues and National Trends*, ed. by Lynton Caldwell and Robert V. Bartlett. Westport, Conn.: Quorum Books, 1997.

Kurlansky, Mark. *Cod: A Biography of the Fish That Changed the World.* London: Jonathan Cape, 1998.

Laferriere, Eric. "Emancipating International Relations Theory: An Ecological Perspective." *Millennium: Journal of International Studies* 35 (1) (1996): 53–75.

Langway, Lynn, and Jerry Edgerton. "The U.S. at Stockholm." *The Nation* 208 (July 10, 1972): 7–11.

Le Prestre, Philippe. "Environmental Learning at the World Bank." In *International Organizations and Environmental Policy,* ed. by Robert V. Bartlett, Priya A. Kurian, and Madhu Malik. Westport, Conn.: Greenwood Press, 1995.

Leggett, Jeremy. "Global Warming: The Worst Case." *The Bulletin of the Atomic Scientists* 48 (5) (June 1992): 28–33.

Leiss, William. *The Domination of Nature.* Boston: Beacon Press, 1972.

———. *The Limits to Satisfaction: On Needs and Commodities.* London: Marion Boyars, 1978. [Originally published in 1976 by University of Toronto Press.]

Levins, Richard, and Richard Lewontin. *The Dialectical Biologist.* Cambridge: Harvard University Press, 1985.

Lewontin, R. C. *Biology as Ideology.* New York: HarperCollins, 1991.

Liberatore, Angela. "The Social Construction of Environmental Problems." In *Environmental Policy in an International Context: Perspectives on Environmental Problems,* ed. by Pieter Glasbergen and Andrew Blowers. London: Arnold, 1995.

Lipschutz, R. D. "Reconstructing World Politics: The Emergence of Global Civil Society." *Millennium: Journal of International Studies* 21 (3) (1992): 389–420.

List, Martin, and Volker Rittberger. "Regime Theory and International Environmental Management." In *The International Politics of the Environment,* ed. by Andrew Hurrell and Benedict Kingsbury. Oxford: Clarendon Press, 1992.

Litfin, Karen T. "Ecoregimes: Playing Tug of War with the Nation-State." In *The State and Social Power in Global Environmental Politics.* New York: Columbia University Press, 1993.

———. "Framing Science: Precautionary Discourse and the Ozone Treaties." *Millennium: Journal of International Studies* 24 (2) (1995): 251–277.

Little, Richard. "International Regimes." In *The Globalization of World Politics,* ed. by John Baylis and Steve Smith. Oxford: Oxford University Press, 1994.

Livingston, John. *Arctic Oil: The Destruction of the North?* Toronto: Canadian Broadcasting Corporation, 1981.

"Lori's War" [interview with Lori Wallach]. *Foreign Policy* (118) (Spring 2000): 28–54.

Luke, Timothy W. *Ecocritique: Contesting the Politics of Nature, Economy, and Culture.* Minneapolis: University of Minnesota Press, 1997.

———. "Sustainable Development as a Power/Knowledge System: The Problem of 'Governmentality.'" In *Greening Environmental Policy: The Politics of a Sustainable Future*, ed. by Frank Fischer and Michael Black. London: Paul Chapman, 1995.

Lutes, Mark W. "Global Climatic Change." In *Political Ecology: Global and Local*, ed. by Roger Keil, David V. J. Bell, Peter Penz, and Leesa Fawcett. London: Routledge, 1998.

MacDonald, Douglas, and Heather A. Smith. "Promises Made, Promises Broken: Questioning Canada's Commitments to Climate Change." *International Journal* 55 (1) (Winter 1999–2000): 107–124.

MacNeill, Jim. "Trade-Environment Links: The Global Dimension." In *Trade, Environment and Competitiveness: Sustaining Canada's Prosperity*, ed. by John Kirton and Sarah Richardson. Ottawa: National Round Table on the Environment and the Economy, 1992.

Maddox, John. *The Doomsday Syndrome*. London: Macmillan, 1972.

Marcos [Subcomandante Insurgente]. *Our Word Is Our Weapon: Selected Writings*. Ed. by Juana Ponce de León. New York: Seven Stories Press, 2001.

Marcuse, Herbert. *The Aesthetic Dimension*. Boston: Beacon Books, 1977.

———. "Art as a Form of Reality." *New Left Review* (74) (July–August 1972): 51–58.

———. *Counterrevolution and Revolt*. Boston: Beacon Books, 1972.

———. "Ecology and Revolution." In *Key Concepts in Critical Theory: Ecology*, ed. by Carolyn Merchant. Atlantic Highlands, N.J.: Humanities Press. [Originally published in *Liberation* 17 (6) (September 1972): 10–12.]

———. *An Essay on Liberation*. Boston: Beacon Books, 1969.

———. *One Dimensional Man*. Boston: Beacon Books, 1964.

———. *Reason and Revolution*. Atlantic Highlands, N.J.: Humanities Press, 1941.

———. "The Responsibility of Science." In *The Responsibility of Power: Historical Essays in Honor of Hajo Holborn*, ed. by Leonard Krieger and Fritz Stern. London: Macmillan, 1968.

———. "Some Social Implications of Modern Technology." *Studies in Philosophy and Social Science* 9 (3) (1941): 414–439.

Maxwell, James H., and Sandford L. Weiner. "Green Consciousness or Dollar Diplomacy? The British Response to the Threat of Ozone Depletion." *International Environmental Affairs* 5 (1) (Winter 1993): 19–41.

McCormick, John. *The Global Environmental Movement*. London: Belhaven Press, 1989.

McKenna, Barrie. "NWT Woos Alaska on Pipeline." *Globe and Mail*, October 5, 2000.

McKibben, Bill. *The End of Nature*. London: Viking, 1990.

Meadows, Donella H., Dennis L. Meadows, Jorgen Randers, and William W. Behrens III. *The Limits to Growth: A Report for the Club of Rome's Project on the Predicament of Mankind*. London: Pan Books, 1972.

Mellor, Anne K. "A Feminist Critique of Science." In *Frankenstein: Contemporary Critical Essays*, ed. by Fred Botting. London: Macmillan, 1995.

Merchant, Carolyn. *The Death of Nature: Women, Ecology, and the Scientific Revolution*. San Francisco: Harper and Row, 1983.

————, ed. *Ecology: Key Concepts in Critical Theory.* Atlantic Highlands, N.J.: Humanities Press, 1994.

"A Message to Our 3.5 Billion Neighbours on Planet Earth from 2,200 Environmental Scientists" [Menton Message]. *The UNESCO Courier* (July 1971): 4–5.

Meyer, John W., David John Frank, Ann Hironaka, Evan Schofer, and Nancy Brandon Tuma. "The Structuring of a World Environmental Regime, 1870–1990." *International Organization* 51 (4) (August 1997): 623–651.

Middleton, Neil, Phil O'Keefe, and Sam Moyo. *Tears of the Crocodile: From Rio to Reality in the Developing World.* London: Pluto Press, 1993.

Molina, Mario J., and F. S. Rowland. "Stratospheric Sink for Chlorofluoromethanes: Chlorine Atom-Catalysed Destruction of Ozone." *Nature* 249 (5460) (June 28, 1974): 810–812.

Morgan, Edward P. "Stockholm: The Clean (but Impossible) Dream." *Foreign Policy* (8) (Fall 1972): 149–155.

Morgenthau, Hans J. *Politics Among Nations: The Struggle for Power and Peace.* 4th ed. New York: Knopf, 1967.

Morrisette, Peter M. "The Montreal Protocol: Lessons for Formulating Policies for Global Warming." *Policy Studies Journal* 19 (2) (Spring 1991): 152–161.

Morse, Bradford, and Thomas Berger. *Sardar Sarovar: Report of the Independent Review.* Washington, D.C.: World Bank, 1992.

Neufeld, Mark. *The Restructuring of International Relations Theory.* Cambridge: Cambridge University Press, 1995.

Newell, Peter. "Environmental NGOs and Globalization: The Governance of TNCs." In *Global Social Movements,* ed. by Robin Cohen and Shirin M. Rai. London: Athlone Press, 2000.

Nicholson, Max. *The Environmental Revolution: A Guide for the New Masters of the World.* Harmondsworth: Penguin, 1970.

Organization for Economic Cooperation and Development. *Economic Globalisation and the Environment.* Paris: OECD, 1997.

Osherenko, Gail, and Oran R. Young. "The Formation of International Regimes: Hypotheses and Cases." In *Polar Politics: Creating International Environmental Regimes,* ed. by Oran R. Young and Gail Osherenko. Ithaca: Cornell University Press, 1993.

Ouattara, Alassane D. "Macroeconomics and Sustainable Development." Address at the World Bank's Fifth Annual Conference on Environmentally and Socially Sustainable Development, Washington, D.C., October 7, 1997. Available at www.imf.org/external/np/speeches/1997/100797.htm.

Ozone Secretariat. "Cairo Ministerial Meeting Links Climate Change and Ozone Solutions." UNEP News Release, 1998/122.

Panitch, Leo. "Globalisation and the State." In *Socialist Register 1994: Between Capitalism and Nationalism,* ed. by Ralph Miliband and Leo Panitch. London: Merlin Press, 1994.

Pasha, Mustapha Kamal, and David L. Blaney. "Elusive Paradise: The Promise and Peril of Global Civil Society." *Alternatives* 23 (4) (October–December 1998): 417–450.

Paterson, Matthew. "Global Warming." In *The Environment in International Relations*, ed. by Caroline Thomas. London: Royal Institute of International Affairs, 1992.
———. *Global Warming and Global Politics*. London: Routledge, 1996.
———. "Radicalizing Regimes? Ecology and the Critique of IR Theory." In *Boundaries in Question: New Directions in International Relations*, ed. by John MacMillan and Andrew Linklater. London: Pinter, 1995.
———. *Understanding Global Environmental Politics*. London: Macmillan, 2000.
Pepper, David. *Modern Environmentalism: An Introduction*. London: Routledge, 1996.
Piddington, Kenneth. "The Role of the World Bank." In *The International Politics of the Environment*, ed. by Andrew Hurrell and Benedict Kingsbury. Oxford: Clarendon Press, 1992.
Porter, Gareth, and Janet Welsh Brown. *Global Environmental Politics*. Boulder: Westview Press, 1991.
Qitsualik, Rachel Attituq. "My Mother Earth Article." *Nunatsiaq News*, April 23, 1999.
Raj, Sebasti L., and Arundhuti Roy Choudhury. *Contemporary Social Movements in India: Achievements and Hurdles*. Delhi: New Delhi Indian Social Institute, 1998.
Read, Daniel, Ann Bostrom, M. Granger Morgan, Baruch Fischhoff, and Tom Smuts. "What Do People Know About Global Climate Change? 2. Survey Studies of Educated Laypeople." *Risk Analysis* 14 (6) (1994): 971–982.
"Report on the GATT Symposium on Trade, Environment, and Sustainable Development." *Trade and the Environment: News and Views from the General Agreement on Tariffs and Trade*. Geneva: GATT, July 28, 1994 (TE 008).
Retallack, Simon. "After Seattle: Where Next for the WTO?" *The Ecologist* 30 (2) (April 2000): 30–34.
———. "Kyoto: Our Last Chance." *The Ecologist* 27 (6) (November–December 1997): 229–236.
Roberts, Paul. "Bad Sports, or How We Learned to Stop Worrying and Love the SUV." *Harper's Magazine* (April 2001): 69–75.
Roche, Douglas. *A Bargain for Humanity: Global Security by 2000*. Edmonton: University of Alberta Press, 1993.
Rolfe, Chris. "Canada's Game: Climate Charade." *Globe and Main*, November 14, 2000.
Roszak, Theodore. *The Voice of the Earth: An Exploration of Ecopsychology*. New York: Touchstone, 1992.
Roy, Arundhati. *The Cost of Living*. New York: Modern Library, 1999.
Royal Society. "The Role of Land Carbon Sinks in Mitigating Global Climate Change." July 2001. Available at www.royalsoc.ac.uk/templates/statements/index.cfm.
Ruggie, J. G. "Territoriality and Beyond." *International Organization* 47 (1) (Winter 1993): 139–174.

Ruggie, J. G., and Georg Kell. "Global Markets and Social Legitimacy: The Case of the 'Global Compact.'" Paper presented at the international conference "Governing the Public Domain Beyond the Era of the Washington Consensus? Redrawing the Line Between the State and the Market," York University, Toronto, November 4–6, 1999. Available at www.unglobalcompact.org/gc/unweb.nsf/content/gkjr.htm.

Sachs, Aaron. *Eco-Justice: Linking Human Rights and the Environment*. Paper no. 127. Washington, D.C.: Worldwatch Institute, December 1995.

Samuels, Andrew. *The Political Psyche*. London: Routledge, 1993.

Saurin, Julian. "Global Environmental Degradation, Modernity, and Environmental Knowledge." *Environmental Politics* 2 (4) (1993): 46–64.

———. "International Relations, Social Ecology, and the Globalisation of Environmental Change." In *The Environment and International Relations*, ed. by John Vogler and Mark F. Imber. London: Routledge, 1996.

Schmidheiny, Stephan. *Changing Course: A Global Business Perspective on Development and the Environment*. Cambridge: MIT Press, 1992.

Scholte, Jan Aart. "Beyond the Buzzword: Towards a Critical Theory of Globalization." In *Globalization: Theory and Practice*, ed. by Eleonore Kofman and Gillian Youngs. London: Pinter, 1996.

Schumacher, E. F. *Small Is Beautiful: A Study of Economics As If People Mattered*. London: Abacus, 1974.

Sebenius, James K. "Designing Negotiations Toward a New Regime: The Case of Global Warming." *International Security* 15 (4) (Spring 1991): 110–148.

Sharma, Devinder. *GATT to WTO: Seeds of Despair*. Delhi: Konark, 1995.

Shelley, Mary. *Frankenstein*. Toronto: Bantam, 1981. [Originally published in 1818.]

Shiva, Vandana. *Biopiracy: The Plunder of Nature and Knowledge*. Boston: South End Press, 1997.

———. "Poverty and Globalisation." Reith Lecture, BBC Radio, 2000. Available at http://news.bbc.co.uk/hi/english/static/events/reith_2000/lecture5.stm.

———. *Stolen Harvest: The Hijacking of the Global Food Supply*. Cambridge, Mass.: South End Press, 2000.

———. "The Violence of Reductionist Science." *Alternatives* 12 (2) (April 1987): 243–261.

Simpson, Sarah. "Climate Change—Kyoto Protocol: Debit or Credit?" *Scientific American* 284 (2) (February 2001): 25.

Sitarz, Daniel. *Agenda 21: The Earth Summit Strategy to Save Our Planet*. Boulder: Earthpress, 1994.

Smith, Steve. "Environment on the Periphery of International Relations: An Explanation." *Environmental Politics* 2 (4) (1993): 28–45.

Smith, Toby M. *The Myth of Green Marketing: Tending Our Goats at the Edge of Apocalypse*. Toronto: University of Toronto Press, 1998.

Sohn, Louis B. "The Stockholm Declaration on the Human Environment." *Harvard International Law Journal* 14 (1973): 423–515.

Soroos, Marvin S. "Conflict in the Use and Management of International Commons." In *Perspectives on Environmental Conflict and International Relations*, ed. by Jyrki Kakonen. London: Pinter, 1992.

———. "The Tragedy of the Commons in Global Perspective." In *The Global Agenda: Issues and Perspectives*, 2nd ed., ed. by Charles E. Kegley and Eugene R. Wittkopf. New York: Random House, 1988.

"Statement of the International Peoples' Tribunal on Human Rights and the Environment: Sustainable Development in the Context of Globalization." *Alternatives* 23 (1) (January–March 1998): 109–146.

Stewart, Christine. "Speech Delivered on the Occasion of the Opening of the Ninth Annual Meeting of the Parties to the Montreal Protocol," September 15, 1997. Available at ww.ec.gc.ca/minister/speeches/protocol_s_e.htm.

Strange, Susan. "*Cave! Hic dragones:* A Critique of Regime Analysis." *International Organization* 36 (2) (Spring 1982): 479–496.

Stirling, Andrew. "Environmental Valuation: How Much Is the Emperor Wearing?" *The Ecologist* 23 (3) (May–June 1993): 97–100.

Strong, Maurice. "One Year After Stockholm: An Ecological Approach to Management." *Foreign Affairs* 54 (4) (1973): 690–707.

———. "A Time of Transition." *World Goodwill Newsletter* (4) (1992): 3.

———. *Where on Earth Are We Going?* Toronto: Alfred A. Knopf, 2000.

Sullivan, E. Thomas. "The Stockholm Conference: A Step Toward Global Environmental Cooperation and Involvement." *The Indiana Law Review* 6 (2) (1972): 267–282.

Swart, Robert J. "A Comprehensive Approach to Climate Policy: Reconciling Long-Term Needs with Short-Term Concerns." *International Environmental Affairs* 4 (1) (Winter 1992): 35–55.

Thomas, Caroline. *The Environment in International Relations*. London: Royal Institute of International Affairs, 1992.

Thompson, Michael, and Steve Rayner. "Risk and Governance Part I: The Discourses of Climate Change." *Government and Opposition* 33 (2) (Spring 1998): 139–166.

Thompson, Michael, Steve Rayner, and Steven Ney. "Risk and Governance Part II: Policy in a Complex and Plurally Perceived World." *Government and Opposition* 33 (3) (Summer 1998): 330–354.

Tickell, Sir Crispin. "A Tract for our Times." *Resurgence* (192) (January–February 1999): 56–57.

Tickner, J. Ann. "An Ecofeminist Perspective on International Political Economy." *International Political Science Review* 14 (1) (1993): 59–69.

Ungeheuer, Friedel. "Woodstockholm." *Time Magazine* 99 (June 19, 1972): 69.

United Nations. *Johannesburg Summit 2002: World Summit on Sustainable Development*. Available at www.johannesburgsummit.org.

Valaskakis, Kimon, Peter S. Sindell, J. Graham Smith, and Iris Fitzpatrick-Martin. *The Conserver Society: A Workable Alternative for the Future*. New York: Harper and Row, 1979.

Victor, David G., with Abram Chayes and Eugene B. Skolnikoff. "Pragmatic Approaches to Regime Building for Complex International Problems." In *Global Accord: Environmental Challenges and International Responses*, ed. by Nazli Choucri. Cambridge: MIT Press, 1993.

Vidal, John. "The Seeds of Wrath." *The Guardian* [weekend supplement] (June 19, 1999): 10–19.

Visvanathan, Shiv. "Mrs. Brundtland's Disenchanted Cosmos." *Alternatives* 16 (3) (Summer 1991): 377–384.

Vogler, John. *The Global Commons: Environmental and Technological Governance.* 2nd ed. Toronto: Wiley, 2000.

Wallach, Lori, and Michelle Sforza. *Whose Trade Organization? Corporate Globalization and the Erosion of Democracy.* Washington, D.C.: Public Citizen, 1999.

Waltz, Kenneth. *Theory of International Politics.* Reading, Mass.: Addison-Wesley, 1979.

Ward, Barbara. "The End of an Epoch?" *The Economist* 243 (May 27, 1972): 66–76.

Ward, Barbara, and René Dubos. *Only One Earth: The Care and Maintenance of a Small Planet.* Harmondsworth: Penguin Books, 1972.

White, Rodney. "Global Warming and the Greenhouse Effect: Implications for International Environmental Policy." In *Greening Environmental Policy: The Politics of a Sustainable Future,* ed. by Frank Fischer and Michael Black. London: Paul Chapman, 1995.

"Why Greens Should Love Trade." *The Economist* 353 (8140) (October 9, 1999): 17–18.

Wijkman, Per Magnus. "Managing the Global Commons." *International Organization* 36 (3) (Summer 1982): 511–536.

Willetts, Peter. "From Stockholm to Rio and Beyond: The Impact of the Environmental Movement on the United Nations Consultative Arrangements for NGOs." *Review of International Studies* 22 (1) (January 1996): 57–80.

Williams, Marc. "Aid, Sustainable Development, and the Environmental Crisis." *International Journal of Peace Studies* 3 (2) (July 1998): 19–33.

Williams, Marc, and Lucy Ford. "The World Trade Organisation, Social Movements, and Global Environmental Management." *Environmental Politics* 8 (1) (Spring 1999): 268–289.

Wilson, E. O. *Consilience: The Unity of Knowledge.* Boston: Little, Brown, 1998.

Wilson, H. T. "Science, Critique, and Criticism: The 'Open Society' Revisited." In *On Critical Theory,* ed. by John O'Neill. New York: University Press of America, 1989. [Originally published in 1976.]

Wiwa, Owens, and Andy Rowell. "Some Things Never Change." *The Guardian,* November 8, 2000.

Wolfensohn, James. "You Can't Beat Us—So Join Us." *Globe and Mail,* April 12, 2000.

World Commission on Environment and Development. *Our Common Future.* Oxford: Oxford University Press, 1987.

Yearley, Steve, and John Forrester. "Shell, a Sure Target for Global Environmental Campaigning?" In *Global Social Movements,* ed. by Robin Cohen and Shirin M. Rai. London: Athlone Press, 2000.

Young, Oran R. "Negotiating an International Climate Regime: The Institutional Bargaining for Environmental Governance." In *Global Accord,* ed. by Nazli Choucri. Cambridge: MIT Press, 1993.

———. "Political Leadership and Regime Formation: On the Development of

Institutions in International Society." *International Organization* 45 (3) (Summer 1991): 281–308.

————. "The Politics of International Regime Formation: Managing Natural Resources and the Environment." *International Organization* 43 (3) (Summer 1989): 349–375.

Young, Oran R., and Gail Osherenko, eds. *Polar Politics: Creating International Environmental Regimes.* Ithaca: Cornell University Press, 1993.

Index

Adorno, Theodor, x, 10, 23, 25n18; on Enlightenment thought, 15, 152

Agriculture: chemical use in, 181, 195; forest use, 180; genetic modification, 84–86; greenwash, 90; in India, 163; in Nigeria, 164

Alliance of Small Island States (AOSIS), 129

Annan, Kofi: and Global Compact, 93–94

Antarctic, 7; and ozone depletion, 122

Arctic: in Berger report, 171–172; National Wildlife Reserve, 134, 152–153; Nunuvut, 164; oil and gas in, 172; Qitsualik on, 174

Arrhenius, Svante: on climate change, 126

Art: Bohm on, 184n14; Knelman on, 167; Marcuse on, 27n41, 184n14; Wilson on, 156

Atkinson, Adrian, 65

Australia: and FCCC, 128

Bacon, Francis, 14, 43, 65, 84, 92, 124, 156

Bauman, Zygmunt, 26n30

Benedick, Richard: on CFCs, 120

Berger, Thomas: report, 171–172

Bernauer, Thomas: on institution building, 106

Bhagwati, Jagdish: on free trade, 68

Bhopal (India), 86

Biodiversity, 190; Hemispheric Social Alliance on, 180, 181; UN convention on, 51

Body Shop, the, 88

Bohm, David: comparison with Marcuse, 184n12, 184n14; on fragmentary worldview, 154–156

Bolivia: protest movements in, 175

Brandt, Willy: and CGG, 90–91

Bretton Woods institutions, 65, 68, 78, 80–83; and CGG, 91; and regime formation, 105

Brody, Hugh, 175

Brundtland, Gro Harlem: chair of WCED, 40

Brundtland Commission. *See* World Commission on Environment and Development

Burson Marstellar, 85–86, 89

Bush, George: at UNCED, 50–51

Bush, George W.: and alternative energy technology, 152–153; and national missile defense, 153

Business Charter for Sustainable Development (Rotterdam Charter), 89–90

213

Business Council for Sustainable Development (BCSD), 87–88; and genetic modification, 85–86; at UNCED, 50. *See also* World Business Council for Sustainable Development

Canada: and carbon "sinks," 132; environmental legislation in, 77; environment minister on incrementalism, 125; Ethyl Corporation court challenge against, 74–75, 77; and FCCC, 128; fish stock, 138; hosts Summit of the Americas, 177; Manganese-Based Fuel Additives Act, 74–75; and NAFTA, 72; Northwest Territories, 171, 172; Nunavut, 164–165; oil and gas pipelines in, 171

Capra, Fritjof: on sustainable communities, 154

Carbon: and Inuit, 171; "sinks," 127–129, 132–133

Cargill, 85

Carson, Rachel, 29, 89; on pesticides, 30

CEC. *See* Commission for Environmental Cooperation

Center for Our Common Future (COCF), 48–49

CFCs. *See* Chlorofluorocarbons

CGG. *See* Commission on Global Governance

Chemical industry: and agriculture, 181; DuPont, 99n47, 121, 139; Ethyl Corporation, 74–75, 77; Methanex, 75; and ozone convention, 121; and ozone depletion, 118; Responsible Care, 89; in the United States, 31–32. *See also* Chloroflourocarbons; Gasoline additives

Chile: hosts Summit of the Americas, 177

Chlorofluorocarbons (CFCs), 27n44, 136; Benedick on, 120; capture device, 119; and DuPont, 121, 139;

and General Motors, 119; Molina on, 119; and Montreal protocol (ozone), 123; and ozone depletion, 119–125; and ozone "fixes," 123–124; Rowland on, 119; Stolarski on, 124; the United States on, 120

Civil society: in CGG report, 92–93; concept of, 55–56; in Hemispheric Social Alliance, 178–179, 182; role of, 58; Strong and, 60n16

Climate change, xii, 148, 156; Arrhenius on, 126; Austrian conference on, 127; and carbon dioxide, 127; Fourier on, 126; Framework Convention on, 52, 127; and GEF, 52; green diplomacy of, 126; and Inuit, 171; and ozone depletion, 125; and regime formation, 103, 112; Toronto conference on, 127; UN convention on, 51. *See also* Framework Convention on Climate Change

Clinton, Bill, on globalization, 11; and Kyoto protocol, 134

Club of Rome, 59n5

Commission for Environmental Cooperation (CEC): and NAFTA, 73, 77–78

Commission on Global Governance (CGG), 90–95; *Our Global Neighbourhood,* 91

Commons, global, 92, 113, 185n37

Convention on International Trade in Endangered Species, 39

Convention on Long-Range Transboundary Air Pollution, 39

Coordinating Committee on the Ozone Layer, 119–120

Cox, Robert: on roles of theory, 8–9

Critical Theory, xi, 4, 8, 13–23, 194; Cox on, 9; and ecological impact of economics, 19; and Frankfurt School, 11; on social uses of science, 152; tools of 12–13

attitudes on intellectual property,
52; and Bretton Woods system, 67;
Bush and alternative technology,
152–153; Bush and Kyoto
protocol, 134–135; and carbon
"sinks," 132; on CFCs, 120;
chemical manufacturing in, 31–32;
and convention on biodiversity, 52;
in *Dolphin-Tuna* case, 78–79; EPA
and ozone depletion, 122, 125;
fast-track legislation in, 73; and
FCCC, 128, 133; and FTAA, 177;
and GCC and Climate Council,
129; Methanex court challenge
against, 75; and missile defense,
153; and NAFTA, 72; NASA
programs and ozone depletion,
122, 125; position on green house
gas targets, 52; Public Citizen, 73;
and regime formation, 104; and
Stockholm conference, 33; and
UNCED, 50–51; at World Climate
Conference, 12
U Thant, 36

Venezuela: protest movements in,
175
Vietnam War, 6, 37; protestors of, 30
Visvanathan, Shiv: on WCED report,
44–45
Volger, John: on ozone depletion
convention, 121

WCED. *See* World Commission on
Environment and Development
Wildlife: conservation of, 39
Wilson, E. O.: on art, 156; on
consilience, 156–157
Wolfensohn, James, 81

World Bank, 158; and environmental
policy, 80–83; and FCCC, 128;
and GEF, 52–53, 81; and Narmada
projects, 163, 169; and oil
companies, 170; and WCED
report, 45
World Business Council for
Sustainable Development
(WBCSD), 88, 139
World Climate Conferences (1979
and 1990), 126–127
World Commission on Environment
and Development (WCED),
40–46, 66, 88; and Bretton Woods
system, 68; on GATT, 78; and
Rotterdam Charter, 89–90;
statement on forest principles, 52;
Strong on, 56; Visvanathan on
report of, 44–45
World Economic Forum, 93, 183
World Industry for the Environment,
88
World Meteorological Organization
(WMO): establishes
Intergovernmental Panel on
Climate Change, 127
World Social Forum (WSF), 183
World Summit on Sustainable
Development, 57
World Trade Organization (WTO), x,
19, 72, 78–80; creation of, 79; and
MAI, 83; protests against, 175,
176

Young, Oran: on regime formation,
105–106, 110

Zapatista (Mexico), 166–168,
172–173, 192, 195

About the Book

Introducing students to global environmental politics from a critical perspective, Lee-Anne Broadhead reveals the yawning gap between the rhetoric of international agreements and the reality of meaningful results.

Broadhead argues that the current emphasis on green diplomacy and regime creation reproduces a dangerous way of thinking about the human relationship with the natural environment—a way of thinking that is at the root of environmental problems. She effectively integrates concepts from critical social theory, international political economy, and international environmental politics to demonstrate that the regimes established to manage the global commons represent no more than a status quo approach, and in fact reinforce inequalities and environmentally destructive practices. Engaging with mainstream debates, her concise, accessible analysis points clearly to the need for alternative international structures that have social justice and ecological awareness as their starting point.

Lee-Anne Broadhead is assistant professor in the Department of Political Science at the University College of Cape Breton, Nova Scotia, Canada.